The Making of the Modern Church

The Making
of the
Modern Church

CHRISTIANITY IN ENGLAND
SINCE 1800

B. G. Worrall

First published in Great Britain 1988
SPCK
Holy Trinity Church
Marylebone Road
London NW1 4DU

British Library Cataloguing in Publication Data

Worrall, B. G.
  The Making of the Modern Church:
  Christianity in England since 1800
  1. England. Christianity, 1800–1987
  I. Title
  209′.42

  ISBN 0–281–04382–5

Printed in Great Britain

Contents

Preface

It is a commonplace observation that great changes have taken place during the last two hundred years. The life and assumptions of the average Englishman at the end of the twentieth century are probably beyond anything which his counterpart early in the nineteenth century could have imagined. Few areas have been so affected by these changes as religion.

The progress of the natural sciences and the disturbing ideas associated with Biblical Criticism, introduced to England from Germany, affected the way people thought about religion. Urbanisation, the rapid change from a mainly rural society to a mainly urban one, affected the practice of religion. Political and social changes, as well as more directly theological ones, affected relations between denominations and the internal lives of denominations. The growth of Britain's imperial power and responsibility helped to inspire and support an extensive Christian missionary movement, and the decline of that power helped to question and partly change that movement.

But Christians did not merely react to changes; they also took initiatives. They explored new understandings of their faith and re-discovered old ones. Some took the lead in social action, others led great movements of evangelism and spiritual renewal. The religious scene has been enlivened by outstanding personalities, intellectual and spiritual giants, charismatic leaders and a few eccentrics. A period which has the Oxford Movement near its beginning and concludes with a renewed interest in the gifts of the Holy Spirit is not lacking in religious vitality.

It is not surprising that examination boards at GCE 'A' level and beyond include sections on this period, nor that it is included in university and theological college courses. It is largely with students preparing for such examinations or taking such courses in mind that this book has been written, though I hope it may also be of interest to a wider readership.

I am aware that many of the issues or people dealt with here in a chapter, or part of a chapter, have been the subject of large and detailed scholarly books. But often the sheer size and complexity of such works is daunting to the beginner or the student who is looking for an introduction or over-view before plunging deeper. My aim has been to provide a treatment which is academic but not too specialist so that the reader can see the main arguments and relate the issues to each other without being overwhelmed by detail. The notes and bibliographies will provide those looking for it with a way in to a fuller discussion of each area. While I have not always hidden my own views I have not obtruded them.

Much of what follows has been used in courses at Avery Hill College and I am grateful to those who have discussed it with me there. I am grateful too to the editors of *Theology* and *Spectrum* for permission to adapt for use here some material which previously appeared in those journals; to my colleague Arthur Rowe, to Dr Jeremy Thornton of Coopers' Company and Coborn School, Upminster, and to my publisher's anonymous reader, all of whom made helpful and perceptive comments on the material in typescript; to the editorial staff of SPCK who endured a number of delays in the preparation of the manuscript; and, above all, to my wife, Sharon, for constant encouragement.

B. G. Worrall
May 1988

I

The Beginning of the Nineteenth Century

To the casual observer of English society at the beginning of the nineteenth century it may well have appeared that the position of the English Church in the life of the nation, and the status of the Christian religion in its thought, were both secure. A more perceptive observer might have noted external and internal forces working upon both which were to lead to revolutionary changes in the century which lay ahead, changes with have continued to have their effects. However, in the early years of the century the religious scene gave every appearance of complacency and security.

Early nineteenth-century England could be described as Christian in a way which it is difficult to imagine when viewed from the late twentieth century. The concept, which had been held since the Protestant Reformation, of the co-identity of Church and state could still be held. The Church of England was the national church. As a great national institution it was a rallying point for national sentiment and, in his *Reflections on the Revolution in France* (1790), Edmund Burke had applauded it as a source of social stability. It certainly appeared popular during the Napoleonic Wars. Parliament functioned as its lay assembly. Its bishops were appointed by the monarch, acting through his ministers, and, as members of the House of Lords, they, and other senior clergymen, had considerable influence in national affairs. Its parochial system covered the country and the parish clergy were often men of considerable influence in local society. The majority of educated men accepted the importance of religion in national life and assented to the general truth of Christianity. The few atheists and free thinkers, men such as Tom Paine, who stood out from this general consensus, achieved notoriety as much by the novelty of their position as by the force of their arguments.

But in spite of the appearance of strength and security the Church was actually in a very weak state. Its place in the establishment partly obscured its spiritual, pastoral and intellectual weaknesses and partly caused them. Men looked upon the clergy as greater or lesser gentry. The higher clergy moved easily among the nobility, the average parish priest was a minor country gentleman with a place in local social life. The Church offered an acceptable career which could sometimes lead to considerable wealth and more often to social acceptance. The novels of Jane Austen give a fairly accurate picture of the situation at the beginning of the century. The wealth, or lack of it, of any particular incumbent depended upon the endowments of his parish church and the generosity of the patron who appointed him to the living. Naturally this led to men seeking to move from one living to another to increase their income, and not infrequently to the holding of several livings at once. Anthony Trollope's Barsetshire novels indicate that the situation had not much changed well into the nineteenth century.

It was not that the Church was corrupt, though its critics could find instances of corruption. Neither should one imagine that there were not deeply spiritual, pastorally energetic and learned clergy within it. We shall meet some later. It was rather that religion, as it was understood by the majority of clergy and laymen, had become formal and was lacking in spiritual vitality and depth. The sincere parish priest was likely to be more concerned with the bodily needs of his parishioners, and with instructing them in conventional politeness, than with their spiritual well-being. Many clergy had little specific training in theology or in their pastoral duties. Their selection and preparation for ordination was in the hands of the bishops, and even the more conscientious of the bishops seem to have given it little care.

Men who considered themselves Christian and loyal members of the Church scarcely allowed their professed faith to affect their lives or gave any thought to their personal relationship with God. In 1797 the evangelical leader William Wilberforce had criticized this attitude in a book with the compendious title *A Practical View of the Prevailing Religious System of Professed Christians in the Higher and Middle Classes in this Country Contrasted with Real Christianity*. Wilberforce criticized the purely formal Christian commitment of most of his contemporaries and pleaded for more 'seriousness'. The 'Real Christianity' which he advocated meant a greater concern by the individual for his own relation to God, more diligence in such matters as prayer and Bible study and an acknowledgement of responsibility to God for all matters of daily life, especially by those who held public office or had influence over others. The book had a great effect upon many, but the fact that it should be written at all, and that so many should be stirred to greater spiritual awareness by its arguments, is an indication that Christian fervour was at a low ebb.

Intellectually, too, the Church was not in a good position to meet the challenges of the new century. Christian theology was largely reduced to deistic arguments for the existence of a Supreme Being and the practical usefulness of morality, a type of thinking which owed more to seventeenth-century rationalism than to the Bible or the Christian tradition. The best example of this type of thinking was probably William Paley, Archdeacon of Carlisle, who is best known for his argument that just as the intricate design of a watch indicates the existence of a watchmaker, so the evidences of design in the universe indicate the existence of a Creator. Such arguments, which have a long history in Christian thinking, were already under attack on the Continent. But, quite apart from any weaknesses in the arguments themselves, this approach reduces religion to the acceptance of certain propositions. It is lacking in warmth and is a long way from the thinking of the New Testament

Forces for Change

We noted that a perceptive observer would have been aware of forces which would lead to change in this apparently settled situation. The chief ones may be fairly quickly mentioned.

There were general political and social forces in the air. Across the Channel the French Revolution of 1789 had shown the possibility of radical social change. In England the democratic ideals with which the revolutionaries in France had begun their work had been widely admired. However, as idealism had given way first to the reign of terror and then to the rise of Napoleon, with consequent warfare thoughout Europe, the initial enthusiasm had waned and generally turned to hostility. Nevertheless, it was now clear that an apparently settled society and an established Church were not unalterable. Henceforth demands for change, which were often accompanied by anti-clericalism, would receive an attentive hearing at least among some Englishmen.

The number of those likely to be impressed by revolutionary thinking was increased by the general increase in the population and especially by the growth of new industrial towns spawned by the industrial revolution. Until recently English society had been largely agricultural, based on the village community. Power belonged to property and inherited social position. The new race of industrialists was an unknown force. The industrial workers, often living in cramped and squalid conditions, were quite beyond the parochial organization of the Church, and had no stake in society. Social constraints and conventions were weakening.

In the more obviously religious realm movements for change came also largely from the Continent, this time from Germany. Behind them was the work of *Immanuel Kant* (1724–1804). Kant not only criticized the traditional arguments for the existence of God, which we saw were basic to conventional English theology, but also raised the question whether such arguments could even be said to be dealing with anything real. For Kant the human mind could have no certain knowledge of truth apart from through sense impression. That means that the questions of theology and metaphysics are simply beyond our mental range. It does not mean that there is no level of reality beyond sense impression, but merely that our minds cannot reach it. Our minds simply operate on what Kant calls the *phenomena* or the outside of things, they cannot reach the *noumena* or the things in themselves.

However, he argues that there is a range of experience in which we do appear to get beyond mere sense impression, that is in the realm of moral experience. In moral experience we believe that we 'ought' to behave in a certain way, we experience what he calls the categorical imperative. It is important to notice that Kant does not argue that all men everywhere and at all times feel that they 'ought' to do the same thing. It is no criticism of his position, therefore, to point out that actions which are accepted as morally correct in one society or historical period may be considered morally reprehensible in another. Neither does Kant argue that men will always do what they feel they 'ought' to do. He simply observes that the feeling that one 'ought' to act in a certain way appears to be universal. This leads him to ask whether this experience gives us any clue to the nature of the world. He argues that if the sense of 'ought' is real it is possible to posit three things – the existence of God, the giver and upholder of the moral law; freedom, since the sense that one 'ought' to do something implies that we can do it; and immortality, since as the perfect obedience which we appear to be called to is not attainable in this life it must be attainable hereafter.

What Kant has done is to distinguish between the realms of knowledge on the one hand and belief or faith on the other. He asserts that as far as knowledge, which he calls pure reason, is concerned, religious questions can reach no conclusions and are in fact meaningless. But he suggests that for man's full life knowledge alone is not enough. Man operates also in the realm of belief or faith, which he calls practical reason, and there religion is a possibility. But it is based on faith experience rather than theoretical argument.

Kant's influence became all-pervasive, but it did so in a piecemeal fashion. His limitation of certainty to the area of sense impression was to lead to scientific positivism. Those who criticized religion in the name of science could appeal to his criticism of the traditional arguments for the existence of God. In contrast to Kant, though consciously taking up his thinking on pure reason and his stress on the *noumena*, or the thing in itself, as opposed to the *phenomena*, or the outside of things, G. W. F. Hegel (1770–1831) argued that everything which is real is knowable and is indeed reducible to reason. These developments came to English religious thinking later in the century.

At the beginning of the century the most influential strand of Kant's thought was the move away from rationalism towards a stress on feeling or emotion. This could take the form of an appeal to a carefully defined sense of dependence, as we shall see was worked out by *F. D. E. Schleiermacher* (1763–1834), but in a more general sense it issued in the mood known as Romanticism. Romanticism was a mood rather than an intellectual movement, but it was certainly a very powerful influence in the early part of the nineteenth century. At first it was characterized by a sense of optimism, of wonder; there was a stress on human freedom and dignity, together with a looking forward to better things just around the corner. In political terms the French Revolution had seemed to herald a new era, and later revolutionary movements in Berlin and Paris in 1848 took up the watchwords of democracy, socialism and humanity, and gave them a crusading ring. There was a reaction against everything formal and rationalistic, and an appeal to inward feelings, to what men knew with their hearts rather than with their minds. Thus the influential English philosopher *S. T. Coleridge* (1772–1834) argued that religion is not a matter of evidences but of deep feeling, or what he called imagination.

While in comparison with the dull and lifeless rationalism which preceded it such a reaction towards a greater stress on emotion is understandable, it led to a breakdown of certainty in religion and a tendency to individualism. It seemed that everyone could follow his own deep feelings, and there seemed to be no objective measurement by which one could say that the dictates of any particular feeling were right or wrong. Thus later, as confidence in the general truth of Christianity crumbled, the Romantic mood often led to a more pessimistic introspection and depression.

Parties within the Church of England

It would be wrong to suppose that all churchmen accepted the status quo in the same way, or reacted to the forces for change in the same way. Looking at the Church of England first, we can see that there were a number of different groups or parties which had different outlooks and characteristics.

Those who were most satisfied with the apparently secure position which we have noticed, and thus the most resistant to change, were what was called the Low Church party. The phrase 'Low Church', as it was used at the beginning of the nineteenth century, did not mean, as it later came to mean, that they were opposed to ritual in worship or that they were particularly evangelical in outlook. In fact they were a group which did not put a high value on the Church's spiritual role, neither were they concerned with questions of dogma – for that reason they are sometimes referred to as Liberals, though that word also was used in a rather different sense later in the century. These people were the relics of eighteenth-century rationalism. They had little patience with, or understanding of, religious fervour. For them Christianity was essentially reasonable, God they saw as the great Creator, to be Christian was to be moral. This mood had flourished during the eighteenth century as a reaction to the fanaticism of the wars of religion. It could accept, indeed support, the place of the Church in society, but it saw it almost as a department of state concerned with morality. Clergy were seen as models and teachers of polite manners, not as mediators between God and man. This group contained men of learning and moral force, but they had little to offer in face of the questions which were about to arise for the Church and for Christian faith. Their typical mood of cool detachment and historical inquiry fitted them more to be observers of theological controversy than participants.

The most numerous and influential of the church parties was the Evangelicals. Their immediate origin was in the evangelical revival of the previous century associated with the names of Wesley and Whitefield. That revival had been a protest against dull rationalism and conventional religion in favour of a more emotional response to the gospel. Theologically it had been a recovery of some of the insights of the sixteenth-century Reformation, especially the doctrine of justification by faith alone. It had stressed the doctrine of the free grace of God, by which alone men could be restored to that communion with him for which they had been made but which had been lost by sin. That grace was uniquely expressed by the coming of Jesus to die on the cross for sinful men, thus bearing the punishment, or paying the penalty, due for sin. Christians were those who, by faith, accepted that this had been done for them and who henceforth gave themselves to Christ and, by the work of the Holy Spirit, were progressively sanctified. This was what Wilberforce meant by 'real' Christianity.

For many of those to whom Wesley had preached, as for the sixteenth-century Reformers, this theology had expressed a deep personal experience. No doubt this experience could still have been found among the Evangelicals of the early nineteenth century, but it is hard to resist the suggestion that the fervour had run down, and that some measure of formality had come in even to their typical criticisms of formal religion. The appeal for conversion and the pattern of the conversion experience had sometimes become stereotyped. The would-be convert was expected to experience a growing awareness of his own sinfulness and of his future plight on appearing before the judgement seat of God. This mood would be followed by repentance, a turning to God in confession of guilt, followed by an awareness of forgiveness through Christ. Finally a strictly disciplined life was expected, in reliance upon the Holy Spirit, which was not intended to earn God's favour but rather to give evidence that it had been received. This scheme encompasses some of the deepest experiences recorded in the history of Christian spirituality, but they are not easily examined. Unfortunately it was possible for the language in which they were traditionally expressed to be used in a trite and conventional way. The possibility of hypocrisy or self-deception was obvious.

In terms of theology they produced little. There was some literature for and against predestination, some speculative works on unfulfilled prophecy and some biblical commentaries of an expository rather than critical nature. They were best characterized by their life-style. Without being learned, they took their religion seriously. The stress was on a life of devotion, humility, obedience to God and service to others. The whole was undergirded by a stress on the life of prayer and an acceptance of Scripture as the word of God which gave little place to criticism. At their best they were men of simple goodness and strict morality. Their leaders were chiefly rich and influential laymen, of whom the so-called 'Clapham Sect', men such as *Henry Thornton* (1760–1815), *James Stephen* (1758–1832), *Zachary Macaulay* (1768–1838) and *William Wilberforce* (1759–1833), were the best known. These were men of social standing, members of Parliament and colonial administrators, who saw it as their Christian responsibility to use their influence to maintain Christian principles in public life, and to use their considerable wealth in works of philanthropy. That their charity seems often to have been accompanied by a patronizing attitude is a feature of their age.

At the beginning of the century Evangelicals did not hold high offices in the Church. The first declared Evangelical to become a bishop was *Henry Ryder*, who became Bishop of Gloucester in 1815. In 1826 the Evangelical *Charles Sumner* was made Bishop of Llandaff, and was translated the next year to Winchester where he remained until 1869. His brother, *John Bird Sumner*, became Bishop of Chester in 1828 and Archbishop of Canterbury in 1848.

Clerical leadership in the earlier period came mainly from *Charles Simeon* (1759–1836), vicar of Holy Trinity, Cambridge, and Fellow of King's College, and *Isaac Milner* (1751–1820), President of Queens' College, Cambridge, and Dean of Carlisle. But perhaps their greatest sphere of influence came through the founding of religious societies, which was a feature of the period. The Religious Tract Society and the Church Missionary Society were founded in 1799, the British and Foreign Bible Society in 1804, and the Church Pastoral Aid Society in 1836. All of these were of Evangelical sympathy.

Their single-minded stress on personal salvation and personal holiness of life seems to have deflected the Evangelicals from much thought about the Church. They accepted the establishment of the Church of England, largely because it gave an opportunity to influence the nation, but they were sensitive to the charge that obedience to Christ should appear subordinate to obedience to the state. They also had no objection to working with Dissenters in any cause which they saw as contributing to the spread of the gospel. The church they saw as a meeting place to hear the word of God, to pray and to praise. It was not usually seen as an object of theological interest or importance. In that sense they were also 'Low Church', but that phrase was not normally used of them until it became useful to distinguish them from the peculiar form of 'High Churchmanship' which came to be associated with Tractarianism.

It could be argued that the Evangelicals lost some of their distinctive spiritual strength when they were 'taken up' by polite society. Such a charge could not be levelled against the 'High Church' party. Once again, the term 'High Church' does not mean precisely the same as it came to mean at a later period when it was often synonymous with elaborate ceremonial in worship.

This was not a numerous group, nor was it as influential socially as the Evangelicals. The High Church party accepted the connection between the state and the Church of England which establishment provided, but saw it merely as the proper acknowledgement of the Church's role as the Catholic Church of the land. High Churchmen were far more inclined to stress the Church's spiritual role and its independence of the state.

9

Theologically they were orthodox and unspeculative, and the religious enthusiasm, or overt reference to spiritual experience, which was found among the Evangelicals was distasteful to them. They saw themselves as successors of Archbishop Laud and the English divines of the Restoration period. They were often men of deep learning, especially in the works of the early church Fathers (an Anglican characteristic until recent times), and they were usually men of simple and deep piety. The Church as an institution was the centre both of their theology and of their spiritual lives. They saw its orders of bishops, priests and deacons as essential to its true life. The sacraments, especially the Eucharist, administered by a priest in apostolic succession, were central to Christian discipleship.

Whereas the Evangelicals were at home in the centres of power, and were able to influence the nation through Parliament and through their places in society, the High Church party was more at home in the country. Their ideal was the devout parish priest among his flock, and they treasured the teachings and the church principles which had been handed down generation by generation in country vicarages.

However, in spite of its size and its generally retiring disposition, this party was powerful within the Church. Among its leading members was *William van Mildert* (1765–1836), Regius Professor of Divinity at Oxford who became Bishop of Durham and was instrumental in diverting some of the enormous wealth of that see to the founding of Durham University. Another Regius Professor who became a bishop was *Charles Lloyd* (1784–1830), who became Bishop of Oxford and was an early supporter of Pusey. Probably most of the intellectual weight of the Church was in or sympathetic towards this party. Nor were they lacking in social concern. A small group of High Churchmen living at Hackney got the name the 'Hackney Phalanx' as a parallel to the 'Clapham Sect'. Their most prominent member was *Joshua Watson* (1771–1855), a prosperous merchant who retired from business in his forties to devote himself to voluntary work. In 1811 he helped to found the National Society, for the provision of elementary education according to the principles of the Church of England.

Of all the groups within the Church this one had probably the most complete and consistent theology. Though they would differ from him on many points, they also had in their stress on spirituality at least some of what Wilberforce meant by 'real' Christianity. The Evangelicals generally suspected them of formalism. At the beginning of the century their chief characteristic was quiet devotion, but when the time came and they thought that the Church was under attack they provided the strength for the Oxford Movement. Yet in spite of their greater vitality and increased influence during the rest of the century, they were also, for the most part, too conservative to meet the challenges of the new age with anything other than a restatement of their traditional position.

Dissent and Roman Catholicism

So far we have spoken only of the Church of England. Its established position gave that Church a prominence in national affairs, and a collection of privileges, which enabled it to overshadow other denominations.

For political and social, as well as theological, reasons both Protestant Dissent and Roman Catholicism presented almost alternative cultures as well as alternative Churches at the beginning of our period. The bond which establishment formed between the state and the Church gave to dissent from the Church of England its political overtones, and, as we have seen, there was such a breadth of opinion within that Church that, to the casual observer, dissent from it must have appeared positively perverse.

The traditional Dissenting churches – Congregational (or Independent), Baptist and Presbyterian – had existed since the sixteenth century, and had experienced political power during the Commonwealth period. Restrictions imposed upon them initially by the Clarendon Code of 1661 were still on the statute book.

The Methodists had, officially, been a party within the Church of England at least until the death of John Wesley in 1791. Now, partly as local magistrates and bishops moved against them and caused them to register their meeting places, and partly as the logic of their own position forced them into open criticism of the structure of the Church of England, they were gradually forced into the position of a Nonconformist Church. But now also a move towards emancipation was about to begin to bear fruit and to carry on throughout the next century. At the same time, incidentally, the descriptions Dissent and Dissenter gave way to those of Nonconformity and Nonconformist. As a recent historian has commented: 'Dissent is querulous, refusal to conform is manly.'[1]

Theologically these were 'gathered' churches. They had two chief distinguishing marks. The first was personal confession of faith. Nobody was born into a dissenting church; one entered by personal choice and that choice, theoretically, was based on an experience of conversion. Secondly, there was an acceptance of moral discipline. Much more than was generally the case in the Church of England, the Dissenters accepted a code of conduct as part of their religious profession. Though it was, as it is, rare to find occurrences of it, excommunication was technically a possibility.

The early fervour of the Dissenters, which had made them stand out on principle against what they saw as the subservience of the Church to the state and had made them assert the 'Crown rights of the Redeemer' in Church affairs, had declined. They had been touched by the Evangelical revival, but not so much as had the Church of England. That was quite natural considering the adhesion of the early Methodists to the Church of England. The Dissenters' traditional stress on individual freedom in matters of religion, and particularly their stress on freedom of thought, had led many of them to doubt traditional Christian orthodoxy. Among Presbyterians particularly there had been a drift to Unitarianism. There was generally too a distaste for religious enthusiasm.

However, while Dissent as a religious force was not strong, Dissenters as a force in society had flourished. Their stress on sobriety and hard work had brought, almost against their principles, considerable material prosperity. It was as if the energies which could not be channelled into political or academic life went with greater force into commerce. Frequently they became successful small businessmen.

Dissenters sometimes wrote and spoke of themselves as being persecuted. When one thinks of the extreme physical sufferings which some Christians have had to endure for their faith, that is doubtless too strong an expression. Nevertheless their exclusion from public life and the inconveniences which they did suffer were serious enough. Together with such things they had to endure a patronizing and insulting attitude from many among the educated, self-consciously cultivated, classes which is well summed up in George Eliot's ironical description of Dissent as 'a foolish habit that clung greatly to families in the grocery and chandlering lines, though not incompatible with prosperous wholesale dealing'. It was time for a change of attitude.

The position of Roman Catholics was similar, though more extreme. The Roman Church in England was at a particularly low point at the beginning of the nineteenth century. It was preserved among a few noble families, who were regarded as somewhat quaint and outside the mainstream of national life, and was found too among Irish labourers, who were apt to be dismissed as ignorant and superstitious. There was a general assumption that an Englishman's religion was Protestantism, which might be further defined as an adherence to the Bible and no popery. Roman Catholicism was seen as an alien force politically hostile to England and likely to be a threat to the nation's security and freedom. This view was fuelled by a collection of myths based on partially understood, or quite misunderstood, theological objections to the authority of the pope, the doctrine of transubstantiation, the role of priests in Roman Catholic life and the attitude to saints and relics in Roman Catholic devotion. The sum was that Roman Catholicism was partly feared as threatening and pseudo-magical and partly despised as superstitious and sinister. The exclusion of Roman Catholics from public life had general support and appeared to be enshrined in the King's coronation oath to preserve the Protestant religion.

That some reassessment of this attitude was overdue had been plain for some time. It became more urgent with the political union of England and Ireland in 1801 by which the Westminster Government became directly responsible for Irish affairs. Since Ireland was overwhelmingly Roman Catholic it was clear that henceforth Roman Catholics could not be treated as quite such a minority in the life of the nation. Nevertheless, the moves which led to the Catholic Emancipation Act of 1829 revealed a great deal of bitter hostility towards Rome and a deep fear of Roman aggression. It also unearthed an instinctive support for the Church of England which was to be significant in the early days of the most important religious movement of the nineteenth century.

Note

1   C. Binfield, *So Down to Prayers* (Dent 1977), p. 7.

2
The Oxford Movement

The middle years of the nineteenth century saw a revival within the Church of England which was comparable in its way with that associated with the Wesleys in the previous century. At first its scope and influence was much narrower. Not only was it deliberately a movement within the Church of England but, as its popular name – the Oxford Movement – implies, it was dominated, at least at the beginning, by men associated with that university. It soon flowed into the parishes of what we have called the 'High Church' party, but it was a long time before its influence passed beyond the clergy and the educated classes. Nevertheless, if by the term 'revival' in its religious sense we mean a deepening of spiritual awareness leading to a greater fervour in religious practice, this was a genuine revival. It was partly based on different, more Catholic, theological presuppositions than those which had motivated the Evangelicals, and it partly helped in the formulation, or public expression, of those presuppositions in England. On the other hand, its affinity with some basic strands of evangelical thinking is shown by the large number of Evangelicals who were attracted to it.

Origins and Aims

Two events are most frequently mentioned as origins of the Oxford Movement. First, on 14 July 1833, John Keble preached a sermon before the Assize judges at Oxford which was later published under the title 'National Apostasy'. In it he criticized the Bill then before Parliament to reform the Irish Church by abolishing ten bishoprics and redistributing the bishops' salaries among the lower clergy. He saw this as state interference in the spiritual life of the Church. Secondly, on 9 September in the same year John Henry Newman published three short tracts which he had circulated among his friends several weeks earlier. The first was addressed to his fellow-clergy of the Church of England and in

15

it he encouraged them to take more seriously their spiritual status and authority derived from their ordination. With these events the public life of the movement had begun. It attracted support for several reasons.

The reform of the Irish Church which so angered Keble was basically a sensible measure. The Irish bishops enjoyed considerable wealth while the lower clergy were often impoverished. The redrawing of diocesan boundaries, which was also involved, made the Church more able to serve its Protestant members. Yet Keble had correctly drawn attention to a constitutional threat to the Church of England and to a significant shift in the nation's political life. In 1828 the repeal of the Test and Corporation Acts had made it possible for Nonconformists to take part in political life. In 1829 the Catholic Emancipation Act had done the same for Roman Catholics. Finally, in 1832, the Reform Act had widened the number of those able to vote in Parliamentary elections. Between them these steps had changed the character of the House of Commons, and particularly its relation to the Church of England. In the first flush of reform there were those who wanted to disestablish the Church of England, ending the official relationship between Church and state completely. They had noted that the bishops, and the clergy generally, had resisted the Reform Bill. Though the fear of disestablishment passed, it was certainly the case that the Parliament which was proposing to reform the Irish Church was no longer solidly Anglican. To some that meant it was no longer Christian.

In such circumstances some of those who had opposed the recent legislation would support what they saw as a movement to restore the Church of England to its previous position for political reasons. The Church of England could be seen as an aspect of the Tory Party, 'the Tory Party at prayer', and so to support it could be seen as a means of resisting the new Whig government and their liberal politics. To this feeling could be added, for many, a vague fear that the liberal politics which had produced the French Revolution, (and more recently the overthrow of the restoration monarchy in France in the person of Charles X), and which were seen to be characterized by anti-clericalism, were now reaching England and had to be resisted. Thus those who were fearful of change might be drawn to a movement which seemed to stand for what was known and understood.

The concept of liberalism has a theological as well as a political connotation. The growth of biblical criticism, well advanced on the Continent and slowly becoming known in England, seemed to be a threat to confident, dogmatic, religious teaching. John Henry Newman, the leading figure of the Oxford Movement in its first phase, later wrote concerning his views at this time, 'my battle was with liberalism; by liberalism I mean the anti-dogmatic principle and its developments.'[1] Such liberalism can tend to the view that any opinion is as good as any other, and that there is no measurement of truth either in Scripture or in the teaching of the Church. Though such a position had not been reached in England, some feared that it was near.

Thus it could be argued that the Oxford Movement gained support for political and reactionary reasons, and that it appealed to those who were fearful of change, or who longed for a lost age of security and settled faith which had probably never existed. A lot of the work which the movement produced, both in its early years and subsequently, could support such an unflattering view of it. Yet such a view omits the most powerful arguments which drove its early leaders and attracted the majority of its supporters.

If there was a single basic aim of the Oxford Movement it was to recover the idea of the Church as a divine institution. Popular teaching and government action showed that the Church of England was generally regarded, even by its members, almost as a department of the state, or as the state in its spiritual or religious aspect. Alternatively it was seen as a convenient gathering place for Christians who were Christians through individual experience quite apart from the Church. Those who rallied to the Oxford Movement were chiefly those who, in their hearts, had never accepted such popular views. For them the Church was divine. To use language from a later period, it was the extension of the incarnation, the instrument of God in the world, the means by which God who had appeared in Jesus Christ continued his activity.

Basic to this claim was the idea of Apostolic Succession, the view that the Church's bishops were the direct successors of the apostles and that they could trace that 'descent' through the rite of ordination. Parish priests were the local representatives of the bishops, who by their ordination had been given a special status. It was by virtue of this status that they could officiate at the sacraments. Such a link with the apostles, and with the early Church generally, was seen to give to the Church a peculiar divine authority which was beyond the reach of secular governments. It also set the Church which could claim it apart from other religious bodies. A validly ordained priest, by this argument, had a spiritual status above that of a Nonconformist minister.

The immediate result of such teaching was twofold. It raised in an acute form the question of authority. This meant not only the authority of the state in spiritual matters, but also the authority of the Church, through its bishops and priests, to teach and to direct the lives of church members. Secondly, it led amongst those who accepted it to a greater stress on holiness of life and spiritual devotion. This was expressed largely through a greater reverence in regard to sacraments and worship generally, but also through a renewal of concern for private devotion and individual holiness which was similar in some ways to that found among Evangelicals.

Some Leaders

We have noted that John Henry Newman emerged as the leading figure of the Oxford Movement. Newman himself reckoned 'the true and primary author of it' to have been John Keble. Though this view is generally held to be flattering to Keble, owing more to personal admiration than to sober assessment, many shared it at the beginning of the movement and there is no doubt that Keble's Assize sermon was seen as a rallying cry.

John Keble (1792–1866) was not fitted by nature to be the leader of a party. He had a shy, retiring and humble disposition, though he was capable of being obstinate and unyielding when he felt that a matter of principle was at stake. He was a man of considerable intellectual ability and for the first part of his adult life, following his ordination in 1815, he alternated between spells at Oxford as a Fellow of Oriel College (1817–23) and Professor of Poetry (1831–4), and periods assisting his father who was a parish priest near Fairford in Gloucester. From 1836 for the rest of his life he was vicar of Hursley in Hampshire.

It was largely at Fairford and Hursley that he exercised his influence, not primarily as a scholar but as the embodiment of the ideals of the Oxford Movement – a learned, humble and devout parish priest. It was his personal holiness and his pastoral concern for those around him which made Keble such an influential figure. Newman records that when Keble congratulated him on his own election to a Fellowship at Oriel he 'felt so abashed and unworthy of the honour done me, that I seemed desirous of quite sinking into the ground'.[2]

Keble had learned from his father to revere the traditions of the High Church party within the Church of England. It came to be his highest expression of praise to say of any theological position, 'it seems just what my father always said'. In line with this tradition he had a deep knowledge of and respect for the writings of the Fathers and also of the Anglican divines of the seventeenth century. From these sources he got his doctrine of the Church and his sense of order. A due sense of order, or of decent reserve, permeated his devotional life as well. He appears as a man of deep feeling and heartfelt devotion. He was convinced that the truths of Christianity are grasped not, primarily, by the intellect but by the heart, and that intellectual cleverness can be a barrier to proper understanding. Yet, in line with his tradition, he had an abhorrence of enthusiasm or over-emotionalism in religion. Thus he taught and practised a piety which had a real place for feeling but which did not allow emotion to run riot and overturn a proper reserve and orderliness.

It was as an expression of, and an aid to, such piety that he produced his best-known work, *The Christian Year*. This consists of a series of verses written for devotional use on each of the Sundays and special feast days of the Church of England. Some have become well known as hymns, but it is important to remember that Keble meant them for private use. The orderliness and unemotional nature of his piety is seen in his translation, from the French of Jean-Pierre de Caussade,

> If on our daily course our mind
> Be set to hallow all we find,
> New treasures still, of countless price,
> God will provide for sacrifice.

The trivial round, the common task,
Will furnish all we ought to ask,
Room to deny ourselves, a road
To bring us daily nearer God.

A more personal devotion is present in

Sun of my soul, thou Saviour dear,
It is not night if thou be near;
O may no earth-born cloud arise
To hide thee from thy servant's eyes.

Abide with me from morn till eve,
For without thee I cannot live;
Abide with me when night is nigh,
For without thee I dare not die.

The Christian Year was published in 1827, though many of the verses are from an earlier period. It established Keble's reputation and, though much of the poetry is not of a very high standard, later earned him the Professorship of Poetry. More importantly it helped to express the theology and religious feeling of his tradition.

Keble's influence was largely of a personal nature on his pupils. One of them was *Hurrell Froude* (1803–36). Froude was a determined and passionate High Churchman and it was Froude who brought Keble into a position of leadership and introduced him to Newman. Froude's High Churchmanship was at least partly political, hence he was a staunch opponent of the Reform Bill which he saw as an attack on the position of the Church of England. In 1827 he became a Fellow of Oriel College and developed a friendship with Newman. In 1833 with *William Palmer* (1811–78) of Worcester College and *Hugh James Rose* (1795–1838), Vicar of Hadleigh in Essex and editor of *The British Magazine*, he agreed to form an association to defend the Church of England. It was to this association that they recruited both Keble and Newman. The basis of the association was the doctrine of Apostolic Succession and the freedom of the Church from interference by the state, but whereas Palmer and Rose wished to proceed politically by petitioning King and Parliament, Keble and Newman were moved more by religious motives. The latter, though they would at first have preferred to keep the connection with the state, were resigned to losing it if that was necessary to maintain their theological position. Froude's other legacy to the movement was a collection of private papers, including a spiritual journal, which was published posthumously by Keble and Newman in 1838. This work, Froude's *Remains*, shows a Catholic spirituality, including the practice of unusual asceticism, and includes the expression of some extremely anti-Protestant opinions. On both accounts the publication proved embarrassing to the movement.

John Henry Newman (1801–90), who was thus brought in to the movement, was possibly the outstanding religious personality of nineteenth-century England. The son of an unsuccessful banker, Newman had experienced an evangelical conversion at the age of fifteen. Though he later disowned the 'Calvinistic' views which he had then briefly adopted, he never denied the importance or the reality of the experience. It was with the reputation of being an Evangelical that he became a Fellow of Oriel College in 1822, and Vicar of St Mary's, Oxford, in 1828. At Oriel, under the influence of *Richard Whateley* (1787–1863), later Archbishop of Dublin, and then of *Edward Hawkins* (1789–1882), he came to question the intellectual foundation of his Evangelical views and developed a higher regard for the Church and for the importance of tradition. He also began to develop a taste for intellectual discussion for its own sake. Later he wrote of this period, 'The truth is, I was beginning to prefer intellectual excellence to moral; I was drifting in the direction of liberalism.'[3]

As his Evangelicalism, and his shyness, faded, he took more interest in church history and liturgy. Chiefly, however, his attention was taken by patristic study. In his own words, he 'learnt to consider that Antiquity was the true exponent of the doctrines of Christianity and the basis of the Church of England'.[4] From the Fathers too he took what became his doctrine of 'economies', that is the possibility of seeing a thing in two ways – what it appears to be and what it is in God's hidden intention, i.e. what it really is. Thus the external world, physical and historical, may be seen also as the outward manifestation of spiritual realities; Scripture may be interpreted allegorically; and pagan learning may be seen as a preparation for the gospel. In all this Newman is working out his own spiritual as well as theological position.

Newman was a complex figure. He was a hypersensitive, often gloomy and over-introspective man, who could say that he was convinced from an early period of his life that only two things really mattered, 'God and my own soul'. He had a very subtle intellect and was a great controversialist, or rather publicist, since he did not always seem able to see other sides of a controversy and was sometimes apt to see opposition to himself as opposition to God. He was a passionate man, deeply religious from an early age and committed to a search for truth and certainty. For him religion and dogma were inseparable. Writing of his conversion experience he says, 'I fell under the influence of a definite creed, and received into my intellect impressions of dogma, which through God's mercy, have never been effaced or obscured.'[5] Later he wrote, 'I have changed in many things; in this I have not. From the age of fifteen, dogma has been the fundamental principle of my religion: I know no other religion; I cannot enter into the idea of any other sort of religion; religion, as a mere sentiment, is to me a dream and a mockery.'[6]

His theological writings and arguments come from, indeed are part of, his own spiritual experience. They exerted their first considerable influence on others through his sermons as Vicar of St Mary's. Though he appears to have had few of the arts of a popular preacher, he drew large congregations of undergraduates and senior members of the university. His published sermons show that his style was usually simple and direct, but that his demands on his hearers and the standards of Christian life which he set before them were both high. He preached for those who were conscious of the reality of a spiritual world and he preached the received doctrines of the Church of England. But he preached those doctrines as awe-ful truths, and he challenged those who were familiar with the language of the Book of Common Prayer to press beyond a conventional acceptance of the language and to come to terms with the realities of it. Such realities – the doctrines of God and the incarnation; of human sin and salvation; of the Church and the sacraments – may not always be easy to grasp intellectually, they are of the 'mysteries' of faith, but they are none the less real. A proper grasp of them, and a proper response to them, demands humility, spiritual commitment and holiness of life. The sermons show great insight into spiritual life and they have been of great value to many who were troubled and seeking certainty as Newman was. Yet they show little, if any, understanding of the non-religious mind, of those who could not believe at all, or who did not see roughly the same questions in roughly the same order of importance as Newman saw them.

Newman had a profound sense of being 'set apart', which he later saw as, in part at least, a divine call to a life of celibacy. It is in this intensely personal religious quest that he works and, as we have seen, it is a quest for certainty of dogma – for him, religion without such clear dogma to which a man can commit himself unreservedly is alien. Such clear dogma, he believes, *must* have been committed by Christ to his Church. It is the possession of such dogma, together with a spiritual appropriation of the religious experiences enshrined in it or based upon it, which mark out the true Catholic Church.

Such a man must oppose liberalism as well as the possibility of state interference in the spiritual affairs of the Church. He could not for long have been satisfied with the rather cool intellectualism of men like Whateley, and he was naturally attracted to the sacramentalism and High Churchmanship of Froude. In the winter of 1832 he set off on a Mediterranean holiday with the Froude family. He ostentatiously turned his back on the French tricolour, symbol of liberalism in all its forms, but was touched by the simplicity and warmth of the Catholic devotion which he found in Malta. While he regarded much of the outward show as superstitious, he was drawn to the richness of sacramental devotion, to the sense of the nearness of the spiritual world and to the feeling of continuity and strength which he sensed in Roman Catholicism. He returned from this journey to be enlisted by Hurrell Froude, who had returned earlier, in what they took to be a defence of the integrity of the Church of England. At this time Newman had no doubt about the catholicity of the Church of England, nor that its bishops were the true successors of the apostles. In this mood, in the first of the Tracts, he reminded his fellow-priests – to whom the tract was addressed – of what he saw as the true ground of their spiritual claims: 'There are some who rest their divine mission on their own unsupported assertion; others, who rest it upon their popularity; others on their success; and others, who rest it upon their temporal distinctions. This last case has, perhaps, been too much our own; I fear we have neglected the real ground on which our authority is built – OUR APOSTO-LICAL DESCENT ... The Lord Jesus Christ gave his spirit to his apostles (cf. John 20.22); they in turn laid their hands on those who should succeed them; and these again on others; and so the sacred gift has been handed down to our present bishops, who have appointed us as their assistants, and in some sense representatives.' Of the bishops themselves he commented, 'we could not wish them a more blessed termination of their course than the spoiling of their goods and martyrdom.'[7]

His published works from this time, especially *Lectures on the Prophetical Office of the Church* (1837) and his *Lectures on Justification* (1838), present the Church of England as the true Catholic Church of the nation. They are hostile both to Dissent and to Rome and see Anglicanism as a *via media* between the two extreme positions. However, the Church of England in general, and the bishops in particular, increasingly refused to accept the roles for which Newman had cast them, and which the logic of his position demanded. Newman himself became disillusioned and began to be concerned with the question of the possible development of doctrine. Once he was able to see that those features of Roman Catholicism which he had previously held to be inconsistent with Scripture, or with the teaching of the early Fathers, could never-theless be accepted as proper developments of that teaching, the way to joining the Church of Rome was open to him.

Together with Keble and Newman the third great name to be associated with the Oxford Movement is that of Pusey. From the late 1830s 'Puseyism' became a popular name for the movement, especially among its detractors, but it is worth noting that Pusey was not one of the first promoters of it.

Edward Bouverie Pusey (1800–82) was perhaps even less fitted by nature for the leadership of a party than was Keble. His two greatest characteristics were his learning and his humble piety. He was one of the few Englishmen of his time to be fluent in German and to have studied theology in Germany. As a young man he attempted to interpret German theological movements to his contemporaries, but later he gave up the attempt. His theological position became increasingly conservative and he was content simply to expound the traditional doctrines which he found in the

Fathers. It was said of him that he wrote like a Greek Father of the fourth century. By the age of twenty-nine he was Regius Professor of Hebrew and Canon of Christ Church, Oxford, and there he remained for the rest of his life. His learning in terms of Semitic languages and Patristic Studies was prodigious, but he increasingly shut himself off from critical biblical studies and from the work of other scholars.

This seclusion was part of his piety. Following the death of his wife in 1839 he lived a semi-monastic life. He practised extreme asceticism, fasting regularly, walking always with downcast eyes, refusing to smile as a matter of principle and giving much time to prayer, contemplation and confession. Later writers have sometimes seen something pathological in Pusey's humility. Those who knew him loved and admired him. Young men who were attracted by his theology and churchmanship came to value him as a friend and confessor. He did not seek to impose his own disciplines on others, but was a keen supporter of the growth in religious communities, especially for women, which later became a feature of the movement. Coming from a relatively well-to-do family he was a generous benefactor of many worthy causes and particularly of plans to build new churches in growing industrial areas.

Pusey, as we have noted, was not at first involved in the plans to form an association to defend the Church of England, nor in the publication of the first Tracts. He did, however, encourage the circulation of the Tracts. In late 1833 he contributed a Tract, No. 17, on Fasting. It was unlike the previous ones in at least two ways. For the first time the author was identified by his initials. It may be that Pusey not only wished to acknowledge his own work, but was also keen to distinguish himself from the movement generally. This Tract also differed from previous ones in length. Whereas Newman had stirred and shocked by brief, trenchant pamphlets, Pusey impressed by the sheer weight of his learning. This was even more apparent in his contribution on Baptism which was about 400 pages in length and was published in three parts (Tracts 77, 78, 79).

Apart from his learning Pusey's chief contribution to the movement at the early stage was the dignity and authority of his position and his reputation. Newman commented, 'He at once gave to us a position and a name. Without him we should have had no chance, especially at the early date of 1834, of making any serious resistance to the Liberal aggression. But Dr Pusey was a Professor and Canon of Christ Church; he had a vast influence in consequence of his deep religious seriousness, the munificence of his charities, his Professorship, his family connections, and his easy relations with University authorities.'[8] Later, as some of the more extreme supporters followed Newman to Rome, Pusey's steadiness comforted many waverers and, though he had to bear much criticism, his devotion could not be denied and probably silenced some who would have been even more critical.

Basic Teaching

We have noted some of the teachings characteristic of the movement. There is the central stress on the nature of the Church as a divine institution free from interference by the state; the appeal to the Fathers and the sense of continuity with the Church of the first centuries; the stress on Apostolic Succession and the importance of priesthood as an order; and there is the stress on the sacraments and a life of discipline and devotion. It is interesting to note that these doctrines were theoretically held by those whom we have described as the High Church party. But that group inspired little response, either of support or opposition, from the majority of their contemporaries. The Oxford Movement can be seen as partly a revival within that High Church party, but the question must be raised: What did the group around Keble, Newman and Pusey have, or teach, which was lacking in the older representatives of the party? Why did the movement of the 1830s attract such attention and prove so effective?

The answer must lie partly in the political and social background of the time. Partly too it must lie in the personalities of the leaders. Much more important than either of these, however, is the question of the spiritual depth at which they operated. The older High Church men had presented their doctrines as intellectual propositions which they held to be true and about which they were willing to argue. Newman and his colleagues were by no means indifferent to intellectual arguments, but the real thrust, the appeal, of their position was not there. They knew that real religion must operate also at the level of the heart, the emotions and the will. In this they were clearly in line with the mood of Romanticism which was so powerful in the literature and general philosophy of their day, but they were not simply adapting their religion to contemporary trends, they spoke from their own feelings and experience.

When they appealed to the Fathers and the liturgies of the early Church they were not bringing forward intellectual arguments from dead philosophers with which they happened to agree. They appealed to the Fathers as part of the Church, in doctrine the normative part, to which they also belonged; and they appealed to the Church of the present as the essential vehicle of contact with the spiritual and the eternal. This all came as a shock to their contemporaries. It stood out from the other options available – the dry appeal to the Fathers by the High Church party; the unemotional moralism of the Low Church; and the rather stereotyped gospel preaching and soft pietism which had become common among the Evangelicals. In contrast they appealed to mystery and experience.

In all this they were aware of the paradoxical two-sided nature of deep religious experience. There must be a sense of awe and fear, a sense of the majesty and distance of God. But at the same time, and without denying what has just been said, there must be a sense of closeness, confidence and peace, a sense of communion with God. The awareness of this paradox was not new with the Oxford Movement, neither is it likely that they worked it out as an intellectual plan, but it is a feature of their work.

There must be a sense of awe and fear. The Oxford Movement reminded men of God as mysterious, high and lifted up, of purer eyes than to behold iniquity. The creator and judge of all the earth is not to be reduced to the end product of man's intellectual arguments. Thus there is a sense of the mystery of God. The word 'mystery' is a favourite with them. They use it in the sense of a truth which is revealed to faith, not merely as something which is puzzling to the human intellect. In this sense the 'mysteries' of religion are beyond human understanding, but they are not vague and uncertain. They are as certain and reliable as the true God who reveals them, but they can only be known in experience, through faith and personal commitment.

With such a conception of God, sin matters and judgement is real. The concept of eternal punishment was accepted. What is involved here, however, is not a judgement on man's opinions alone, or even, chiefly, on his deeds. It is rather his character, the sort of person he is in relation to God, which is important. Thus the preacher, and even more the parish priest, while he will not ignore his hearers' or parishioners' views, is much more concerned with promoting holiness of life. Such holiness is not merely outward. Hence there is in their writings a strong note of moral earnestness in face of the deep things of God.

This strand in their teaching led them to some criticism of Evangelical thinking, as they understood it, and to one of the fiercest disputes which the movement caused. It seemed to those who were inclined to stress the mystery of God and of his ways with the world that the typical Evangelical stress on the cross and the doctrine of atonement was lacking in reverence. In two of the Tracts (80 and 87), *Isaac Williams* (1802–65) wrote *On Reserve in the Communication of Religious Knowledge*. He was critical of the Evangelicals for what he saw as a one-sided stress on atonement which threw the whole pattern of Christian doctrine out of balance, and he accused them of ignoring other doctrines. Behind this was a sensitive nature which was hurt by what he saw as their undue familiarity with holy things, and a pastoral concern which believed that men and women at different stages of spiritual understanding need to be approached in different ways. Above all he thought it was cheapening the wonder of what God had done through the cross that it should be handled lightly in slogans, and that a stress on the cross should be accompanied by teaching on repentance and discipline.

For their part the Evangelicals denied the charge which was made against them, but assumed that Williams, and the Tract writers generally, were in favour of permanently holding back some of the promises of God for a spiritual élite. The whole approach seemed to them to tend towards their understanding of Roman priestcraft as dabbling in secrets and dividing Christians into first and second class citizens in the Kingdom of God. It may be that neither side fully understood the other, and that both were willing to judge the other party by its least commendable members and characteristics.

The teaching of the Oxford Movement also spoke of a sense of closeness and communion with God. As God is moral so man, made in his image, is also moral. It is the proper end of man's nature to find communion with God. Sin has so disrupted that communion that man can hardly imagine what it would be like, but it remains his true good and he has occasional intimations of it. In the fullest sense such communion with God lies in the future, beyond this life, but even fallen man can have some genuine foretaste of it in his present communion with the Church and particularly through the sacraments.

This is a genuinely high view of the Church. It is not that High Churchmanship which magnifies the Church's political role, but it attributes to the Church a high spiritual value and magnifies its spiritual role. It is to see the Church as continuing the work of Jesus during the incarnation of bringing God to man and, on God's behalf, asking for repentance and offering forgiveness and direction. Within the Church the priest, by virtue of his peculiar status, and the sacraments as peculiar vehicles of grace, make this presence, offer and direction of God available to individuals. Man for his part is to make use of what God has provided and thus share the communion with him which is available. To do this he is called to a life of obedience and a struggle for holiness within the communion of the Church.

Such emphases led to disputes with Evangelicals on at least two grounds. The typical Evangelical stress was far more individualistic. The Evangelical stressed the individual's personal relationship with God through faith and was suspicious of anything which seemed to get in the way of that. Particularly Evangelicals were wary of such a stress on the Church, which seemed to them to veer to Romanism.

At a more basic level there was a dispute about the nature and means of justification. It was most important for the Evangelical to argue that man was put right with God (justified) purely by grace, and that the sinner himself added nothing to this act. He simply accepted by faith what had been done for him. In technical terms the righteousness of Christ was *imputed* to the sinner at conversion. It really remained Christ's righteousness to which man, of himself, had no claim. In apparent contrast to this, Newman and his supporters insisted on holiness of life in such a way that it seemed to their opponents that justification was being earned by works. Much of the language they used seems to support this criticism, but it is likely that they were in fact using a different notion of grace. For the Evangelical grace is God's will, a decision which he makes and effects through Christ. For their opponents it is God's assistance to men which is available even before conversion to those who ask for it and co-operate with it. The advantage for Newman is that he can argue for a new quality of life in the believer. In technical terms the righteousness of Christ is *imparted* to the sinner continually through his life in the Church. In his *Lectures on the Doctrine of Justification* (1838) Newman reviews various approaches to the subject and argues that his own position is that of the Church of England, and that it steers a middle course between what he sees as the errors of Rome on the one hand and extreme Protestantism on the other.

Progress and Effects of the Movement

When the first Tracts appeared they were warmly received in some quarters as expressing what many thought. Pusey commented, 'The Tracts found an echo everywhere. Friends started up like armed men from the ground. I only dreaded our becoming too popular.'[9] We have noted some reasons for this popularity. As time passed and more Tracts appeared many of those who were committed to the movement became even more passionate in their adherence. Others, including some who had at first been willing to welcome the movement, or at least to suspend judgement, became hostile. In the minds of its critics the movement was over censorious and unnecessarily combative. There seemed also to be a decided and inevitable drift to Rome.

In 1836 R. D. Hampden (1793–1866) was nominated Regius Professor of Divinity at Oxford. The nomination was opposed by some for political reasons. Keble, Newman and Pusey opposed it because they distrusted Hampden for his supposed sympathy to Dissenters and for his theological liberalism. Their opposition failed, but they had appeared small-minded and their reputation had been damaged.

On a more obviously theological level we have noted that the publication of Froude's *Remains* (1838) had caused criticism of their Roman tendencies and their hostile attitude to the Reformation. A number of the Tracts, especially Pusey's, also seemed to lean towards Roman Catholicism and were criticized for that reason. In 1841 came the, for them, most disastrous publication of all, Tract 90. In this Newman set out to show that the Thirty Nine Articles, theoretically the doctrinal standard of the Church of England, were not anti-Catholic.

The Thirty Nine Articles were published in their final form in 1570. They were intended to unite the Elizabethan church and it had always been acknowledged that they allowed some liberty of interpretation. In subsequent years that liberty had been extended in practice but without formal acknowledgement. However Newman's treatment of them – even allowing for the fact that for him the word 'Catholic' did not yet mean 'Roman Catholic' – was offensive to many of his fellow churchmen. Broadly he admitted that the articles were not suitable for the Church of his own day, and that they had been intentionally uncatholic in their own day. Nevertheless, he argued that a strict interpretation of the actual words did not rule out Catholic belief. His attempt was seen as an attack on the Protestant nature of the Church of England, and his opponents accused him of dishonesty and deviousness in his use of words. Even allowing for some intended vagueness in the Articles themselves, it is hard not to agree with his opponents.

Following Tract 90 both the University and the bishops began to move against the Tractarians. Later in 1841 Newman opposed the idea of a joint Anglican-Lutheran Bishopric of Jerusalem. That merely strengthened the view that he was truculent and censorious without materially affecting his position. His own bishop, Bagot of Oxford, asked that no further Tracts should be published. In 1843 Newman moved from Oxford to the village of Littlemore on its northern outskirts where he lived in a small monastic community with a few friends and disciples. Finally, on, October 1845, he became a Roman Catholic.

Though October 1845 was a great landmark for the movement, many would say the end of it, at least as far as it could properly be called the Oxford Movement, it had in fact been without Newman's effective leadership for the previous two years. During those years others had made the Romeward tendency of the movement more pronounced. There had also begun a stress on ceremonial, though the extreme ritualism which is popularly associated with the movement comes rather later. Among the new leaders *W. G. Ward* (1812–82), of Balliol College, was probably the most extreme in his Romanism. His *The Ideal of a Christian Church* (1844) explicitly named Rome as the ideal, and he boasted that he believed all Roman teachings while remaining within the Church of England. Ward was stripped of his degrees and he joined the Roman Church, also in 1845. Both his behaviour, which appeared eccentric and attention seeking, and the attacks upon him were an embarrassment to the movement. It was a tribute to the personal influence of Keble and Pusey that more of their supporters did not follow Newman to Rome and that so many of the characteristic emphases of the movement remained within the Church of England.

Turning to the effects of the movement some are obvious and easily stated. The most immediate was a revival of religious and theological debate within the Church of England. In this way both admirers and opponents were affected. Within this there was a recovery of interest in the doctrine of the Church as an institution. This involved a recovery of the experience of being within the Church, coupled with a retreat from the excessive individualism of previous years. Parallel with the contemporary movement of Romanticism, though not necessarily dependent upon it, there was a recovery of warmth and feeling in religion.

At a more contentious level the Oxford Movement forced the Church of England to look again at the question of authority, and thereby to consider its role as a Catholic church, though not a Roman one. During his Anglican period Newman had made much of what he took to be the typical Anglican appeal to the Scriptures and the teaching of the Fathers of the first four centuries, what he called the period of the undivided Church. From this standpoint he had challenged both Roman Catholics and Protestants to justify their doctrines (a line of argument, incidentally, which had been used in the form of a 'Challenge Sermon' by Bishop Jewell in the Elizabethan period). In taking this line Newman had forced the Church of England to ask itself whether it was to take its stand with the Reformed Churches of Europe which appealed, in theory at least, to Scripture alone, or, if not, what status it would give to the Fathers and to Christian tradition. Most obviously there arose the question of Apostolic Succession and the status of the priesthood, questions which continue to face the Church of England in the ecumenical debates of the late twentieth century.

Almost as a by-product there was a renewal of interest in church architecture. This was a natural development of the move towards sacramental worship and the greater interest in symbolism which the movement encouraged. As long as Christian congregations were encouraged to regard the sermon as the central act of a service of worship, and saw that as directed to their minds and wills, a central pulpit in a bare meeting house might be adequate. But, as the Tractarians moved the activity of the priest as celebrant at the Eucharist to the centre of interest, and particularly as they stressed the place of mystery and the symbolism of actions and furnishings with a greater appeal to emotion and imagination, the different emphases had to be recognized in the shape and decoration of church buildings.

The leading figure in this development was *J. M. Neale* (1818–66), a Cambridge man. Neale founded the Cambridge Camden Society in 1839. Through its journal, *The Ecclesiologist*, the society aimed to restore medieval principles of architecture which, its members believed, preserved the best principles of sacramental worship. Since the mid nineteenth century saw a great movement to build more churches to meet the needs of the rapidly expanding urban population the time was ripe for them to put their ideas into action. As far as possible they wanted to sweep away the custom of reserved family pews for the wealthy, with its overtones of patronage of the church by the rich and powerful. More significant, for them, was the restoration of Gothic architecture, especially the decorated style, with its stress on the vertical dimension of worship. At the same time they encouraged anything which restored a sense of mystery and which might teach through symbolism, such as rood screens, stained glass windows, decorated woodwork, candles and, of course, colourful vestments. Much of this was soon to arouse the opposition of the Evangelicals who suspected a tendency to copy Rome.

On a more personal level the Oxford Movement clearly set before the clergy a pattern of spiritual and moral commitment more searching than they had known for several generations. Many learned to take their priestly role as mediators between God and man far more seriously than had become the custom. Services were more regular and more reverently conducted, with a greater prominence given to the sacraments. Pastoral duties were undertaken more scrupulously and the practice of confession was frequently introduced – another offence to the Evangelicals.

A further indication of a deeper religious seriousness was the founding of a number of Anglican religious orders. A movement which consciously looked back to the Middle Ages and sought to practise religious discipline would naturally be attracted to the idea of Christian community life under something like a monastic rule. The group which lived with Newman at Littlemore from 1842 may be seen as a forerunner. Later, with the encouragement of Pusey, a number of communities were founded. It was Pusey's hope that some parish churches would develop as centres of communities for priests. As we shall note later, there was some success in a number of slum parishes, but these were more like orders of mission priests. Much more successful were the communities for women such as that founded at Park Village West, in London, at Easter 1845 under Pusey's spiritual direction, and the Society of the Most Holy Trinity founded by Priscilla Lydia Sellon at Devonport in 1848. These communities, or sisterhoods, gave the opportunity for women to live in community following an ordered religious life. In the main they were not cut off from the world, but engaged in nursing, teaching and various charitable works, often in the most difficult circumstances and among the poorest of the people, as part of their Christian vocation.

Among the obvious weaknesses of the movement was the fact that it appealed mainly to the educated classes, and among them chiefly to clergy. There was a danger that it would, though doubtless unintentionally, downgrade the apparent worth of the life of the devout Christian layman. Furthermore, in its appeal to the educated it could be presented as always asking them to look backwards and as presenting a romantically distorted version of the pre-Reformation Church. It did not obviously have anything to say to the masses of working people in the growing industrial cities for whom all religious questions were increasingly remote.

In time it did move from university circles into the parishes – first into the rural areas in which the old High Church party had always been strong, and then increasingly into the urban areas.

Had its original leaders been more conciliatory, more politically adroit, more in touch with the world, these wider influences might have come earlier. But it was their gift to influence by personality and quality of life. As it was, later in the century the immediate and more distant disciples and admirers of Keble, Newman and Pusey served the Church of England nobly in slum parishes and on the mission field as well as in the academic world. But those are considerations for later chapters.

Notes

1   J. H. Newman, *Apologia Pro Vita Sua* (Fontana 1959), p. 132.
2   ibid., p. 108.
3   ibid., p. 105.
4   ibid., pp. 114 f.
5   ibid., p. 97.
6   ibid., p. 132.
7   Tract 1. The whole text is printed in E. R. Fairweather, ed., *The Oxford Movement* (New York, Oxford University Press 1964), pp. 55–9.
8   op. cit., p. 141.
9   cited A. R. Vidler, *The Church in an Age of Revolution* (Penguin 1961), p. 52.

3
The Church and Social Problems

While the University of Oxford and much of the religious and intellectual world of nineteenth-century England was concerned with the teaching of the Oxford Movement, the 'defections' of some of its leaders and others to Rome, and the general development of Tractarianism, another world had come into being among the poor and the labouring classes, especially in London and the growing manufacturing towns and major seaports. In that other world the concerns of Newman and his friends were largely meaningless and apparently irrelevant. There men and women were grappling with harsher and seemingly much more real problems.

Social upheaval

Throughout the century official and unofficial reports presented a grim picture of grinding poverty, hard and often dangerous work, overcrowded and insanitary living conditions, disease, malnutrition and crime. Lord Shaftesbury harangued the House of Lords on the plight of women and children working twelve hours a day, often with dangerous and unguarded machinery and in poorly ventilated conditions. The Report of the Select Committee on the Health of Towns (1840) and the Report on the Sanitary condition of the Labouring poor (1842) spoke of crowded lodging houses, sometimes with whole families living and sleeping in one small attic or cellar, and inadequate sewage – one lavatory to forty houses was apparently quite normal. In case of death the body was often kept in the room because relatives could not afford a coffin and simply did not know how to dispose of it or get it removed. In any case the cemeteries of the growing towns were unable to meet the demands of overcrowding and became such a hazard to health that by the Public Health Act (1848) and the Cemetery Acts (1852 and

36

1853) the government was compelled to close many of them. Rubbish was thrown into the streets to rot, and the provision of water was sometimes even in private hands and dispensed at profit. In such circumstances outbreaks of disease were common, and cholera, smallpox and typhus sometimes reached epidemic proportions in the large cities. Among the unofficial records one of the most passionate and widely quoted was an anonymous penny pamphlet entitled *The Bitter Cry of Outcast London* which appeared in October 1883. Its author was probably Andrew Mearns, the secretary of the London Congregational Union. Its opening words may be taken as a summary of the situation from a Christian point of view: 'Whilst we have been building our churches and solacing ourselves with our religion and dreaming that the millennium was coming, the poor have been growing poorer, and the wretched more miserable, and the immoral more corrupt. The gulf has been daily widening which separates the lowest classes of the community from our churches and chapels, and from all decency and civilisation.' It goes on to point out that, in spite of some valiant efforts to counter it, 'We must face the facts, and these compel the conviction that *this terrible flood of sin and misery is gaining upon us. It is rising every day.*'

Material poverty and distress were, almost inevitably, accompanied by an increase in drunkenness and crime. It has been commented that 'the quickest way out of Manchester is through the door of the public house', and, in view of the prevailing conditions, it is not surprising that many in Manchester and elsewhere took that route. Petty crime, usually stealing for immediate gain, was equally an obvious means of seeking to escape desperate poverty. Occasionally the poor resorted to mob action, almost it seems from desperation. Sometimes the actions of the mobs were orchestrated by the Chartists and others for political ends, but this was probably not very common. The very poor were usually too dejected to consider long-term political ends and too concerned with their own immediate distress to unite for action.

The reasons for such extreme social problems are complex. At least four closely interrelated causes may be mentioned. First, the nineteenth century saw an immense growth in the population. Malthus' *Essay on Population* in 1798 had warned that the population was growing faster than the means to feed it. The population of England had doubled in the Hanoverian period and did so again in the Victorian era, rising from about five and a half million in 1700 to about twenty-nine million in 1900. For our period the end of the Napoleonic Wars not only removed a crude but effective means of population control but also, through the return of men from the army, added to the numbers of those seeking employment.

Secondly, the movement known as the industrial revolution, already well into motion as the century began, became its dominant influence. The arrival of machinery deprived many small craftsmen of their livelihood and decreased the number of labourers needed, at least in some trades. More positively it made England the centre of the industrial and commercial world. The development of railways and canals made possible the rapid movement of people and goods within the country, while the Empire and the Merchant Navy provided a world dimension to English trade.

Thirdly, largely because of the industrial revolution, this was the period of urbanization. England began the nineteenth century as still largely a rural society, but by the end it was largely an urban one. It is estimated that by 1850 only 22% of the working population was engaged in agriculture, and by 1900 this figure had dropped to 9%. It must have seemed natural for the unemployed rural worker to move into the growing towns where the new factories needed 'hands'. But the move was accompanied by the breakdown of familiar social patterns. The village life which had been left behind should not be falsely idealized. Agricultural work was hard and not always well rewarded, and village life had its social gradations. Nevertheless even the poor had had a place in such societies, and the Poor Law, which until 1834 was still operating on a statute of 1601, was framed with a rural economy in mind and was based on the parish system. The new manufacturing towns and the major seaports grew rapidly and without planning; the parish system was irrelevant within them as the sheer number of people involved overwhelmed a system devised to deal with much smaller numbers.

Finally, this was the period of *laissez-faire* economics. It was widely believed that the laws of supply and demand and the freedom of the individual were sacrosanct, and that to interfere with them would cause more problems than it solved. For this argument, if matters were left alone they would find their own level – enough goods would be produced to meet the demand for them and if too many were produced the price would fall. On the human front it was argued that a labourer could sell his labour or skill to those who needed it and that if it was not needed he could learn another one. This harsh and simplistic philosophy gradually gave way as the century progressed and the sheer enormity of the need and the distress of the poor became known. Nevertheless the individualism at the heart of it, and the suspicion that the poor were poor because they would not work, and that the recipients of charity were 'sponging' on the benevolence of others rather than helping themselves, persisted. One manifestation of it was the heartless and tasteless display of wealth by some of the 'new rich' represented by some factory owners and prosperous merchants who were ostentatious in their display of luxury.

The Churches were unprepared for the growth and movement of the population, and for the rapid development of the slums – then picturesquely described as 'rookeries'. It is sometimes suggested that at some undefined period the Church, or Churches, 'lost the working classes'. The truth is that, in spite of heroic and sacrificial efforts by some individuals and groups, neither the Church of England nor the older Nonconformist bodies could ever claim to have much hold on the poor in the new towns.

In the village, church or chapel was a centre of social as well as religious life and attendance at worship was habitual. The vicar or minister knew his flock and was known by them. Such circumstances never prevailed in the towns where both buildings and clergy were often lacking. Labourers who moved from village to town and who wanted the spiritual or social benefits which church or chapel had provided had to make a positive effort to seek them. When they did so they often found the social atmosphere was strange to them. In the towns it had never become customary for working people to attend any form of worship in great numbers. Most of those who moved from village to town soon lost the habit, most of those born in the town never acquired it. What was involved was not so much a loss, or change, of belief as a loss, or change, of habit caused by environment. Those on the social scale below the skilled artisans or the middle classes simply did not usually attend any place of worship. The working people and the very poor were a mission field which organized institutional Christianity rarely reached.

The Church of England was hampered by the parish system and an outlook more suited to rural conditions. The parish system as it existed in the first part of the century was not suited to such density of population, and the provision of many more churches in the second half of the century was too late to be effective. The clergy were usually related by family education and general outlook to the upper classes and had difficulty relating to the slum dweller. The autocratic, paternalist, style which could be successful for a country vicar dealing with farm labourers and secure in the support of the local squire was inappropriate in the new conditions. That some clergy did manage to bridge the gap was a considerable achievement.

The older Nonconformists, the Presbyterians, Congregationalists and Baptists, were not tied to the parish system and might have been expected to be more successful. They, however, tended to be middle class. Their chapels depended on the contributions of members, and the style of church government, involving lay people in the organization and direction of church life, demanded the ability to verbalize and organize. Neither the money nor the education were easily found among the very poor. The Baptists did better than the others and their tabernacles and mission halls were found in some poor areas. The Congregationalists on the other hand prided themselves on their middle-class status and seem genuinely to have believed that they had a mission to that stratum of society.

Of the major denominations only the Methodists, still genuinely evangelistic though growing nearer to the older Nonconformists, could claim some hold on the poor, at least in some places. The impact of Methodism on the mining communities of the North East and the South West was profound, and the practice of putting each member into a class, which involved among other things a small regular contribution which might be used for the relief of the poor, has some place in the history of the development of the Welfare State.

In some cases, notably in Liverpool, the Roman Catholic Church kept a hold on the Irish working class immigrants.

However Roman Catholics were still generally outside the mainstream of English social life.

The potential of the Church to combat serious social problems was limited by the excessive individualism of most of its theology, especially among the Evangelicals. For Evangelicals the chief concern was the individual's relation to God. On the one hand this led them to great concern for individual souls and, as they became aware of the distress and need of many of their fellow-citizens, philanthropy became central to the Evangelical life-style. However, on the other hand, they did not usually ask whether there were underlying social causes for the distress which they sought to ameliorate. Thus they were moved by the plight of factory workers, drunkards, orphans, prostitutes, the sick and many other suffering groups; but they were more concerned to help the individual and his family than to change the political system which produced the evils. Broadly speaking, they believed that individual salvation would be the beginning of social reform, and that as individuals adopted the life which God intended for them their material circumstances would improve. Many instances of dramatic conversion followed by social improvement seemed to support their argument. But there were also many instances where men and women wanted to live godly, virtuous and sober lives but were simply overwhelmed by their circumstances.

Nevertheless the achievements of individual Christians from the Evangelical school in improving social conditions should not be overlooked. The most prominent among them was *Lord Ashley,* later *Earl of Shaftesbury* (1801–85). A Tory aristocrat of determined Evangelical convictions, Shaftesbury sacrificed the political honours which he would have loved, and which would probably have come to him through his ability and his family connections, to dedicate his life both to the spread of his religious views and to social reform. He is best known for his advocacy of shorter working hours in factories, leading to the Ten Hours Act of 1847. In addition he was also active on behalf of lunatics, cripples, the blind and many other weak and disadvantaged groups. Neither was he slow to criticize British treatment of native labourers in India or British profit from the opium trade. Other names worthy of note are *Dr T. J. Barnardo* (1845–1905) the founder of orphanages; the

Rev. Benjamin Waugh (1839–1908), the South London Congregational minister who was instrumental in the founding of the
National Society for the Prevention of Cruelty to Children; and
Josephine Butler (1828–1906) who campaigned for the rights, as
well as the reformation, of prostitutes.

The Slum Ritualists

From the 1840s the Tractarian priest working in a slum parish
became a feature of English religious life. This meant a reworking
of the Tractarian ideal. The ideal picture of the parish priest
ministering to the flock which he knew, and encouraging among
them a deeper earnestness in accepted religious practices, was out
of place in the slums. Church attendance never became habitual for
most of the urban working classes. Instead there developed an
alienation from clergymen and established religion. It was not that
the majority of working-class people were consciously opposed to
Christianity. It was rather that they saw the clergy as representing
the wealthy and the factory owners, and thus as having a vested
interest in social inequality. For their part few clergy were willing
or able to adapt to the life of the slums. Among those who did were
a number of Tractarians who earned respect for their devotion and
who, almost incidentally, earned for the Tractarian movement its
reputation for excessive ritualism.

The increase in the number of men of Tractarian sympathies
being ordained, and the parallel increase in the number of
churches built in the new cities, would inevitably have meant that a
considerable number of young Anglo-Catholics worked in slum
parishes. Since, in spite of the Oxford Movement, or because of it,
ritualism was still suspect in the Church of England, most of those
who were keen to introduce it into worship were unwelcome in
more established parishes. Thus the Tractarian curate in a slum
parish became something of a tradition. Often the inevitability of
such a parish was welcomed as a sphere of service and witness. The
theology of the movement stressed the incarnation of Christ as
God's amazing condescension to mankind. It was a natural coroll-
ary that his representatives should also be seen to throw in their lot
with the poorest and meanest elements in society.

It was accepted that the clergy were bound by their ordination
vows to visit the sick and care for the needy. The tradition of the

Church of England had made it natural that the vicar should be concerned with the material as well as the spiritual welfare of his parishioners. By their performance of these duties in the slums a number of Anglo-Catholic priests earned the respect of their people, and a number of parishes came to be known as strongholds of Anglo-Catholicism. In London during the 1850s and 1860s Charles Lowder and Alexander Mackonochie worked sacrificially at St George's-in-the-East, a church which served an area of dockland notorious for its poverty and immorality. At St Saviour's in Leeds, a church built by the generosity of Pusey, a community of celibate priests established soup kitchens, provided other material relief for the poor of the city, and earned the gratitude of the poor for their ministry to the sick and dying during the cholera epidemic of 1849. George Rundle Prynne in Plymouth and, slightly later, Robert Dolling in Portsmouth did similar work.

Such parishes shared two characteristics. The priests lived a community life. Pusey, who encouraged his followers to work in slum areas, strongly urged the formation of such communities both for the greater effectiveness of their work and for the spiritual development of the members. This move was copied both from the Roman Catholic religious communities and from experience on the mission field. It was in effect a recognition that the Church in the slums was in a missionary situation.

A second and more obvious characteristic was the stress on the centrality of the sacraments, especially the Eucharist, and the ritual which came to accompany it. Eucharistic worship was central to the lives of the communities of priests. In Plymouth, during the cholera epidemic of 1849, Prynne was assisted by the recently formed Sisters of Mercy who visited in the parish and helped to care for the sick. It was they who asked for a daily communion to strengthen them in their work. There, and in the similar situation in Leeds, provision was made for both communion and the possibility of sacramental confession for the dying. Such practices were unusual in the Church of England and led to accusations of popery.

But it was in the normal weekly services of the parish that ritual was most clearly seen and most vehemently opposed. The early Tractarians had spoken of reserve and had valued sobriety in all things. The slum priests were moved by different considerations.

They saw that the decent and orderly reading of the services of the Book of Common Prayer did not convey any sense of awe or feeling of worship to their small and largely illiterate congregations. They turned, therefore to ritual and the language of the senses. By means of movement and colour, by sung services, by processions, candles, vestments and incense they sought to inculcate reverence and give, amid the drabness of the slums, a sense of mystery and the worship of heaven. Furthermore they believed themselves to be both carrying on the work of the Oxford Movement in recovering the worship of the medieval Church, and not infringing the strict interpretation of the Book of Common Prayer. It is worth noting that Pusey himself gave no support to such activities. He did not care for ritual and his biographer noted that he even had to ask what a cope was.

To some observers the ritual practices which were introduced symbolized what they held to be false doctrine and a resurgence of Roman practices within the Church of England. To others they were merely an excuse for riots. Anti-ritualist riots occurred in several places, notably in St George's-in-the-East. Lowder and Mackonochie, whom we have mentioned, were curates. The rector was Bryan King, a staunch Tractarian, devout but unsuited to the area. His ritualistic innovations had disturbed some of his parishioners. A more moderate man might have compromised as many Tractarians did, but King refused to do so. The parishioners had the right to elect a 'Lecturer' and, in 1859, they elected a committed Protestant, Hugh Allen, who preached against the innovations. For about a year there were riots in the church each Sunday, ostensibly in support of the Protestant cause against ritualism. The mob interrupted the services by coughing, hissing and stamping. They slammed pew doors, set loose dogs which had been maddened by drugs and occasionally even attacked the clergy and choristors. Even after King had been persuaded to take a 'holiday', from which he did not return to the parish, the riots continued for some time.

St George's-in-the-East was not typical. However, events there, and some less serious disturbances in other places, persuaded Protestants that Anglo-Catholicism meant ritualism, and persuaded Anglo-Catholics that Protestantism was opposed to reverence in worship. Attempts were made to establish through the courts how much ritual was legally permitted in the Church of England. For the Anglo-Catholics such attempts were led by the English Church Union, established in 1856, and for the Protestants by the Church Association, established in 1865. However, such was the complexity, and perhaps the intentional broadness, of the Prayer Book rubrics, that all such attempts proved inconclusive. They did little to persuade the slum dwellers that either side had much to offer them.

F. D. Maurice and Christian Socialism

The work of the slum ritualists was deeply impressive in places. It drew the attention of churchmen to the conditions of the poor, but it did not greatly affect either Church or society. Anglo-Catholic clergy tended to be paternalistic and authoritarian. They taught and served their working-class parishioners, but they did little to produce working-class leaders. They did not provide any criticism of society as it was, nor try to draw upon their faith to put forward a different 'model' of society as they thought it ought to be. For such attempts we must look to the work of F. D. Maurice and the movement of Christian Socialism which looked back to him and which was found in various forms for most of the rest of our period.

Frederick Denison Maurice (1805–72) was one of the most influential and controversial Christian leaders of the nineteenth century. In his own day and since he has provoked widely differing estimates. To friends and admirers he is a prophetic thinker with an all-embracing theological vision. To critics he is a confused and muddled dreamer who gathered ideas from many sources but was unable to combine them into a coherent whole. But all agree that he inspired many of his contemporaries and that his influence was considerable.

From his own self-estimation Maurice was a theologian at heart and his theology informed all that he did. His involvement in the Christian Socialist movement was, for him, the natural expression of his theological principles in the social situation of his day.

Maurice's theology arose from his personal quest and was influenced by his own experience. He was the son of a Unitarian minister. In his youth he experienced both the exclusiveness of a small sect and the petty persecutions and social ostracism suffered by its members. Later he was an opponent of sectarianism and argued that no idea which has nourished the spiritual life of any individual or group can be totally without value. He saw his mother and his sisters, influenced by suffering and by the example of friends, move away from his father's faith. They were moved first to an appreciation of the compassion and friendship of Jesus and then to an acceptance of the orthodox understanding of his deity and of the Trinity. Though not without feeling, Maurice's own journey had a greater intellectual content. He was helped by his Cambridge tutor, later his brother-in-law, Julius Hare, and particularly by Hare's exposition of Plato. He grew dissatisfied with the Unitarian picture of God as a cold absolute reigning serenely above the struggles of humanity, and he speaks of his relief in the possibility of seeing in Jesus the incarnation of that principle in warm human terms.

Nevertheless, he keeps the strong Platonist sense of unity and of a unifying principle. For him God is everywhere and in everything. In language reminiscent of that later used by Paul Tillich, he speaks of God as the root or underlying ground of all things, 'He himself is the root from which all human life, and human society, and ultimately, through man, nature itself are derived.' Later, in the same letter to J. M. Ludlow, he explains that his own vocation 'is not to build, but to dig, to show that economics and politics . . . must have a ground beneath themselves, that society is not to be made anew by arrangements of ours, but is to be regenerated by finding the law and ground of its order and harmony, the only secret of its existence in God.'[1] In other words, Christian Socialists, like Christian theologians, were not, in his view, propounding anything new, they were simply discovering divine principles which were always true, whether men chose to see them or not, and seeking to live by them.

This basic theological position made him critical of the contemporary Evangelical position which satisfied his mother and sisters. He believed that the Evangelicals began in the wrong place, or from the wrong end. For Maurice the basic feature of the world and everything in it, especially mankind, is that God made it and that he made it basically good; through Christ God had restored the world to its right relationship to himself, because it was originally his. Maurice argued that the Evangelicals were wrong in starting their thinking from ideas of sin and the fall, because that made man's misuse of the world and his disobedience to God more important than God's original intention. In his view Christian preaching should not concentrate so much on rescuing individuals from their supposed fate, but rather on promoting a realization of the one-ness of humanity in Christ which already exists in principle. In other words, instead of beginning from the first Adam and the evil fruit of his disobedience, it should begin from Christ, the second Adam, and take seriously the change in the status of mankind and creation which he had brought about. Individual men may deny the work of Christ, and the attitudes and actions which arise from such a denial are serious, but such denials do not outweigh the truth of that work or make it less true. The grace of God is greater than the sin of man.

Signs or foretastes of the unity of humanity may be recognized, according to Maurice, in the divine institutions of the family and the nation. There men are trained and directed in earthly things and prepared for heaven. But the chief sign of the divine order is the Church. For Maurice the Church is the sphere in which men recognize God's presence, his claims upon them and his plans for them, and live accordingly. 'The World is the Church without God; the Church is the World restored to its relation to God, taken back by him into the state for which he created it.'[2] While there is a sense in which there is One Holy Catholic Church, it is manifested differently for each nation. The Church of England is the Catholic Church for the English nation.

As he worked out his theology Maurice had found his intellectual and spiritual home in the Church of England. His most important and lasting work, *The Kingdom of Christ* (1838), is an explanation and defence of the theological position of the Church of England as expressed in the Thirty Nine Articles, as Maurice understood it. The book is in the form of a series of letters to a Quaker in which the Church of England is compared with, and defended against, Roman Catholic and other Protestant positions. The chief argument is that the Church of England contains all that is best in those other positions, while they have to be maintained by excluding some other view which may contain something of value. He goes on to criticize not only all the main historical presentations of Christianity but also the various parties within the

47

Church of England. In each case he attempts to set out the truths for which they stand while arguing that their exclusiveness always denies some truth. He argues that theological parties are generally right in what they assert but wrong in what they deny.

Maurice became Chaplain of Lincoln's Inn and Professor of History and Theology at King's College, London. He had a comfortable and secure position within the ecclesiastical and social establishment of early Victorian England. The state of the poor and the idea of socialism must have seemed a long way away. Some Christian leaders, partly appalled at the suffering of the poor and partly frightened by the agitation of the Chartists and the Luddites, had been attracted by the concept of socialism as practised by Robert Owen in his New Lanark factory. However, when Owen appeared to come out against Christianity the attraction faded. When, in 1848, socialism seemed to lead to riots in Berlin and Paris, and even to an abortive march on London, it seemed clear that socialism was an evil force, destructive of society. In the same year Maurice became a socialist.

The instrument of his conversion to the cause was *J. M. Ludlow* (1821–1911) an English barrister born in India and educated in Paris. In Paris he had witnessed the risings of 1848 and the attempts to form communes. He persuaded Maurice that 'Socialism was a real and very great power ... and that it must be Christianised or it would shake Christianity to its foundations, precisely because it appealed to the higher and not to the lower instincts of men.'[3] The result was the 'Christian Socialist Movement'. In its early form the Movement lasted six years only (1848–54), but its influence lasted much longer.

Maurice and Ludlow gathered around them a group of like-minded friends. Among them was *Charles Kingsley* (1819–75), who under the *nom-de-plume* 'Parson Lot' was the popularizer of the group. Through a number of novels, such as *Alton Locke* (1850) and *Yeast* (1851), he drew attention to the plight of working people. Another was *Thomas Hughes* (1822–96), best known as author of *Tom Brown's Schooldays*. Hughes, who had been known in his youth as an amateur boxer, became Principal of the Working Men's College, perhaps the most enduring memorial of the movement, and was later a High Court Judge and a Member of Parliament. A friend from Maurice's early days in London was

Daniel Macmillan (1813–57) who, with his brother Alexander was later to establish the famous publishing firm. As early as 1841 Macmillan had approached Maurice with a view to persuading him to produce some clear and simple Christian teaching for those outside the Church. A slightly later member of the group was *Edward Vansittart Neale* (1810–92), the wealthiest of the group who poured large sums of money into their operations.

The group aimed to publicize the lot of the poor and to attempt to persuade the workers, including the Chartist leaders, that some churchmen sympathized with their aspirations. On 11 April 1848, the day after the failure of the proposed march on London, they published a placard addressed to the 'Workmen of England' assuring them of support and understanding. During the next month they began a series of tracts, consciously based on those produced by the Oxford Movement, called *Politics for the People* and dealing with the problems of the working men. Later they produced a series of *Tracts on Christian Socialism* and a journal under the title *Christian Socialist*. Gradually they broke down the suspicion of some of the Chartist leaders and of the working men. Maurice and his friends showed genuine sympathy and willingness to learn, and they found among the working men a deep respect for Christianity coupled with great hostility to the Church as an institution.

But more was needed than publicity and sympathy. They identified the root cause of low wages and unemployment as *laissez-faire* capitalism, with its appeal to profit and competition. In contrast, adopting ideas which Ludlow had learned from Louis Blanc in Paris, they set up associations of workers in various trades known as workers' co-operatives. An association of tailors was first, followed by others for shoemakers, bakers and needlewomen. More followed, and in January 1850 Maurice and his friends formed themselves into a *Society for Promoting Working Men's Associations*. He asserted that human society is a body of many members, not a collection of warring atoms, that workers must co-operate not compete, and that a principle of justice not selfishness must regulate exchanges.

Meanwhile Maurice, Kingsley and others were using every opportunity to put forward their views in the pulpit, often to the distress of fellow-clergymen. They had no difficulty in finding biblical texts criticizing the rich and urging justice for the poor. The decent ordered calm of many churches was disturbed by working men demanding that all clergy should preach in a similar vein. Sadly, the advocates of Christian Socialism too often antagonized those whom they wanted to convince because of their over enthusiasm and one-sidedness. Too many simply assumed that Christianity should be equated with socialism, that all Christian doctrine could be reduced to demands for Liberty, Equality and Fraternity, and that services of worship should be political meetings only. Maurice's opponents, a growing number, pointed out that a large number of the leaders of the working men were avowed atheists.

Interestingly it was Ludlow, the only real socialist thinker among them, who wanted to limit the Society of Promoters to Christians and who frequently reminded Maurice of the spiritual basis of their thinking. Maurice was uneasy in face of such criticisms. His basic theological position forced him to believe that there was some underlying presence of God in all men to which he could appeal, but he had no practical suggestions when there were divisions between members of the group as there often were between Ludlow and Neale.

For a time the co-operatives flourished, but one by one they failed. Sometimes their lives were lengthened by injections of money from Neale but they became unworkable on their original premisses. It had been unrealistic economically so to ignore the laws of supply and demand. The associations simply produced goods which they could not sell and so they could not pay wages. It had been unrealistic too to expect so much from producers' co-operatives working on such a small scale. They were better fitted to a pre-industrial age. Ludlow had spoken and written of action by the state, but this had been overlooked by his more optimistic friends. In fact those of the co-operatives which survived more than a few years did so by adopting competitive methods. The co-operatives of consumers, as opposed to producers, which are the forerunners of the modern co-operative movement, accepted the ethic of competition but adapted it to their own advantage.

Maurice was severely attacked for his activities and was eventually dismissed from his chair at King's. Articles in the religious and secular press poured scorn on his Christian Socialism and criticized his friendship with Kingsley, who was dismissed as a firebrand. They were accused of fomenting unrest and there were fears at King's for the good name of the College. Maurice defended himself vigorously, though not always clearly, in a long correspondence with the Principal, Dr Jelf, and a Committee of Inquiry cleared him of serious fault, though regretting that he had allowed his name to be connected with 'questionable publications'. It was the publication of his *Theological Essays* in 1852 which gave his enemies the weapon they had been looking for. One of the essays was a discussion of the traditional doctrine of eternal punishment for the wicked. Maurice pointed out that eternal, in its scriptural use, does not mean the same as everlasting, which was the usual understanding. He was accused of denying the doctrine altogether. That is, in fact, a possible interpretation of what he had written, though his meaning is not clear and he asserted that he did not want to deny the doctrine completely. Interestingly, he was not in fact dismissed for teaching false doctrine but because his opinions were 'calculated to unsettle the minds of the theological students at King's College'. Presumably it was thought that the doctrine of everlasting punishment was a stimulus to moral living which should not be removed. An attempt, led by W. E. Gladstone, to have the matter considered by a group of theologians rather than leaving the decision to the largely lay Council of King's was defeated in the Council.

Shortly after his dismissal from King's Maurice was appointed Principal of a proposed Working Men's College. He helped to draw up a scheme for its management and teaching, and it was officially opened in October 1854. It was probably the most effective effort of the Christian Socialist Movement. Maurice and his friends were teachers at heart, and often by profession. They gathered a most distinguished group to teach at the College. Those already around Maurice were joined by such figures as Ruskin, Alexander Munro, Brewer, Lowes Dickinson and D. G. Rossetti. Maurice was in his element. His son wrote, 'The name "college" attracted him greatly. It seemed to him to imply an association of men as men – an association not formed for some commercial purpose and not limited by coincidence of opinion, and to represent, therefore, that union which he was always striving to bring about.'[4] The students, though not always aware of the worth of their teachers, set a high value on learning and were keen to learn. Many, too, had higher than average intellectual gifts and responded to the unpatronizingly high standard of material offered to them. Both the cultural and social side of the College flourished. In time students were introduced to the governing body and the essential equality and unity which Maurice had taught for so long was, in part at least, realized. Later, however, we find Ludlow complaining that the College had lost its distinctively Christian base and tone, and that Maurice was failing to give strong spiritual leadership.

As their attention moved to the College, and to other educational interests, the original group seem to have lost interest in the workers' co-operatives, which either changed their character or failed. Thus it can be argued that Christian Socialism itself, at least in this phase, failed. Maurice and his friends can be dismissed as a group of fairly rich, high-minded, Christians who were basically too unworldly to make much impression on the needs of the poor. More hostile critics could say that they were merely hypocritically 'buying off' their consciences.

However the successes of this early phase, and those which flowed from it, should not be overlooked. They had drawn attention to the needs of working men and had aroused a sense of responsibility and compassion in many churchmen. They had established relations between at least some of the leaders of the working men and some churchmen. They had given the working men some vision of what they could achieve through co-operation, and though producers' co-operatives were to be replaced by co-operatives of consumers they had given an impetus to the co-operative movement. They had assisted, and continued to assist in the developing Trade Union movement. Perhaps their greatest achievement, though least measurable, was the vision they gave to others. It is remarkable how many Christians who later became leaders of various movements of social concern looked back, directly or indirectly, to the influence of Maurice.

The Settlement Movement

A later attempt to bridge the gap between the Church and the working-classes was the Settlement movement. Its exponents were not only concerned about the material and spiritual impoverishment of so many of their fellow citizens in the slums. They also recognized that few of the educated classes, even if they were sympathetic to the plight of the poor, had any real knowledge of working class life, and that offers to help were likely to appear patronizing and to be ill-directed. Settlements, therefore, had a twofold aim.

The usual pattern was the establishment of a large building in the poor area of a major city. This could be used as a centre for charitable work which would include the provision of educational and recreational facilities as well as the relief of poverty. It would also be used as an hostel for undergraduates, or men just down from university, who would both assist its charitable work and have the opportunity of seeing for themselves the living conditions of the slums.

The outstanding figure in the early history of the movement was *Samuel Barnett* (1844–1913), Vicar of St Jude's Whitechapel from 1872. Wealthy and well connected, Barnett attracted the support of some of the leading figures in Oxford for his social work in East London. One of them was the historian Arnold Toynbee and on Toynbee's death a Settlement was established and named after him as a memorial tribute. Toynbee Hall was opened in January 1885, with Barnett as its Warden and a number of young Oxford men living on the premises to act as his assistants. It became a centre for local activities, a meeting place for various working men's clubs and a base for Trade Union activities.

Barnett had insisted that Toynbee Hall should be open to Nonconformists as well as Anglicans. A number of other Settlements more distinctive either of Anglicanism or of Nonconformity were established in London and other major cities in the later years of the century.

In spite of their distinctively Christian origins the influence of the Settlements was probably more social than religious. In the social realm too their influence was palliative, ameliorating some evils and showing the good will of the churchmen, rather than working towards a fundamental change in society. The labour leader George Lansbury was one of a number critical of the movement. He commented, 'My sixty years' experience in East London leaves me quite unable to discover what permanent social influence Toynbee Hall or any other similar settlement has had on the life and labour of the people.'⁵ That is a hostile verdict and may indicate that Lansbury was looking for the wrong things. Men like Barnett were not full-blooded socialists and should not be criticized for failing to do what they did not set out to do. They had set themselves more limited aims. They wanted to spread understanding between classes, to create opportunities for poor people to improve their own situations, and to stir rich Christians into an awareness of their responsibilities to others. By those standards they could claim a modest success. Biographies and autobiographies of a number of later leaders, both those from the universities and those from the working men, pay tribute to lessons learned in the Settlements.

Stewart Headlam and the Guild of St Matthew

A much more committed socialist position is found in the work of *Stewart Headlam* (1847–1924), an influential Anglo-Catholic in the tradition of English eccentric clerics. A wealthy old Etonian, son of an ardent Evangelical underwriter, he spent most of his life in Bethnal Green, earning a reputation for his support of radical causes, his criticism of the ecclesiastical and social establishment, and his bohemian life-style.

Headlam was by nature an extremist who took up causes wholeheartedly and found it difficult to compromise. There were three main influences in his thinking which he seems never quite to have brought into harmony. Thus at different times he took up different positions which, while not exactly contradictory, did not fit easily together.

Probably the most basic influence was the theology of the Tractarians. He was passionately convinced of the truth of Catholic Christianity in its Anglican form and a devoted sacramentalist. Thus he was opposed to both secularists and members of non-Anglican Churches. His sacramental ritualism was one of several reasons which brought him into conflict with his bishop.

Secondly, his Anglo-Catholicism was influenced by the theology of Maurice and its social implications. He believed that the sacraments were expressions of God's concern for, and involvement in, the world at every point. Following Maurice he saw the movements to improve the condition of working people as an expression of Christianity, and thought of everything which contributed to the wholeness and well-being of men as essentially the work of God. He spoke of Jesus as 'a carpenter, who became a radical reformer both in social and religious matters',[6] and he considered it to be as much his duty as a priest to lead campaigns for public health and education, or for a local playground or swimming bath, as to celebrate the Mass. Indeed, one of his complaints about the secularist speakers and societies which flourished in the early days of his ministry was that they spent too much time criticizing what he saw as the less important features of the Bible, such as some of the miracles of the Old Testament, and did not give enough time to genuinely secular activities which would improve the living conditions of the poor. Nevertheless, he opposed any attempts to prevent secularists from speaking freely or criticizing the Church.

The third influence came from the American economist *Henry George* (1839–97), whose views, expressed in *Progress and Poverty* (1879), were very popular in England at the time. George argued that real wealth lay in the possession of land and the rent which came from it. He pointed out that the great increase in productive power which had marked recent times had not greatly reduced poverty. This, he believed, was because landowners took the profit in increased rent. Rent he saw as the cause of social unrest. His solution was that the state should take all rent as tax, leaving the land with the owner. The income from the 'single tax' would be devoted to public works for the good of all. Furthermore it would be so great that other taxes could be abolished leaving the benefits of work and thrift with the workers and savers. This theory was expressed in biblical terms and Headlam was one of many Christian Socialists who was attracted by it. The importance is not the theory itself so much as the fact that Christian Socialists were advocating such intervention by the state.

The chief vehicle by which Headlam put forward his views was the Guild of St Matthew which became a force in the national Church almost by accident. It was founded in 1877 and was originally limited to communicants of St Matthew's, Bethnal Green, where Headlam was curate. Headlam had the title of Warden. Its objects were:

1 To get rid, by every possible means, of the existing prejudices, especially on the part of Secularists, against the Church, her sacraments and doctrines, and to endeavour to 'justify God to the people'.

2 To promote frequent and reverent worship in the Holy Communion and a better observance of the teaching of the Church of England, as set forth in the Book of Common Prayer.

3 To promote the study of social and political questions in the light of the incarnation.[7]

In the next year Headlam wrote an article in defence of music halls which so angered his previously long-suffering rector Septimus Hansard that he was dismissed from his curacy. The result was that the Guild of St Matthew became a national movement. As well as London, branches were established in Oxford and many provincial cities. There were even off-shoots in America and Australia. Membership increased among clergy and laity, reaching a peak in the mid 1890s and lasting until 1909. At the height of its influence it published, largely at Headlam's personal expense, its own newspaper, the *Church Reformer* (1884–95). Without losing its Anglo-Catholic tone, and drawing its membership almost exclusively from that school of thought, the Guild became more devoted to campaigning on social issues and criticizing what it saw as the excesses and irresponsibility of the rich. It attracted some of the ablest radical High Churchmen of the day, including *T. Hancock* (1832–1903), *H. C. Shuttleworth* (1850–1900), and *W. E. Moll* (1857–1932).

In 1884 the Guild committed itself to
support such measures as will tend
(a) to restore to the people the value which they give to the land;
(b) to bring about a better distribution of the wealth created by labour;
(c) to give the whole body of the people a voice in their own government;
(d) to abolish false standards of worth and dignity.[8]

These issues were brought before Church Congress and members lectured to interested groups throughout the country. They show a greater willingness to campaign for definite socialist principles and practice than had previously been found, going much beyond Maurice. Headlam himself was a member of the Fabian Society, and was a member of the committee which drew up its basis in 1886. He wrote a number of articles for it, but the somewhat arid intellectualism of the Fabians contrasted unfavourably for him with the more passionate involvement in the real social conditions suffered by the poor which he found among the slum ritualists.

For a time the Guild of St Matthew caught the imagination and won the support of many Christian Socialists. However, it did not look beyond the Church of England, and was only really congenial to the High Church party there. Most of its leaders were frankly hostile to other denominations. It also reflected the impulsiveness and autocratic style of its leader, and it was the latter which caused dissension within it.

Headlam was an ardent supporter of public education. In 1891 he issued a manifesto which appeared to commit the Guild to that position without, apparently, consulting other members. In fact many Anglo-Catholic clergy believed that the Church should still control education and were opposed to the idea of state inspection of education. Headlam's action caused great offence. Even more controversial was his attitude to the Independent Labour Party (ILP). He was opposed to the formation of any working-class political party. In his view it would be wrong 'to vote for a man simply because he is a carpenter and will try to improve carpenters' wages',[9] and he opposed the Fabians' support of this idea. His argument was that such a party would increase rather than diminish class consciousness and class division. Once again he did not carry all Guild members with him and there grew a dissatisfaction with his despotic manner. The personal affection in which he was generally held seems to have been undiminished.

Headlam's bohemianism has been somewhat exaggerated both by friends and critics. Nevertheless he showed unusual interests and behaved in an unconventional way for a Victorian clergyman of his class. At a time when the theatre and dancing were considered vaguely immoral he supported the music hall and scandalized his bishop by his friendship with female ballet dancers. He tried to promote better understanding between the

Church and the acting profession through the 'Church and Stage Guild', founded in 1879, but without conspicuous success.

The Christian Social Union

Long before Headlam dissolved the Guild of St Matthew in 1909 a rival organization had appeared in the Christian Social Union, founded 1889. Among its members were many who had been, and continued to be, leaders of the Guild. However, it exhibited a different tone and responded to a different situation in the Church of England.

Headlam and his group have been described as the 'shock troops' of Christian Socialism in the Church of England. They had made it a topic of interest and concern. However, they were considered to be extremists and Headlam in particular was regarded with suspicion. Many who welcomed the growing place of social concern in the thinking of the Church did not want to be associated with his impulsiveness. That there was, and continued to be, a growing interest in this area is indicated by the fact that Christian Socialism was a major theme of the Church Congress of 1887, and the fact that the Lambeth Conference, the gathering of all Anglican bishops, meeting in 1888 positively encouraged discussion of the subject and urged clergy in their teaching to show 'how much of what is good and true in Socialism is to be found in the precepts of Christ'. From that time, at least until the 1920s if not longer, the Church of England frequently spoke in its official pronouncements as if there was an accepted and natural relationship between the Church and socialism. While the sort of social concern they had in mind may not have been what Headlam and his friends advocated, and while it may not have permeated to the thinking of the average parish priest and layman, the change in attitude is considerable, and it is largely due to the Christian Social Union.

The origins of the Christian Social Union are to be found in two groups of Oxford academics, all Anglicans. One, calling itself the 'Holy Club', a humorous reference to the group around the Wesleys in the previous century, began to meet about 1875 to discuss matters of theological interest in the light of the most recent thought. Its most significant product was the collection of essays *Lux Mundi*, published in 1889 under the editorship of

Charles Gore (1855–1932), at that time Principal of Pusey House and a leading High Churchman. Some of the theological implications of that book will be considered later, here we must notice its sub-title, 'A series of essays in the religion of the Incarnation', which links it both with Maurice and with the aims of the Guild of St Matthew. Many of the contributors had been pupils of the Oxford Hegelian *T. H. Green* (1836–82). From him they had learned a stress on divine immanence, and the belief that the individual can only find fulfilment in society and that society should provide the necessary means for his development by giving him liberties and reminding him of rights and duties. Their discussions naturally turned to questions of ethics and society, which concerns are reflected in *Lux Mundi* by essays on 'Christianity and Politics' by W. J. H. Champion, and 'Christianity and Ethics' by R. L. Ottley.

The second was a smaller group led by *Henry Scott Holland* (1847–1918), founded in 1879 and called PESEK (standing for 'politics, economics, socialism, ethics and Christianity'), which met to discuss social questions. There was considerable overlap in membership between the two groups.

Convinced of the need for a Christian Socialist group, free from the influence of Headlam and attracting members from a broader spectrum of the Church, they formed the Christian Social Union in 1889, the year of a serious dock strike in London which concentrated their minds on questions of Christianity and social ethics. The aims of the Union were:

1 To claim for the Christian Law the ultimate authority to rule social practice.

2 To study in common how to apply the moral truths and principles of Christianity to the social and economic difficulties of the present time.

3 To present Christ in practical life as the living Master and King, the enemy of wrong and selfishness, the power of righteousness and love.[10]

From the beginning the Christian Social Union was successful in attracting some outstanding men who would never have joined the Guild of St Matthew but who had greater influence in the

Church. Charles Gore was an aristocrat by birth who later became a Canon of Westminster and Bishop successively of Worcester, Birmingham and Oxford. He was one of the outstanding theologians and churchmen of his generation. Scott Holland also had an aristocratic background. From Oxford he became a canon of St Paul's where he stayed for twenty-six years (1884–1910) before returning to Oxford as Regius Professor of Divinity. Perhaps even more outstanding was *B. F. Westcott* (1825–1901), appointed the first President of the Union in 1889, the year before he became Bishop of Durham. Westcott was a major New Testament scholar and theologian as well as a writer on the social implications of Christianity. He was also an honorary chaplain to Queen Victoria and a man of great prestige and influence in the Church.

With such support it is not surprising that the Christian Social Union was soon accepted as a respectable body within the Church of England. Thinking of the quite different membership of the Guild of St Matthew, particularly in its early days, Headlam was no doubt correct to remark, 'I can well understand that it would be perhaps for many reasons a little difficult for some of these distinguished gentlemen to come and join our little society.'[11]

But how successful was the Christian Social Union, and how socialist? At one level, as we have noted, it was very successful. In the years immediately before the First World War many of the most influential men in the Church were also members of it. Gore and Holland consistently campaigned in its name on behalf of the poor. They supported demands for a 'minimum wage' and for improvements in the living conditions of the working classes. Gore particularly called both the Church and Nation to penitence for the neglect which had allowed such wretchedness to exist alongside such ostentation in the richest nation in the world. The Lambeth Conference of 1908 was dominated by the concerns of the Union.

Yet there remains a softness about the movement, especially when compared with the Guild of St Matthew. Its influence came through its writings, more numerous and more academic than those of the Guild, and through the social standing of its leaders. But for all their genuine passion and sincerity neither Gore nor Scott Holland established such personal relations with working men as Headlam had done. Interestingly Westcott, austere academic and mystic though he was, did seem to establish a more personal relationship with the Durham miners, as is evidenced by his mediation in the coal strike of 1892. But Westcott died before the movement reached its peak.

In accordance with their aims they studied, lectured and wrote, but they did not act. Critics commented that their typical reaction was, 'Here is a social problem, we must write a paper about it.' Perhaps all that could have been expected was that they should have persuaded the Church of England, still rich and influential in national life, to have instituted some national action. In fact, while bishops and leading churchmen were willing to call themselves socialists they did not affect the rank and file of the church members, and they did not, as a body, support the ILP. For all their agitation they remained progressive liberals at heart, concerned for charity and improvement, rather than committed socialists in a political sense, committed to radical changes in the structure of society. It is a sign of Gore's greatness that he went beyond most members of the Union and did involve himself in the practicalities of Trade Union organization and mediating between employers and Trade Unions in industrial disputes.

Some of those who were unhappy about the Christian Social Union's lack of commitment to positive socialism, in its political sense, united, following a conference at Morecambe in 1906, to form the Church Socialist League. It is significant as the first Anglican society definitely committed to socialism. It attracted a number of able radical thinkers and activists, especially from the North of England where it drew much of its strength from the Community of the Resurrection at Mirfield near Leeds, a monastic community set up by Gore largely to train men from working-class backgrounds for the Anglican priesthood. Apart from this definite socialism some of the attraction of the League appears to have been a revolt against the social, intellectual and southern tone of the Union.

After a brief period of growth, during which it nearly affiliated with the Labour Party, the League divided into a number of different groupings on theological and political grounds. It was the last major manifestation of an organized Christian Socialist group within the Church of England. After the First World War, though socialist groups of various kinds continued, none achieved anything like the influence of the Christian Social Union, and the concept of Christian Socialism was never again as prominent in the Church of England.

Notes

1 F. Maurice, *Life of Frederick Denison Maurice* (Macmillan, 2nd edn 1884), vol. 2, pp. 136 f.
2 F. D. Maurice, *Theological Essays* (Macmillan 1852), p. 403.
3 F. Maurice, op. cit., vol. 1, p. 458.
4 ibid., pp. 220 f.
5 cited S. Mayor, *The Churches and the Labour Movement* (Independent Press 1967), p. 323.
6 ibid., p. 190.
7 ibid., p. 188.
8 ibid., p. 193.
9 cited P. d'A. Jones, *The Christian Socialist Revival* (Princeton University Press 1968), p. 141.
10 Mayor, op. cit., p. 196.
11 Jones, op. cit., p. 164.

4
Religion and the Advance of Science

The Victorian age is sometimes presented as a period of confident and settled religious faith. Certainly church attendance, at least among the upper and middle classes, was high. Missionary societies flourished. Theological and devotional literature was produced and sold in great quantities. The Church, and the Christian faith generally, had considerable influence in public life. Even those among the new working-class leaders who were most critical of the Church as an institution frequently made a distinction between the Church which they criticized and what they took to be genuine Christianity, which they believed themselves to hold.

It would be foolish to dismiss totally this apparently lively and widespread allegiance to Christianity as sham and hypocrisy. Yet, behind it, it is also clear that for many, at least among the educated, this was a time of growing doubt about the very foundations of Christianity. Among the Christian Socialists whom we considered in the last chapter, some engaged in social and political activities because of their Christian faith. Others, including some clergymen, appear to have thrown themselves into practical Christian work in order to avoid growing doubts about the truth of Christian theology – a phenomenon also found in later ages.

The most common reasons given for this growing doubt were the suspicion that scientists had disproved Christianity, and the suspicion that biblical critics had disproved the Bible. The citadel of faith thus appeared to have been assailed from without and betrayed from within. Very few of those who harboured such suspicions would have been able to state very clearly why they felt as they did. Nevertheless, such ideas were in the air and their influence was powerful. Science and biblical criticism were closely related in the mood of growing doubt, but they may be separated for convenience of discussion.

Some Underlying Questions

The religion and science debate of the late nineteenth century is often reduced to the single question of evolution. There is good reason for that since evolution, or Darwinism as it was often called, was the central issue in the public mind. But the evolution debate illustrated and became a focus for a number of underlying questions on which religion and science, or theologians and scientists, appeared to be on opposite sides. At least four such questions are worth mentioning.

The first and most obvious is the question of factual truth. The Bible, and therefore the Christian Church, appeared to be putting forward as statements of fact assertions which science was showing to be untrue. Did God create the world more or less as we know it now in a period of six days, as the book of Genesis asserts, or did it evolve over many millennia? Was there a universal flood in the days of Noah or not? More controversially, is man unique among all living beings through a special act of creation and a special relationship with God or is he simply part of the animal kingdom?

Secondly there is what might be called the question of success. Science in its applied form, what would later be called technology, had made great strides in ways which might be expected to improve the lot of men long before Darwin and evolution were widely discussed. The inventions which lay behind the industrial revolution may have led initially, as we have noted, to unemployment and social unrest, but they had manifestly succeeded in improving means of production. Men knew that such inventions had something to do with science and believed that ultimately they were good. It seemed that if science could be properly harnessed, much of the drudgery could be taken out of life and a golden age of ease and prosperity might quickly be ushered in. As the nineteenth century progressed and gave way to the twentieth it also became clear that science in the form of medicine could conquer much disease and in its application to husbandry and agriculture could improve production in those areas beyond men's wildest dreams.

Looked at in such ways science embodied what was new, progressive and liberating. The effect of science was to make life better, more enjoyable and free, or more free, of pain in this world. Religion, by comparison, could easily be seen as a bulwark of conservatism and reaction. It promised happiness in the next world but had failed to provide it in this one. As religion appeared to be in opposition to science it could also appear to be standing in the way of progress. Religion, men might say, had been tried, but in two thousand years it had failed to succeed in the way that science had succeeded in a few generations.

More complex than either of those was the question of the status of science in intellectual and social life. To an extent which later generations find difficult to comprehend the Christian religion had dominated the intellectual life of Western Europe and had set the limits within which men thought. Theology had been accepted as the Queen of the sciences. The Bible had been accepted as containing divine revelation. Theologians, relying on divine revelation, could comment on anything. This attitude had lasted throughout the age of the enlightenment. It was not generally questioned that scientists were 'thinking God's thoughts after him'. As they discovered the regular working of the planets or the intricacies of plant and insect life, such discoveries only brought to light more of the wonders of God's creation. They were incorporated into the books of natural theology where they illustrated the argument that evidences of design in the world pointed to the existence of God the great Designer. But scientists were not expected to go beyond revelation, much less to appear to contradict it.

Now the relation between theology and science was to change. Science was to assert its independence, and scientists were to refuse to be limited in their conclusions by what was to be found in the Bible. The fact that the Bible seemed to be under attack from the biblical critics added strength to this move. The change can be seen in relation to the 'laws' by which the world appeared to be governed. In many hymns praising God for his work in creation they had been hailed as 'laws of God'. Now, almost imperceptibly, they became 'laws of Nature' and took on an identity of their own. The change became more complete as men discovered more about them and learned to manipulate them for their own ends. Then there was the danger that they should become the scientists' own 'laws'. To reach that point is to come perilously near to idolatry. Certainly before the end of the nineteenth century the connection with God had been severed. For some science had almost been deified and the declarations of scientists were given the respect which had once been given to those of bishops.

Finally there was the question of method. Science appeared to have a very clear methodology, to proceed on the evidence and therefore to be unarguably correct in its conclusions. There was observation, classification and measurement of the facts followed by the framing of hypotheses to account for the facts. Such hypotheses could theoretically be checked by experiments and the experiments could be repeated. That such methods brought results was indisputable. The question was whether such methods were the only ones which could reach valid conclusions. Alternatively, are there different types of knowledge and different ways of knowing?

Such questions were not always distinctly formulated. In particular the distinction between science as a quest for truth and applied science as a useful aid to improve man's lot was not always made. But unspoken questions such as those mentioned contributed to the uneasy relationship between religion and science against which the debate about evolution took place.

The Theory of Evolution

We have noted that the Bible had for a long time been accepted as providing a framework for thought. In some editions of the Authorised Version of the English Bible, beside the first verse of the Book of Genesis, appeared the date 4004 BC as the date of creation. This date had been calculated by *James Ussher* (1581–1656), Archbishop of Armagh, who had arrived at it through the various dates and chronological lists of the Old Testament. Though it was realized that this was not part of the text and that Ussher's calculations were not sacrosanct, an age of some six thousand years for the world appeared about right.

Problems for this position first appeared through the study of geology and the existence of fossil remains which suggested a longer period of development. The accepted explanation was known as 'catastrophism'. This was the view that the world had been subject to a number of catastrophes, possibly divine judgements, after which God had created new species while preserving some of the old. The most recent of such catastrophes was the flood in the days of Noah. This also explained what appeared to be marine deposits well above sea level.

Gradually, and reluctantly, geologists were forced to abandon that view. An illustration of the change which came about can be seen in the Professor of Geology at Oxford, *William Buckland*, later Dean of Westminster. Buckland first argued for 'catastrophism' but came to see that the accepted date for Noah's flood was too recent to allow for the development of the known rock strata. Nevertheless, he still tried to harmonize his geology with the book of Genesis. He suggested that the single phrase 'In the beginning . . .', with which it opens, covers a very long period, and that the six 'days' of the creation narrative are not periods of twenty-four hours but immense epochs. In spite of such efforts he was still roundly criticized for not accepting the truth of Scripture.

The new orthodoxy was 'uniformitarianism', the belief that the present geological structure of the earth had come about over millions of years through natural causes such as sedimentation and erosion. This view was argued by *Charles Lyell* whose *Principles of Geology* appeared between 1830 and 1833. Lyell built on the work of previous scholars but provided more argument and more illustrations of the way changes had taken place. Though he was consciously arguing against 'catastrophism', which seemed at the time to have biblical support, he still apparently believed that his position could be harmonized with Genesis.

Men such as Buckland and Lyell were basically still in the tradition of natural theology, arguing from evidence of a design to a Designer. They were unwilling to believe that there could be a conflict between God's word in the Bible and God's work in creation. A particular manifestation of this type of thinking, in part occasioned by the new developments in geology, was the publication of the *Bridgewater Treatises* between 1833 and 1840. These eight volumes were financed by a bequest of the Earl of Bridgewater who died in 1829, having left £8,000 to the President of the Royal Society for the publication of a work or works 'On the Power, Wisdom and Goodness of God, as manifested in Creation . . .'. Posterity has not rated these works very highly. One of them, *Geology and Mineralogy* was written by Buckland. Perhaps the most interesting of them was by the Scottish divine Thomas Chalmers. The interesting feature of his contribution was that, in spite of the terms of the bequest, Chalmers drew attention to the limited role of natural theology, as he did in his better-known *Astronomical Discourses*. He argued that it could at best predispose men to a relationship with the God of the Bible, and that it could not replace the knowledge of God which came from revelation.

It was with the science of biology that the real conflict began. The geologists, as long as they kept to their own discipline, did not appear to disturb the accepted view of the fixity of species. This was the view that each species had been separately created by God with its own peculiar characteristics. If 'catastrophism' was accepted this idea could be traced back to the story of the flood, where Noah was depicted as having taken a pair of each species into the ark and thus preserved them. The 'prehistoric' creatures such as the giant mastodon, whose existence was now being talked about by geologists, could be understood as species which had not been rescued at that time. When the Swedish naturalist Linnaeus had worked out his system of botanical classification he had accepted the fixity of species, assuming that the distinctions of species depend on separate lineages which do not change. The 'uniformitarian' position did not immediately change the basic view. It simply pushed the fixity of species firmly back to the original creation. However, reflection on Lyell's position showed that the accepted static view of nature could no longer be held. All plants and animals were in a state of development or evolution. It was the further idea that species evolve from each other that was to be so disturbing.

The possibility of development between species had previously been suggested by, among others, Erasmus Darwin (Charles Darwin's grandfather) in 1794, and by Jean Baptiste de Lamarck in 1809. It was thrust upon the public in a more sensational way in 1844 by the publication of an anonymous work, *The Vestiges of the Natural History of Creation*, which was later found to be the work of Robert Chambers, an eccentric Scottish publisher who was also responsible, with his brother, for Chambers' Encyclopedia. Chambers' book argued that man should be included in the evolutionary process. Unfortunately it also contained a great deal that was fanciful and quite unscientific. It was easily, and quite savagely, criticized, by scientists more than theologians. The result was that the theory was made to look ridiculous.

Religion and the Advance of Science

Charles Darwin (1809–82) was the son of a doctor. His father hoped that Charles would follow the same profession but, finding that he was unhappy with the medical course at Edinburgh, he sent him to Christ's College, Cambridge, with the intention that he should take holy orders. After some initial hesitation Charles seems to have accepted this plan. He read some of the current theological works, including Paley the arch-proponent of natural theology, and was not only happy to call himself a Christian but appeared to have no more qualms about becoming a parson. However, at Cambridge he came under the influence of John Henslow, a clergyman who combined his parish duties with the Professorship of Botany. Henslow encouraged his interest in botany, and it was Henslow who arranged for him to sail as naturalist aboard HMS *Beagle* on a scientific expedition to Tierra del Fuego.

Between 1832 and 1836 the *Beagle* charted the coastline of South America, crossed the Pacific to Australia and New Zealand and, most importantly for Darwin, visited the Galapagos archipelago. It was on this voyage that Darwin began collecting the material on which his later work was based.

On his return to England Darwin's first scientific works were geological. He had taken a copy of Lyell's *Principles of Geology* with him on the *Beagle*. Later he published works on zoology and botany. He became well established as a scientist by the extent and thoroughness of his work, and in 1853 he received the Royal Medal of the Royal Society. All this was later to mean that when his work on evolution appeared it came as the work of a recognized and established scientist and not as a dabbler or a crank. From as early as 1837 he kept notebooks on the evolution of species, and his friends knew that he was preparing a major work on that subject, provisionally entitled 'Natural Selection'.

At last he appears to have been forced into publication by an article by Alfred Wallace 'On the tendency of Varieties to depart indefinitely from the Original Type', which he received in June 1858. Wallace was working in the Moluccas and, knowing that Darwin was studying in the same field, he sent his article for comment. Darwin realized that Wallace had given in a nutshell the position at which he had arrived. Papers from both men were lodged with the Linnean Society in London. The next year

69

Darwin published his major work. It was called *On the Origin of Species by Means of Natural Selection, or the Preservation of Favoured Races in the Struggle for Life.*

Darwin's work was unlike any that had preceded it on the subject of evolution. As we have seen it came from an established scientist. Most importantly it amassed such a wealth of data that henceforth the theory had to be taken seriously. Darwin's great strength was his capacity for observation and classification.

His theory of natural selection began with the observation that there were in fact random variations among individual members of the same species. This had struck him in comparing the wildlife on different islands in the Galapagos chain where he had found that such variations existed and were passed on, though there was little difference in environmental conditions between the different islands. Secondly he knew well that animals and plants produce far more young than survive to reproduce the species. There is in fact a struggle for food and living space. Finally it is clear that some variations give advantages in the struggle for survival. Those individuals which possess such advantages usually live longer and produce more, and stronger, progeny. They also pass on the variation which has given the advantage. Over many generations the individuals within the species which have the advantage become the majority within the species. Those without it become less and are finally eliminated. In this way a gradual change in the species has occurred. Those who are fittest, or best adapted, to survive have survived.

In the years between the voyage of the *Beagle* and the publication of the *Origin of Species* Darwin had tested the theory. He had observed the natural development of plants, insects and animals. More significantly he had considered the selective breeding methods applied to pigeons and dogs. He was able to point out that the breeders had deliberately selected variations which they wanted to enhance. His argument was that variations also occurred in nature but there they came by chance.

The last sentence introduces what is sometimes seen as a problem, or at least a paradox, in Darwin's thinking. It can be seen by comparing his views with those of Lamarck. Lamarck had argued that changes came through the efforts of individuals to survive. He gives the example of the giraffe and argues that its long neck came by the perpetual effort to stretch up to get food from trees. Darwin almost reverses this. He suggests not that the long neck developed in order that the animal should survive, but rather that those animals which had developed long necks did in fact survive. The development of the giraffe's long neck, or of any other helpful organ, is purely random. To that extent evolution by natural selection is by *chance*. However, chance here does not mean chaos. It simply means that there is no causal connection between the helpful development and its use. In another sense Darwin does talk about a *law* of natural selection. It is the law that those members of a species which are best adapted to survive do so and continually lead to new species, in other words the survival of the fittest. It becomes important as the debate continues to see that Darwin held both random selection (chance) and law together, and that they are not contradictory.

In the *Origin of Species* he seems to have studiously avoided speaking at length about the evolution of man. However, earlier evolutionists had included man in their theories and it was clear that Darwin's work would lead to the same conclusion. In fact the work was denounced or defended on the supposition that man was included in the evolutionary process. In 1871, in *The Descent of Man*, Darwin did discuss human origins and showed how man could have descended by natural selection immediately from ape-like creatures but ultimately from even lower forms of life. In other words he sought to establish the continuity of man and the rest of nature. Some who had followed him thus far, including A. R. Wallace, were unwilling to follow him so far. But, strangely, the second volume caused far less furore than the first. He was simply saying what he had been assumed to intend. By this time too the theory of evolution had achieved scientific respectability. The religious world had to come to terms with it.

Evolution and Christian Belief

That Darwin's work had widespread implications for Christian belief is clear. The *Origin of Species* was an epoch-making work. But we must remember that basically evolution is a theory in the science of biology. Though Darwin was aware of some of the implications of his work for traditional theology, and must have known that he was widely criticized, he appears to have been reluctant to draw any conclusions outside the scientific sphere. He continued to work as a scientist, publishing works on plants, flowers and vegetables. His last published work, in the year before he died, was *The Formation of Vegetable Mould, through the Action of Worms, with Observations on their Habits*. It may be salutary for those who approach Darwin from the perspective of the history of religious thought to be reminded that he was not an *agent provocateur* who deliberately set out to antagonize the faithful. He was a professional scientist who went quietly about his own business. Within the scientific community others have gone on to develop, criticize or correct some aspects of his work, but, as far as evolution is concerned, the central thrust of it has been accepted.

Turning to its effects on Christianity we have noted that the theory of evolution became a kind of focus or rallying point for a number of areas of uneasiness between science and religion, or scientists and theologians. Some reactions from both sides owed more to personal animosities than to a careful consideration of the issues involved. It is worth noting that by no means all scientists were in opposition to religion and that not all theologians and religious leaders reacted violently to Darwin's work. Among scientists Lyell, though he finally gave his support to Darwin's work in 1868, remained a practising member of the Church of England, and many others, such as Faraday and Kelvin, seemed to feel no conflict between science and faith. In 1864 a group of leading scientists issued a declaration expressing 'sincere regret that researches into scientific truth are perverted by some in our own time into occasion for casting doubt upon the truth and authenticity of the Holy Scriptures . . .'[1] The devout pointed with satisfaction to the large number (716) who had signed this declaration. Others pointed out that it was a relatively small number in proportion to the actual number of professional scientists who could have signed. Many in fact had declined to sign because they doubted the value of such gestures.

From the religious side some, such as F. J. A. Hort, welcomed the *Origin of Species* and encouraged others to read it. Charles Kingsley, himself a naturalist, commended it strongly to Maurice and engaged in a warm correspondence with T. H. Huxley, Darwin's self-appointed popularizer. The Tractarians, such as Pusey and Liddon, took a moderate line. Perhaps because their faith had never leaned too heavily on natural theology, they were not too disturbed by changes in that area. Finally it is worth noting that on Darwin's death it was Canon Farrar who suggested that he should be buried in Westminster Abbey.

But if the above paragraphs indicate that the conflict between science and religion was by no means total, it remains the case that acceptance of evolution had a number of serious and far-reaching implications for theology. The working out of these implications took several generations and is still going on. Some issues which seemed the most important at the time turned out to be less significant. Others which received less public attention at the time have been found to be much more far-reaching. We shall meet many of the effects in later chapters, but it will be helpful to list some of them here.

(1) The first and most obvious effect was on the question of *Scripture*. We have said that what seemed to many to be the attack of science came at the same time as English Christianity was being forced to come to terms with new approaches to Scripture. This question will be taken up in the next chapter. Here we may note that there is a clear conflict between a literal interpretation of the words of Genesis concerning creation and the theory of evolution. Was creation a series of related acts by God over a period of six days, or is the world as we know it the end of millions of years of evolution?

Not all Christians were equally affected by this question. Lyell seems to have been willing to accept the Genesis accounts of creation as myth or poetry, in any case not as giving historical information. Buckland was one of many who tried to ease the problem by suggesting that the 'days' of Genesis were in fact geological epochs. Gladstone argued, incorrectly, that even if the time scale of creation as given by Genesis needed some attention the order of the account was correct. All of these approaches show an abandonment of a literalist reading of Genesis. But, at the time, that was an unusual attitude. The majority of people saw only the apparent contradictions.

For over a generation the best theological minds in England had been aware of the problems and of the movement of biblical criticism taking place in Germany. Pusey is a good example. Yet the changes in outlook involved did not reach the average man in the pew until it came either as a threat or as a compromise. Christian leaders were at least as much to blame as scientists for the real anguish of many simple believers.

(2) With the apparent attack on the authenticity of Scripture, the *doctrine of man* was also clearly questioned. For the Bible and the Christian tradition, man was seen as a special creature, separately created and capable of a peculiar union with God. In Catholic theology, especially Roman Catholic, this uniqueness is represented by teaching about the immortal soul. Man is therefore, to a large extent, distinguished from the rest of nature. His intelligence and his moral sense could be seen as indications of this distinctness.

Evolution appeared to threaten that position. Darwin accepted that man has a superiority over other creatures, much as organic life is superior to inorganic dust, yet he also asserted the continuity of man and the animal kingdom. Primitive tribes, he suggested, almost closed the gap between man and the apes. Huxley claimed there was less difference between man and the highest apes than there was between the highest and lowest apes. Many exponents of evolution drew attention to the similarity in physical characteristics between man and apes, including the shape of the brain.

This was taken as an affront to human dignity and seems to have been greeted with fear and reproach rather than with argument. It is the question of human dignity or worth which lies behind the celebrated exchange between Huxley and Bishop Samuel Wilberforce at the Oxford meeting of the British Association in 1860. This confrontation has been extensively quoted but, strangely, there are no contemporary reports. Wilberforce argued against evolution and in favour of the fixity of species. He is said to have sarcastically asked Huxley whether he was descended from an ape through his grandfather or his grandmother. Various accounts are given of Huxley's reply. His own version is, 'If . . . the question is put to me, would I rather have a miserable ape for a grandfather or a man highly endowed by nature and possessed of great means of influence and yet who employs these faculties and that influence for the mere purpose of introducing ridicule into a grave scientific discussion – I unhesitatingly affirm my preference for the ape.'[2]

The point of Wilberforce's comment is that descent from an ape is degrading. A similar view lies behind the reported comment of a Christian critic to a supporter of evolution, 'If you will leave me my forefathers in heaven, I will leave you yours in the Zoological Gardens.'

There were, and are, of course, arguments against the position of Darwin and Huxley. A. R. Wallace, whose paper had forced Darwin into publishing the *Origin of Species*, and who continued to take a very similar line, could not follow Darwin at this point. He drew attention to the differences between men, even of savage tribes, and the apes. Particularly he pointed out that the brain of even the lowest savages is much larger than that of the highest apes, and is much larger than is needed. 'They possess a mental organ beyond their needs. Natural selection could only have endowed savage man with a brain a little superior to that of an ape, whereas he actually possesses one very little inferior to that of a philosopher.'[3] We may note in passing that, in typical Victorian fashion, nobody saw anything odd in talking of 'lowest savage' or 'highest ape'.

Wallace also drew attention to man's use of language, to his moral qualities and to his aesthetic sensibilities. Interestingly Darwin, late in his life, expressed regret that in his own case concentration on his scientific work had led to the atrophy of his aesthetic appreciation.

A further point is worth making. On both sides of the argument there was a tendency to accept a description of man's origin and development as making a judgement about his worth. It was as if his descent determined his nature. That is a fallacious argument. To say that a man may have descended from an animal, as a scientific description, is not the same as to say that he is an animal, as a description of his nature and worth.

A more recent writer has drawn attention to what he calls the fallacy of 'nothing-buttery', the idea that to explain any part of a phenomenon is to explain it away.[4] In the case we are discussing, to explain the descent of man from the animal kingdom is not the same as to say that man is 'nothing but' an animal. Other aspects of his personality need to be examined. Many observers would say that Wallace, and others, have made a case for the distinctiveness of man which must at least be allowed to stand beside Darwin's case for the continuity of man and animals.

(3) A further dispute arose over the doctrines of *sin and the fall*. The book of Genesis describes how Adam and Eve sinned against God, both by not believing what he said and by not obeying what he commanded, as punishment for which they were banished from paradise and the close presence of God. In many ways this had proved a satisfying account. It explained the evil in the world as the result of God's curse. It also explained the sense which many sincere people have that they do not always have the moral strength and purity of heart to choose the highest when they see it. Man not only has a conscience he has a guilty conscience. The weakness behind this could be traced to Adam.

Long before Darwin there had been involved theological debates concerning what exactly Adam had lost at the fall, and what exactly was the relationship between his sin and the sins of his successors. But what was not in dispute was that man was a sinner and liable to the judgement of God.

The theory of evolution appeared to cast doubts on that picture of the human condition and some followers of Darwin ridiculed it. The Victorian age was a time of optimism, confidence in man and belief in inevitable progress. As we shall see later this mood affected theology at several points. Evolution appeared to some to support it. It was taken from its place as a scientific theory in the field of biology and extended to cover every field of human endeavour. Thus in politics, culture, religion and ethics man was believed to be getting better and better. Ideas of sin and the fall appeared offensive in such an atmosphere. At worst there might be occasional slips back into animal behaviour, but these could not be seen as sins against God. The path was securely set upwards. Thus Huxley is reputed to have declared that man must be a very peculiar creature because when he fell he fell upwards. Though one must also point out that Huxley himself did not believe that standards of behaviour could be derived from and explained by evolution, as Darwin had suggested.

In fact to extend the theory of evolution so far is invalid. It may be that the human race has progressed ethically, though by no means all observers would accept that view nor would all the evidence support it. What is clear is that the theory of evolution does not logically undergird such a view. The philosopher *Herbert Spencer* (1820–1903) is the best example of one who tried to build an all-embracing philosophy on evolutionary lines. *Karl Marx* (1818–83) was also willing to see links between evolution and his own views, though, as he clearly realized, he had a quite different starting point.

(4) An unexpected side effect of evolution and the criticism of the doctrine of sin and the fall was a questioning of the *person and work of Christ*, though the conclusions were not always drawn. Several elements are involved. As far as the person of Christ is concerned, the concept of God becoming incarnate and Jesus living as both God and man has never been an easy one for Christian theology to express. It was particularly difficult to fit it in to a view which began with such a stress on the animality of man. Furthermore, if, as evolution and the prevailing mood seemed to suggest, man was getting better and better, it could be asked why the supreme example of man appeared some two thousand years ago. It seemed more appropriate that he should be at the end of the evolutionary process.

As far as the work of Christ is concerned, traditional Christian theology saw his death as a means of dealing with man's sinful state and making possible the restoration of communion with God. But if man's state was not as sinful as had been supposed the need for his death seemed to have gone. Thinking such as this caused great offence to many, especially to traditional Evangelicals with their stress on the death of Christ, and it led to many reinterpretations of Christ's person and work.

(5) By far the greatest effect of evolution on the traditional theological position was the challenge to the *argument from design*. We have noted on many occasions the centrality which this argument had obtained. While he was preparing for holy orders Darwin himself had been impressed by Paley's work in this area. However, in the form it had taken with people like Paley the argument depended on a static view of the universe. It drew attention to the apparent appropriateness of design to function. Thus the hand or the eye appear to be superbly designed for the functions which they perform. Natural selection, however,

appeared to replace beneficent design by chance. Those beings which had not developed in advantageous ways had simply not succeeded in the struggle for survival.

But it was possible, and is possible, to maintain the appeal to design in a modified form. It can be widened from the particular instances and the whole process of evolution can be cited as indication of a great design with the 'laws' of natural selection working throughout it and the whole dependent on God. A number of Darwin's followers and interpreters drew attention to what they took to be the overall purpose displayed in the process of natural history. One of the most prominent and persuasive of these was *Asa Gray* (1810–88), Professor of Natural History at Harvard, who was Darwin's chief American interpreter. Gray was convinced that the evolutionary process could and should be interpreted so as to show divine purpose on a large scale. Reluctantly he had to concede that Darwin himself had declined to accept that position.

The appeal to design has always been a tantalizing argument for theism. Many observers, sometimes almost in spite of themselves, have been impressed by the many apparent traces of purpose in the universe. In the nineteenth century it was particularly difficult to throw off what had been an accepted argument for many generations.

Interestingly, Darwin's own development shows the difficulty of finally abandoning the argument from design, especially when to do so was seen as virtually equivalent to abandoning Christianity. The indications are that Darwin was reluctant to appear as an opponent of Christianity and that he only gradually moved from a theistic position. His own home background had not been religious, but he had been deeply impressed by the parson botanist Henslow, whom he appears to have admired as a Christian as well as a scientist. Added to that his wife, who was also his cousin, Emma Wedgwood, was a devout Christian. His later background, therefore, would incline him to Christianity. It is interesting to note that when Karl Marx wanted to dedicate the English translation of *Das Kapital* to him, he declined on the grounds that his family might not like it.

However, there was a gradual abandonment first of Christianity and then of theism. In his autobiography he speaks of his gradual realization that the history of the Old Testament was unreliable, that the attitudes attributed to God were those of a revengeful tyrant, that he was unable to accept miracles and that he had doubts about the historical reliability of the gospel narratives. He concludes: 'By such reflections as these, which I give not as having the least novelty or value, but as they influenced me, I gradually came to disbelieve in Christianity as a divine revelation ... This disbelief crept over me at a very slow rate, but was at last complete. The rate was so slow that I felt no distress, and have never since doubted even for a single second that my conclusion was correct.'[5]

Clearly his convictions moved 'at a very slow rate'. Parts of the *Origin of Species* speak of the laws of the Creator, and that book is prefaced by a quotation from Bishop Butler. He appears to have been deeply impressed by indications of the harmony of nature and, if he never doubted for a single second that he was right to reject Christianity as he knew it, he was not so sure that he should reject the idea of a creator. In some moods he felt he should be called a theist. In the end he appears to have suspended judgement with the reflection, 'Can the mind of man, which has, as I fully believe, been developed from a mind as low as that possessed by the lowest animals, be trusted when it draws such grand conclusions?'[6]

The Question of Miracles

A result of evolution, of the growing confidence in the orderliness of nature and of the growing expectation that science would soon explain all things, was the tendency to criticize the biblical miracles. This was a considerable change of outlook. From New Testament times the miracles of Jesus had been part of the preaching about him. In the eighteenth century they, together with the argument from prophecy, had been a major weapon in the apologist's armoury. The argument was simple – Jesus performed miracles, it was prophesied in the Old Testament that the Messiah would perform miracles, therefore Jesus was the Messiah. The fact that he had indeed performed miracles, and that miraculous events had occurred in the Old Testament and in connection with the preaching of the gospel, was accepted because there appeared to be eye-witness corroboration.

There is of course a strong tradition of miracles throughout church history. Interestingly the non-biblical miracles were generally viewed with some reserve in Protestant England. The miracles recorded in the lives of the saints or associated with certain shrines were usually rejected or ignored. After all, Luther had been critical of them and they were tainted with Romish superstition. Biblical miracles were tacitly accepted as being in a different class.

In 1865 J. B. *Mozley* (1813–78), who was, incidentally, Newman's brother-in-law, delivered the Bampton Lectures, *On Miracles*. He defended the biblical accounts largely on the grounds that as the uniformity of nature cannot be proved but is merely an assumption, the possibility of miracles cannot be ruled out *a priori*. Though his argument is valid, the interesting point is that he still regards miracles as evidences of Christianity but realizes that the case is not so widely accepted as it had been.

Four lines of argument developed about miracles which, in various combinations or separately, have gone on ever since.

The first, and probably the most pervasive, is the one with which Mozley dealt. It was widely held that the 'laws of nature' ruled out miracles. An exponent of this view was the Oxford mathematician *Baden Powell* (1796–1860), father of the founder of the Boy Scout movement. Powell was convinced that the order of nature was the surest indication of the existence and the beneficence of God. He accepted evolution and saw it as part of God's design. As far as he was concerned the orderliness of nature ruled out miracles and he could see no point in further discussion. Basically this closing of the question on dogmatic grounds is open to Mozley's criticism. It assumes a greater knowledge of the 'laws of nature' than is warranted, and sees them as prescriptions of what can or cannot happen rather than as descriptions of what has been observed. Powell's attitude was, and is, a common one. It is not as certain as he thought that it is genuinely scientific or that it rests on the grounds he thought it did.

The second line was the general criticism of Scripture. Miracles had been 'read off' from Scripture but now that it was becoming possible to criticize Scripture it appeared that they could be discarded. For many this was a circular argument. Those who were embarrassed by the miracles because they did not fit in with what they wanted to find were pleased to drop them. They were left, as they wanted to be left, with a picture of Jesus as a moral example and teacher stripped of the encumbrances of miracles. Later biblical criticism is generally agreed that, however one regards the miracles, one cannot have Jesus without them. Miracles are an integral part of the Gospels. This, of course, is not to assert that miracles must have happened, it is merely an observation on the limits of biblical criticism.

An age which was unhappy about miracles had to explain why they had previously been so prominent. This brings us to the third general line of argument. It was widely assumed that the ancient world was particularly credulous and that it would therefore accept as miraculous what later ages would explain as natural, or even invent miracles to attach to the story of a great leader. Because it became such a widely accepted assumption it is important to disentangle the element of truth from what can only be called arrogance in this argument. It is true that later ages do know much more than former ones about the world, and thus have generally less sense of wonder about it. It is probable for instance that a modern psychiatrist would have a different interpretation for some instances of demonic possession. However it was a false application of evolution, of the notion of development and progress, which led many to believe that the 'modern' world is wise and the 'ancient' one credulous. The ancients were also wise and there is simply no justification for simply 'writing off' the biblical miracle stories as products of credulity.

Fourthly, there was a suspicion that to rest faith on miracles was unsatisfactory from the point of view of faith itself. No doubt the miracles had been overstressed in the past. Often they were used as if they could compel faith. It was right that men should be invited to see the work of God in the natural as well as in the supernatural. This was part of the thinking which led to the stress on God's immanence which was the chief feature of English theology until the 1930s. However, its best representatives, men such as Charles Gore, did not forget to balance immanence with transcendence and they did not categorically deny miracles.

In the face of the tendency to dispute miracles it was often pointed out that a person's attitude to the gospel miracles at least depended on his attitude to Jesus. Those who accepted him as the incarnate Son of God were, and are, more ready to accept the miracles.

It may also be added that much also depends on a person's estimate of the humanity of Jesus and of what might be considered 'natural' to humanity. The critics' attitude is usually based on a consideration of the humanity of men and women such as ourselves and what might be considered 'natural' to that. If account is taken of the possibility that Jesus had a unique relationship with God which freed him from the limitations which other men experience, it might be that our concept of what is 'natural' could be extended.

Such a reflection might also provide a standpoint from which to view some other well authenticated accounts of, for instance, miracles of healing within the Church. It could be natural that those who go some way to sharing Jesus' relationship with God might also share some of his freedom from the limitations which others experience.

Notes

1   O. Chadwick, *The Victorian Church* (A. & C. Black 1970), Part 2, p. 7.
2   Cited ibid., p. 11.
3   J. Dillenberger, *Protestant Thought and Natural Science* (Collins 1964), p. 225.
4   D. Mackay, *The Clockwork Image* (Inter-Varsity Press 1974), pp. 42 f.
5   cited J. C. Greene, *Darwin and the Modern World View* (New York, Mentor Books 1961), p. 16.
6   cited I. G. Barbour, *Issues in Science and Religion* (SCM Press 1966), p. 90.

5
Biblical Criticism

A major change in English religious thought between the early or middle years of the nineteenth century and the later years of the twentieth lies in the different attitude to the Bible. English Protestantism claimed to be based on the Bible. In contrast to Roman Catholicism, it was claimed that 'the Bible and the Bible alone is the religion of Protestants'. For its part the Church of Rome, while giving authority to the Church and the place of tradition, had essentially the same attitude to Scripture. The Bible was accepted as giving information which was not available to reason, and this information was accepted as historically correct. It was this position which appeared to come under attack.

But more was involved than a debate among theologians. The Bible had helped to form the way of thinking of English civilization. For many it was the only book they had read, or heard read. Among the upper and middle classes it was often read daily at family prayers. Many working-class families were also proud of the 'family Bible', in the front of which was kept a list of family baptisms, marriages and funerals. The words and phrases of the Authorised Version of 1611 were part of common speech. Its stories were well known, feeding the imagination and conveying spiritual truth. The complaints of some critics that some of the stories are of doubtful moral worth were overcome by preachers who, with what later generations would call a falsely spiritualizing or moralizing treatment, were able to set them against the broader background of the whole of Scripture. Devout men and women could say with the Psalmist, 'Thy word have I hid in mine heart, that I might not sin against thee' (Psalm 119.11 AV). Thus the reality of God and his claims upon men were mediated through Scripture.

Yet there was a strange 'flatness', a two-dimensional nature, about the understanding and use of Scripture. Generally it was accepted, learned and passed on. The history, or what appeared to be history, was unquestioned. That the Ten Commandments had been given to Moses; that David had composed the Psalms as we have them, or Solomon the Proverbs; that the prophets had foreseen the coming of Jesus as the Messiah and his birth from the Virgin Mary; and that Paul had preached the gospel, founded churches and written letters; all these were accepted. They were all scriptural and somehow all on the same level because they were all in the Bible.

Of course some men had seen that there were problems. They had recognized for instance that there are two accounts of creation in the opening chapters of the Book of Genesis, or that what appears to be the same history is given in a slightly different form in the Old Testament Books of Kings and Chronicles. It was clear too that there are discrepancies even in the Gospels. Nineteenth- and twentieth-century biblical criticism did not bring such things to light for the first time, as is sometimes implied. Intelligent and pious men had not pondered over Scripture for so long and so earnestly without noticing things so obvious. But usually their piety had ruled their intellect. They had assumed that if there seemed to be a problem or a discrepancy it must be in their own understanding, and that further study, more prayerful meditation, would show that, properly understood, the Bible was correct after all.

They were also often surprisingly lacking in historical judgement or imagination. At one level they knew that Jesus and the Apostles had lived nearly two thousand years ago, that Isaiah was some eight hundred years earlier and Moses before that, and that the events recorded in Scripture took place in Palestine, Egypt, Babylon, etc. But, knowing those things, they frequently wrote and preached as if such differences of time and place did not exist. For all the reverence with which they approached Scripture they had in some ways 'domesticated' it and made it more manageable.

The work of biblical criticism was to change that picture. At its best it made the Bible even better known than it had been. It added extra depth and breathed new life into the flat two-dimensional picture. As a result it made it possible for readers to know the characters and the world of the Bible in a much richer and more living way. Many factors contributed to this new look at the Bible – a new attitude to history; reports of travellers; the work of

84

archaeologists; a growing knowledge of parallel cultures, their literature and religions; new ways of handling the literature of the Bible itself; and better texts. Through all these factors, and by a combination of them, the Bible was brought to life in a new and exciting way.

But for all this there was a price to pay. Chiefly it came through a loss of security, a feeling that the old confidence in the Bible was being shaken. When the new approaches were described as 'scientific', as they were when scholars spoke of the scientific approach to history, or literature, or sources, many people felt threatened. After all they had heard that science was opposed to religion. Sometimes the critics, or more frequently their popularizers, were impatient or clumsy in presenting their work. Great claims were sometimes made for what appeared to be its negative elements. It seemed to be dismantling an old, even venerable, view of Scripture without supplying a better one to replace it.

Partly as a reaction to what was perceived as frightening and destructive, and partly from sheer conservatism or timidity, some sought to 'defend' the Bible against its critics. Too often the result was that men took sides and argued. They seemed to be arguing about the work of criticism and its results; in fact their divisions often arose from prior philosophical or emotional decisions about whether such approaches to Scripture were permissible for Christians at all.

Such divisions on this subject have been with the Church ever since. The situation is made worse by the range of meaning in the word 'criticism'. At its best, as far as this context is concerned, it means a serious, scholarly approach to the Bible. At its worst it can mean the acceptance of a denigratory attitude which delights in shocking the faithful and overturning accepted views. Serious scholars should accept the first, worried conservatives feared the second. Some mischievous souls, knowingly or not, have appeared to move freely between the two.

History and Archaeology

The nineteenth century and early twentieth century saw an upsurge of interest in the study of history among English scholars. There had been notable historians before but history had become a branch of literature. Particularly in respect of the ancient world historians had tended to accept what evidence they could get, which was usually in a documentary form, and tell the story of the past in an uncritical, often somewhat moralizing, tone.

Now a new mood became evident. It began in Germany and its most notable exponent was *Georg Niebuhr* (1776–1831). Niebuhr and his followers believed in testing historical documents and not accepting traditional accounts of events unless they were confirmed from impartial sources. The result was a pendulum swing from a willingness to accept everything to a desire to doubt everything unless it could be proved. Niebuhr applied his methods to classical studies in his *History of Rome* (1812), the revised version of which was translated into English by Connop Thirlwall and Julius Hare, two prominent English 'Broad Churchmen', in 1828 and 1831. The critical approach to sources was claimed to be 'scientific'. Attention turned to comparison of texts, counting, storing, collecting and rearranging 'facts', to such an extent that, for some, it appeared immature and 'unscientific' to accept anything but such facts. Once such techniques had been applied to classical literature it was clearly only a matter of time before they were also applied to the Bible. It was argued that the Bible must be studied like any other historical book and set in the light of the growing knowledge of the ancient Near East. Its accounts of nature and history should be compared with those which come from other sources and from the natural sciences. The Bible was not to be immune from criticism because it was 'sacred'.

An important contribution to the growing knowledge of the ancient Near East came from archaeology. Archaeological interest in the lands of the Bible began rather late. For generations travellers to Greece and Rome had brought home souvenirs from the ruins, and the romance of the recovery of the city of Pompeii, destroyed by an eruption of Mount Vesuvius in AD 79, had begun in 1594. But the beginning of systematic archaeology in the lands of the Bible is generally attributed to the geographers and surveyors who went to Egypt with Napoleon in 1798. In the following years progress was made with increasing speed. Ancient languages were discovered and deciphered. Ancient civilizations were brought to light. Scholars learned to date remains of rediscovered cities, principally through pottery. Artefacts of all kinds illustrated the lives of the people. Of greatest importance was the discovery of

ancient texts. Until the middle of the nineteenth century the Bible
was virtually the only written source available for the life and
history of the peoples it mentions. Now other texts became
available, making possible that critical comparison which historians were now demanding.

In 1865 the Palestine Exploration Fund was set up in London.
Previously the work had been done by gifted amateurs and
enthusiasts, sometimes slightly eccentric. Since that time many
similar organizations, French, German, American and, of course,
Israeli, have come into existence. Excavations have been carried
out on specific sites and occasionally, as in the finding of the Dead
Sea Scrolls in 1947, chance discoveries have been made. The result
is a wealth of material giving a far greater knowledge of the ancient
history of the biblical lands.

The first reaction of many biblical scholars to archaeological
studies was to look for confirmation of the biblical record. In some
few cases it appears that there is such direct confirmation. The
Moabite Stone, discovered in 1868, was erected by Mesha, king of
Moab, around 830 BC. It tells how Moab having been humbled by
Omri and Ahab, kings of Israel, successfully rebelled against the
next king, Jehoram. Thus it tells the story told in 2 Kings 3 from
the Moabite point of view. It is probable that the Siloam inscrip-
tion, discovered in a water tunnel in Jerusalem in 1880, refers to
Hezekiah's redirection of the waters of Gihon into Jerusalem in
about 701 BC as recounted in 2 Chronicles 32.30. The Lachish
ostraca, discovered in 1934 and 1935, come from the last days of
the Babylonian siege of Jerusalem and consist of letters relating to
the defence of outposts of that city. They reflect incidents
recounted in the Book of Jeremiah and may contain a reference to
the prophet (cf. Jeremiah 34.7).

Many other attempts have been made to link archaeological
discoveries to incidents mentioned in the Bible, but such links do
not amount to the 'proof' of biblical accuracy which is sometimes
claimed for them. We know for instance, from work at Ras Shamra
and Mari in the 1920s and 1930s, that some customs described in
the patriarchal narratives correctly reflect the culture of the time
and period. But they do not 'prove' the stories of Abraham, Isaac
and Jacob. The Tell el Amarna tablets, discovered in 1888,
mention the '*Habiru*' people who troubled Egyptian authorities in

the dependent city states of Canaan early in the fourteenth century BC, but this does not 'prove' a date for the Exodus. Finally, it seems likely that the walls of the city of Jericho did fall at some time, but the most likely date does not fit in with the time of Joshua and the account could not amount to 'proof' of the story in Joshua 6.

The great contribution of archaeology to biblical studies is not really in this kind of attempt to identify, or confirm, specific historical incidents. It is rather in the placing of Israel within the wider culture of the region. The writers of the Old Testament had seen the previous inhabitants of Canaan largely as a threat to the purity of their religion and had judged them by their hostility to Yahweh. Thus there is a dismissive ring to such comments as 'Hereby ye shall know that the living God is among you, and that he will without fail drive out from before you the Canaanite, and the Hittite, and the Hivite, and the Perizzite, and the Girgashite, and the Amorite, and the Jebusite' (Joshua 3.10; cf. 9.1; 12.8). But now we know that at least some of those named were advanced civilizations. Even such nations as the Assyrians and Babylonians had previously been known to scholars largely from their contacts with Israel, and thus from Israel's point of view. Now it is possible to know something of them from their own point of view.

Great interest and controversy were aroused by the similarities which emerged between some of the religious stories and customs of the surrounding nations and those known from the Old Testament. There is for instance a Chaldean account of creation probably dating from early in the second millennium BC. It is known as *Enuma Elish*, from its opening words 'When from on high . . .' (Note that the book of Genesis also takes its name from the first word in the Greek text.) In this work the world is seen as emerging from a conflict between the god Marduk, representing order, and Tiamat, representing chaos. An even earlier Egyptian creation story represents the god Ptah creating by thought and word. There was also a Chaldean account of the flood, known as the *Gilgamesh Epic* in which Ut-Napishtim tells the story to Gilgamesh the King. The Code of Hammurabi, an Amorite king of the seventeenth century BC, has resemblances to some of the law codes of the Old Testament.

The first reaction was to exaggerate the similarities between these texts and parts of the Old Testament. The *Gilgamesh Epic*, for instance, was first hailed as corroboration of the flood story. Later scholars have been more cautious. They have been less inclined to make links with the Old Testament. Instead they have pointed to many differences in detail and, above all, to the different, monotheistic, 'tone' of the Old Testament. Nevertheless, the effect was to show the similarity between Israelite culture and that of surrounding nations and thus to minimize the uniqueness of the Old Testament.

The Revised Version

Perhaps the most important and permanent achievement of British biblical scholarship in the later part of the nineteenth century was the production of the Revised Version of the Bible. By that time a number of early manuscripts and parts of manuscripts were available which had not been available to the translators of the Authorised Version of 1611. This was particularly true of the New Testament. The translators of 1611 had used manuscripts which were themselves largely copies of a Greek version of the New Testament which can be traced back to the fourth century. The edition of the Greek Testament which they used later came to be known as the 'Received Text', though that title was given to it by a publishing house in Leyden and it has, as a description, no more authority than a good advertising slogan. Among other manuscripts now available two were particularly important, both also from the fourth century. One was the *Codex Vaticanus* which had been in the Vatican Library in Rome but had not been available to the translators of the Authorised Version for political reasons. Now, though often grudgingly, the Vatican authorities began to allow non-Roman Catholic scholars access to it. The other was the *Codex Sinaiticus*, which the German scholar Tischendorf had rescued from St Catherine's Monastery on Mount Sinai in 1844. It had been in a box of old manuscripts which the monks were using to light fires. The edition of the Greek New Testament produced by Westcott and Hort in 1881 was very largely based on Vaticanus and Sinaiticus.

Gradually it became clear that the Authorised Version could no longer claim to be based on the best available manuscripts. In 1870 the Convocation of Canterbury set up two committees, one for the Old Testament and one for the New, to produce a new translation.

Even at that stage a number of leading churchmen were afraid that alterations to the familiar text of the Authorised Version might undermine the faith of some. Therefore a number of conditions were imposed on the committees which included directions that they should make as few alterations as possible and attempt to retain the style of the Authorised Version. Changes from the Authorised Version were to be noted in the margin. The one major change which was urged upon the revisers was the use of paragraphs and a scrutiny of the use of italics and punctuation.

At the suggestion of the Convocation the committees which were set up included scholars from all denominations. Newman was invited to represent the Roman Catholics but declined. At the same time two parallel committees were established in the United States with the intention of producing one agreed version. However, the conditions imposed on the British committees were not acceptable in America. The American committees were responsible for the American Standard Version in 1901.

The New Testament in the Revised Version appeared in 1881, a few days after the publication of Westcott and Hort's edition of the Greek New Testament. The Old Testament came in 1885. The introduction of paragraph divisions was generally accepted as helpful. But another change from the Authorised Version was an aim at greater consistency in translation – that is always to render a particular Greek word or expression by exactly the same English equivalent. That was generally seen as leading to a loss of style and an impression of 'woodenness'.

At the time, however, most interest and concern was aroused by the fact that some different readings had been accepted and some familiar words had been questioned, either relegated to marginal notes or omitted entirely. For instance it was noted in the margin that Jesus' words from the cross, 'Father, forgive them; for they know not what they do' (Luke 23.34), are not present in all the ancient manuscripts. The Ethiopian eunuch's confession of faith before baptism (Acts 8.37) was omitted completely as was the apparent scriptural confirmation of the doctrine of the Trinity, 'For there are three that bear witness in heaven, the Father, the Word and the Holy Ghost' (1 John 5.7 AV).

Both because of the changed or omitted words and because of the style the new version received some criticism. It has since been accepted as a much more accurate version than the Authorised Version, and therefore of greater use to students who cannot use the original languages. Nevertheless it has never achieved the popularity and widespread acceptance of the Authorised Version. Since its publication the discovery of even more texts and a greater knowledge of the biblical languages have tended to give it a somewhat 'dated' tone. Furthermore the twentieth century has seen the production of many other versions of the Bible which have generally paid more attention to style, intelligibility and accuracy of meaning rather than to absolute consistency of translation.

Development of 'Higher' Criticism

The establishing of a correct text is a technical and complex matter. It involves comparing ancient manuscripts and quotations from them in other works and making judgements about their comparative value. But scholars do have the manuscripts before them on the basis of which they can argue about possible readings. There is little ground for theorizing. However, other types of criticism, already quite well known in Germany, were gradually becoming known in Great Britain. These often did seem to be theoretical. They were generally put together under the not altogether helpful title of 'Higher Criticism'.

The custom of speaking of 'Higher' or 'Lower' criticism caused confusion. The terms were misunderstood. 'Higher' criticism seemed to imply that those practising it adopted an attitude of superiority to Scripture. In fact the picture behind the terms is that of a river. The 'Lower' part of a river is where it passes the observer. Hence 'Lower' criticism of the Bible is concerned with the actual text and asks whether the text we have is the best one. The 'Higher' part of a river is where it begins. Thus 'Higher' criticism of the Bible is concerned with the source of the biblical material. The 'Higher' critics attempted to get behind the text as we now have it and to ask such questions as: Who wrote it, when did he write it, for what purpose did he write it, and did he use any sources?

Of course such questions were not new, but in the late nineteenth and early twentieth centuries they were asked in a new intellectual climate. The biblical critics of the period brought at least three peculiar characteristics to their work. They had a growing knowledge of ancient Near Eastern religion and culture, so they were likely to set the Bible and especially the Old Testament against that background; they accepted the current critical 'scientific' approach to history and texts, so they did not approach the material with quite the same reverence as previous scholars had done; and they approached Scripture from an intellectual atmosphere deeply influenced by the progress of science and particularly by the theory of evolution translated to mean inevitable progress, so they were predisposed to find an evolutionary development of religious ideas in the Bible.

There was first a great interest in distinguishing underlying sources. In certain books repetitions or inconsistencies had already been noted. Now, as attention was given to the historical background and comparisons were made with contemporary or near contemporary cultures which had become known from other sources, scholars began to suspect that the historical background of some passages was different from the one traditionally accepted. It was tacitly assumed that a difference in historical background, or in the religious ideas expressed, or sometimes even in literary style pointed to a different author. Thus scholars sought to distinguish and label the different sources.

The result was a number of theories questioning the accuracy of some traditional views on the date and authorship of some biblical books. It was soon accepted, for instance, that the Pentateuch, the first five books of the Old Testament, could not be attributed to Moses as was the accepted view. Instead it was argued that there were a number of sources coming from different historical periods. In the same way it was argued that some of the prophetic books were in fact compilations of distinct sources. For similar reasons, implied differences in historical background, it was argued that the Psalms were of varying dates and could certainly not all have been written by David, and that the Book of Daniel came from the second century BC and not, as had been supposed and as the book itself implies, from the sixth century BC.

Most of this kind of criticism concentrated on the Old Testament rather than the New. Because of the wider time span covered by the Old Testament more dislocating in the traditional dating was likely. As far as the New Testament was concerned particular attention was paid to the Synoptic Gospels. It had been accepted that Matthew was the first to be written. Now, as the result of a series of studies, it came to be generally accepted that Mark's Gospel was the first to be written and that Matthew and Luke had used Mark together with a source which both had used, known as 'Q', and that both Matthew and Luke had their own source not known to the others, known as special 'M' and special 'L' respectively. As far as the rest of the New Testament was concerned it was argued that the Fourth Gospel was not written by John the son of Zebedee, though this conclusion was accepted much later in England than in Germany, and that some works attributed to Paul, notably the Pastoral Epistles, were not in fact written by him. In both cases it was suggested that the contents of the books indicated a later period for their composition.

Later scholars attempted to get behind the supposed sources and to ask how the material had existed before it came into written form. This type of study, known as Form Criticism (from the German *Formgeschichte*, better history, or tradition of forms), began with the basic assumption that much of the material existed in oral form long before it was written down. It also assumes that it is possible to identify certain key 'forms' or 'shapes' in which it was preserved. More important is the suggestion that in those forms the material was used in the life of the community which preserved it. Careful study indicated the forms in which laws were preserved, or in which a prophet may have delivered his message, or in which the community which preserved the Psalms may have worshipped. In all these cases parallels were drawn between the life and literature of Israel and that of the nations among whom they lived. Turning to the Gospels it was argued that the teaching of Jesus and the stories about him which have been preserved may also fall into recognizable forms and may have been used in the life of the early Church for preaching, teaching or argument.

It was an extension of Form Criticism when scholars, having accepted that a lot of the material once existed in relatively small units, began to ask why it was put together in the way in which we now have it. The presumption is that the biblical writers had some end in view when they collected and arranged the material, and that their particular end has influenced the way in which the material is presented. In other words it may be more accurate to think of them as arrangers or editors of the material rather than as authors. This is known as Redaction, or editorial, Criticism.

Methods such as these are very helpful in throwing light on how and why the material we now have in the Bible was preserved. They may help to throw light on the communities which kept the material and help to illustrate the problems they had. However, when they were first made widely known such more positive aspects were not the first ones seen. Two particular problems worried more conservative Christians. First, it looked as if the critics were reducing the teaching of the Bible and the biblical communities, both Israel and the Christian Church, by drawing parallels between them and the cultures in which they lived. Secondly, there was the suggestion that the communities may have made up the material to suit their own ends. The questions of the Bible's uniqueness and truth, normally understood as literal accuracy, were the main sources of argument between the biblical critics and those who saw themselves as defenders of Scripture.

There was, and is, some suspicion that traditional views were set aside too easily. Christians of a more conservative type sometimes felt that the whole process of biblical criticism was destructive. Certainly some extreme positions were adopted from time to time, as they have been subsequently when new approaches have been initiated, but the most extreme ones have usually been abandoned as a result of further study. As we shall see, the greatest confusion arose when the questioning of traditional views on such matters as the date, authorship or original purpose of parts of Scripture was seen as a rejection of its authority.

6

Reactions to Scientific and Biblical Criticism

We have noted that the Victorian age witnessed a growing sense of religious doubt among the educated classes in England. The progress of science and the growing awareness of biblical criticism did not so much create it as confirm it and focus it. For those who were aware of it, and it is important to remember that many were not, it came as an uneasy feeling that the foundations on which previous generations had been able to rest securely were being undermined.

Christianity has always been subject to attack. In every age there have been critics and scoffers and there were such people now. The late nineteenth century saw a growth of secularist agitation in England. *G. J. Holyoake* (1817–1906) began the London Secular Society in the early 1850s. He was joined in a somewhat uneasy alliance by *Charles Bradlaugh* (1833–91), and after some internal wrangling Bradlaugh emerged as leader of the party and re-launched it as the National Secular Society in 1866. Other similar societies were formed and numerous journals were published. But in a strange way these groups were hardly a threat. Their intellectual arguments were stylized and well known, as were the orthodox replies. Their criticisms of the wealth, the social and political influence of the Church and the hypocrisy of some of its leaders were not only known but shared by many Christians. Men like Stewart Headlam established working relationships, friendships really, with a number of the secularist leaders. Their opposition to Christianity was so well known as to be almost comfortable for both sides.

The new threat was more insidious. It was a growing agnosticism among self-consciously intellectual people which did not so much oppose orthodox belief as simply assume that much of it was false, and that intelligent men must naturally throw off much which had previously been accepted by orthodox Christians. Paradoxically many of the doubters had a remarkable confidence about their doubting. At the heart of it was an appeal to the conscience as well as to the intellect. On one level they were sure that doctrines such as the eternal punishment of the wicked, or the death of Jesus as a substitute for sinners to appease the wrath of his Father, were immoral. It was therefore a moral duty to reject them. On another level they were sure that doctrines such as the creation as recorded in Genesis, or the incarnation, or miracles, could not be accepted by intelligent modern men. They were relics of a superstitious past which were now known to be untrue. It was therefore, in another sense, a moral duty to reject them. On the other hand they were convinced that at the heart of Christianity there was an irrefutable moral ideal, and that it was in this ideal that its real value lay. As far as they were concerned they were more true to the ideal than those who clung to orthodoxy.

In the face of such confident agnosticism, and conscious of the twin threats of science and biblical criticism, what response could the orthodox make? Some merely drifted from a conventional, relatively unthinking, acceptance of Christianity into a conventional, relatively unthinking, agnosticism. A steady trickle of educated men and women 'went over' to Rome, though it would be too easy to say that they went simply in search of security. The vast majority continued in their faith, with varying levels of enthusiasm and commitment, unaware of any threats. Others sought both to defend the faith and, incidentally, to preserve that majority from the threats by appeals to authority. In the case of High Churchmen and Tractarians, that meant an appeal to bishops; in the case of Evangelicals, now increasingly becoming known as Low Churchmen, by appeals to Scripture.

Increasingly, however, a third group was emerging, the so-called 'Broad Church'. It was through them that the new knowledge and its effects on orthodoxy were to become widely known and notorious. In particular that happened through the book *Essays and Reviews* (1860).

The Broad Church and 'Essays and Reviews'

The title 'Broad Church' was one which men used of others more readily than they accepted it of themselves. It was a mood rather than a party, and was in fact suspicious of parties. F. D. Maurice expressly rejected the application of the description to himself on the grounds that the Church of England did not need parties. Yet he could be described as the archetypal Broad Church man. Certainly many to whom the title has been applied had affinities and often personal links with Maurice. They include his brother-in-law, *J. C. Hare* (1795–1855), *Connop Thirlwall* (1797–1875) the historian Bishop of St David's, *A. P. Stanley* (1815–81) the Dean of Westminster, and the writers of *Essays and Reviews*. In the background is the influence of Coleridge with his stress on truth experienced through deep feeling as opposed to being defined by external authority. Those included under the title did not always agree with each other, but they share some general characteristics.

First there is the appeal to toleration of breadth of opinion within Christianity. They opposed any attempt to limit too strictly what opinions might or might not be held by churchmen. In any case they insisted that orthodoxy could not be compelled and they stressed the value of private judgement. Hence they generally opposed the demand that clergymen of the Church of England should subscribe to the Thirty Nine Articles of Religion and the Book of Common Prayer, and they supported the relaxation of this demand in 1865.

Secondly they were all to some extent influenced by German theology. German theology was not widely known in detail in England until late in the nineteenth century, but it was generally thought to be rationalistic and hostile to traditional faith. Those who had any experience of Germany knew that ministers of the German Protestant churches did not have to subscribe to any statement of belief. They would know too of the influence of Schleiermacher who seemed to combine a fervent sense of dependence on God with an acceptance of the most critical attitude to Scripture and traditional orthodoxy.

Their willingness to adopt a critical attitude to Scripture may be taken as a third characteristic. To others it seemed that they were denying not only the authority of the Church, through their attitude to subscription, but also that of the Bible. Their answer was that modern science had made it impossible to accept parts of Scripture, especially the miracles, and that biblical criticism had shown different ways of regarding the literature. They tended to speak of only some parts of the Bible as being inspired, or of degrees of inspiration so that some parts were more authoritative than others.

To avoid the obvious difficulties of their position, and to provide some fixed point to which reference could be made for authoritative guidance, they had their fourth characteristic, the appeal to morality. Here, it could be said, is the heart of their position. Everything was to be judged by the appeal to morality. At the heart of Christianity, they believed, was a moral ideal, and at the heart of every man was the possibility of responding to that ideal. As they saw it traditional appeals to the evidence of miracles or to an authoritative Scripture were immoral in that they forced men to accept certain propositions as true, they did not appeal to the moral sense. As they understood it Christianity had the duty of setting before men and women an ideal to which they would, and could, respond. It was not an easy ideal. It demanded clear insight, strenuous moral effort and the assistance and fellowship of the Church. If that assistance was to be offered and men were to be attracted to the fellowship the demand that they should accept the literal truth of Scripture, or the truth of traditional orthodoxy, had to be put aside.

Finally the Broad Church was characterized by a remarkable optimism and belief in progress. Its exponents believed that if private judgement was allowed, and if men were encouraged to follow 'the moral law within' they could conform more closely to the Christian ideal. What was needed was education which would free them from superstition and fear of authority. Then, far from losing faith, they would emerge with a purer more confident faith.

It is temptingly easy to present the position of the Broad Church men as somewhat flabby and pompous. They had a romantic notion of a fearlessly critical approach, and seemed to have an heroic picture of themselves following the argument wherever it might lead and shaking of the conventions of the past in a noble search for truth. This is all intoxicating stuff, but not all who tried it had the head for it. One may occasionally detect an intellectual arrogance which seems to delight in facing problems which other – lesser – men did not know. There is a danger in a mood which is for ever searching and never coming to the truth, or which even prefers to be searching and is fearful of being committed. The

Broad Church was noticeably clearer about what it doubted or rejected than it was about what it asserted. There was also a clear tendency to suppose that morality and Christianity were somehow the same thing and that the highly moral man was the genuine Christian.

There is truth in such a picture but it is not the whole truth. There were serious problems in belonging to a Church about whose stated doctrines one has reservations. The problems for a minister would be greater. It was clear too that problems about the nature and authority of the Bible, and about the status of traditional orthodoxy, would have to be faced in England as they were being faced in Germany. The Broad Church was trying both to make the results of modern scholarship more widely known, and at the same time to keep within the Church those who were drifting into agnosticism. In effect they were redefining Anglicanism, and to some extent English Christianity, as adhesion to a living and moving tradition rather than as intellectual acceptance of static creeds. The difficulty in what they were attempting made it easier for those who accepted more rigid positions to attack them.

They were also unfortunate in incurring guilt by association. It was accepted that the moral ideal for which they strove was to be found in the person of Jesus. A notable presentation of Jesus as an ideal was made by the German *David Friedrich Strauss* (1808–74) whose *Life of Jesus* was published in Germany in 1835. In spite of the title Strauss left little of the gospel accounts of Jesus intact. Instead he spoke of the figure of Jesus found in the Gospels as a myth representing the ideal union of the natural and the spiritual. He does not deny that there was an historical Jesus. He also admits that, as far as our accounts are concerned, the union of which he speaks is presented through the story of one man and in terms of Old Testament messianic prophecies. However, as far as Strauss is concerned, it is axiomatic that such things as miracles do not occur, messianic thinking has been outgrown, and the important feature which remains is the ideal towards which the whole of mankind is tending. Strauss' position, especially his critical handling of the texts, was extreme. Few Englishmen would have gone so far. But when his book appeared in English, first in an anonymous translation of 1842 and then translated by the novelist George Eliot in 1845, it was seized upon by agnostics as an admission from within the Church that the gospel was false. This, it appeared, was the direction in which Broad Church tendencies would lead. The Broad Church men appeared to be agnostics at heart and the movement was feared.

The aim of the volume *Essays and Reviews* (1860) was to introduce modern ideas, especially on biblical criticism, to a wider public. The contributors wished to demonstrate both the inevitability of changes in the accepted views and also the benefits to real religion which would come from such changes. In a much quoted letter to Stanley, Jowett, the most distinguished contributor, affirmed their desire to remain 'within the limits of the Church of England', and added, 'We do not wish to do anything rash, or irritating to the public or the University'.

There were seven essays, uneven in length and quality. *Frederick Temple* (1821–1902), Headmaster of Rugby School and later Bishop of Exeter and London and Archbishop of Canterbury, wrote on 'The Education of the World'. This had previously been used as a sermon. It draws a parallel between the development of the race and that of the individual, a not uncommon use of the idea of evolution. The thrust was that just as an adult throws off the restraints of childhood, so the human race had reached a stage of development where it could take more responsibility upon itself. This could be shown in a more independent and critical attitude to Scripture, though it is assumed the Bible will continue to exercise authority through its moral appeal. Curiously, roughly a hundred years later ideas of man 'come of age' could still cause a stir in English religious life.

Rowland Williams (1817–70), Professor of Hebrew at Lampeter and Vicar of Broad Chalke in Salisbury, contributed a review of the biblical work of Baron Bunsen, a Prussian diplomat and scholar much admired by the Broad Church. Williams was already known to have controversial views on Scripture. He took the opportunity to list some of the conclusions of German biblical criticism and to argue for the idea of progressive revelation. Though the positions he reviewed were commonplace in Germany he knew that they would come as a surprise to English readers. Nevertheless he presented them in an aggressive way. He appeared scornful of a number of traditional doctrines, such as atonement through the substitutionary suffering of Jesus, and caused offence by the comment that the Bible should be understood as 'the written voice of the Congregation'.

Baden Powell wrote on miracles. He developed the argument that religion and science should be separated. For himself the orderliness of nature was a sure argument for God, miracles were unnecessary. While he did not specifically deny them, he argued that they could not be used as evidences to force belief or confirm faith.

H. B. Wilson (1803–88) is sometimes described as editor of the volume. He was Vicar of Great Staughton in Huntingdonshire and had been a tutor at St John's Oxford where he had been one of the four tutors to protest about Tract 90 in 1841. His theme was the National Church. In previous works he had shown his concern that the Church of England was losing the allegiance of many Englishmen. He felt that the reason for this was that modern men could not reconcile traditional Christian doctrine with their moral sense. In particular he felt that much of the Old Testament was immoral. He argued for a comprehensive Church with no definition of dogma and freedom of opinion among clergy, a rather extreme statement of a central Broad Church position. Like Williams he denied that the Bible was 'word of God' in the accepted sense and suggested that men should test it by its moral appeal. They would then find that though parts of it were primitive and could not meet the test, other parts would impose themselves by their moral authority.

Charles Goodwin (1817–78), an Egyptologist, was the only Cambridge man and the only layman in the group. He wrote on the Mosaic cosmogony. He argued that the creation stories of Genesis could not be reconciled with modern geology. However, he suggested that was no great loss since they were intended to give religious not scientific truth.

Mark Pattison (1813–84) wrote on 'Tendencies of Religious Thought in England 1688–1750'. He argued that theology should not be a matter of providing arguments for a given position, as it had been with the Deists, but that it should recognize its true basis in spiritual intuition. This was something which modern theology needed to learn from Coleridge. By implication this raised the question of authority and Pattison clearly preferred to locate authority in the individual's spiritual or moral experience rather than in any external source such as Scripture or the Church.

The final essay was by *Benjamin Jowett* (1817–93), tutor at Balliol and Regius Professor of Greek at Oxford. Jowett had previously written critically of the Evangelical understanding of atonement and original sin. His subject in *Essays and Reviews* was the Interpretation of Scripture. It is a long and involved piece which gives the impression that Jowett is often arguing with himself. His was a reverent and religious mind. He seems to want to find the 'word of God' in Scripture in some sense. However, on another level, he is convinced that modern scholarship has made the exclusive claims of the Hebrew Christian tradition untenable, religion is historically conditioned and the final court of appeal is the moral consciousness of modern man. To the question 'what then of the Bible', his answer is that it must be approached like any other book and its meaning will be plain. Certainly the Bible could not be immune from criticism.

From a distance of over a century *Essays and Reviews* appears somewhat trite. At the time, in England as opposed to Germany, it was certainly unusual in making public the differences in view which had grown up between the scholar and the layman. The fact that six of the seven contributors were Anglican clergymen, and the deliberately provocative tone with which they sometimes wrote, made it sensational.

Its appearance in February 1860 caused little comment. The furore about it began in October with a review in the *Westminster Review* by the agnostic *Frederick Harrison* (1831–1923). Harrison welcomed it, but suggested that the logic of the essayists' position should lead them to leave the Church, as he had done. Other writers of various shades of opinion agreed. Petitions and appeals were sent to the bishops and eventually a declaration was issued on behalf of them all saying that denial of such doctrines as atonement or biblical inspiration was not consistent with the Articles of the Church of England. It did not mention *Essays and Reviews* but clearly had it in mind. The fact that the declaration was signed by such people as Thirlwall, earlier known as a supporter of the Broad Church, and Tait the Bishop of London, a close friend of Temple, meant that personal disagreements were added to theological ones.

The outcry continued and eventually Williams and Wilson were prosecuted before the ecclesiastical Court of Arches for teaching which was inconsistent with their subscription to the Thirty Nine Articles. Those two were picked upon because they were the only incumbents of parishes and thus more directly under the bishops' jurisdiction. Of the others, Goodwin was a layman, Baden Powell had died, and the rest held university posts. Both the accused were suspended from their livings. However, they appealed to the Judicial Committee of the Privy Council and in February 1864 the earlier decision was reversed and they were legally reinstated. The debate inevitably widened to take in not only questions of doctrine and authority within the Church, but the question of the right of the secular state to sit in judgement on the affairs of the Church of England. It was further confused by another controversy, that of Bishop Colenso of Natal.

Bishop Colenso

J. W. Colenso (1814–83), a Cornishman by birth and a mathematician by training, became Bishop of Natal in 1853. A colonial bishopric was not a great prize. Colenso accepted it as an opportunity to serve his Church and the Zulu people. He earned a good reputation among the Zulus, who subsequently remained loyal to him throughout his legal difficulties. With the help of two Zulu assistants he set out to translate the Bible. As he did so they asked whether he accepted the stories he was translating as literally true and, though he evaded the questions at the time, he came to realize that he did not.

In 1862 he published the first of a number of books under the title *The Pentateuch and the Book of Joshua critically examined*. It borrowed heavily from German works in the same field, drawing attention to duplications and inconsistencies, casting doubt on certain stories and suggesting redating of some parts. In some respects it resembled the approach of *Essays and Reviews* but there were significant differences.

In the first place, unlike the essayists, Colenso does not speak of finding spiritual or moral truth in accounts which are unhistorical. The essayists had implied that the question of historical accuracy was not the most important one. But that is the question upon which Colenso fastened. Either the accounts are historically accurate or they are not, and he is convinced they are not. Then there is an 'oddness' about his argument in that he is so concerned with mathematical accuracy. He calculates the number of men, women and children who are supposed to have passed through the Red Sea, and how long it would have taken them; he is interested in the amount of food they would have needed, the possible rate of growth of the flocks, and he even speculates on the amount of dung likely to be found in the Israelite camp. His interest is in facts, literal not spiritual truth. Finally there was the fact that he was a bishop, albeit a colonial one, and hence must be taken more seriously.

His work appeared when Williams and Wilson, the essayists, were under suspicion. The English bishops, with the exception of Thirlwall who seems to have suspected that the tactics were wrong, wrote a collective letter suggesting that he should reconsider his position or resign his post. When Williams and Wilson were reinstated, the bishops were less confident about their position and Colenso more confident. His metropolitan, Gray, Bishop of Cape Town, called a Synod of the South African Church to consider the matter and Colenso was officially deposed as a heretic.

There then occurred a change in the general view of the matter. Colenso now appeared as a persecuted champion of religious freedom. He argued that the right of private judgement had been at the heart of the Protestant Reformation and accused his opponents of being disloyal to the Reformation principle. Public opinion had been against him, as far as his treatment of the Bible was concerned it probably continued to be against him, but now he began to appear in a more romantic, crusading, light, and public opinion became more sympathetic. The English bishops now appeared as representatives of harsh and oppressive authority.

Colenso appealed to the Privy Council. In 1865 judgement was given in his favour on the technical grounds that the Crown had no jurisdiction to create a bishopric in a colony which had its own legislature. This was not a reference to Natal directly, but to the Letters Patent which had been given to Gray when he had been appointed Bishop of Cape Town. It was on that authority that Gray had called the Synod which had deposed Colenso. The effect of the Privy Council decision was to restore Colenso to the temporal possessions of the see of Natal. The Privy Council had not pronounced on a matter of doctrine but simply on Gray's right to dismiss Colenso from his job and the salary and benefits which went with it.

Against the advice of the English bishops Colenso returned to Natal where he remained technically bishop until his death. In 1866 the Convocation of Canterbury declared that the Church of England was in communion with Bishop Gray. This, by implication, gave support to his excommunication of Colenso, though an earlier resolution to include a positive statement that the Church of England was not in communion with Colenso was toned down. W. K. Macrorie was consecrated Bishop of Natal and so there were two bishops until Colenso's death.

The legal disputes concerning *Essays and Reviews* and Colenso raised difficult problems, both theological and constitutional, for the Church of England. The complaint against Williams and Wilson, and here they stood for all the essayists and, indeed, for the Broad Church, was many-sided. There was the question of whether official teachers of the Church could accept and publicize the principles of biblical criticism. There was the further question, which came up more fully rather later, of whether or not such criticism did lead to the conclusions the defendants had reached. There was the underlying question of whether the essayists, and the Broad Church in general, had not departed from historic Christianity by reducing their understanding of it to morality and enlightened common sense. Finally there was the question whether logic and honour should not have led men who professed to put morality above all else to have left the Church if they could no longer subscribe to its teaching.

This welter of questions was in the air, but for the courts it was necessarily reduced to one: was the teaching contrary to the Thirty Nine Articles of religion and the Book of Common Prayer? The sixth of those Articles asserts the sufficiency of the Holy Scriptures for salvation, 'so that whatsoever is not read therein, nor may be proved thereby, is not to be required of any man that it should be believed as an article of the Faith, or be thought requisite or necessary for salvation'. But, as Wilson pointed out, it does not define inspiration nor argue that all parts of Scripture should be regarded as equal in value. In fact the Articles had been framed in a quite different intellectual background to deal with different problems. The point at issue had been to assert the authority of Scripture against other possible authorities. In suspending Williams and Wilson the Court of Arches probably correctly reflected the thought of most churchmen that the essayists were in error doctrinally. In reversing that judgement the Judicial Court of the Privy Council was asserting that their position was not contrary to the law as interpreted by the state. The bishops of the Church of England 'by law established' had to accept the decision or forfeit establishment.

The Colenso affair threw up some of the same questions. In that case the decision of the Privy Council was a personal triumph for Colenso and a setback for Gray and the English bishops. But the very technicality which led to Colenso's apparent victory could be seen as an opportunity for the exercise of episcopal authority and independence. In this case the bishops did not accept the secular court's decision as having any bearing on the Church's spiritual authority. The consecration of Macrorie showed that the bishops represented an authority independent of the state. However, it was noticeable that it was deemed prudent that the consecration should take place in Cape Town rather than in England. It was one thing for the bishops to assert their independence of the state but quite another to flaunt that independence. It was also unclear whether this assertion of the independent authority of the bishops could be taken as any kind of episcopal pronouncement on the propriety of ordained clergymen propounding unusual views of Scripture.

Gore and the 'Lux Mundi' Theology

It was the question of Scripture which caused most distress. English Christians had assumed that the Bible was inerrant and, for most of them, the question of its authority was bound up with the question of its inerrancy. They felt instinctively that if it contained factual error, or even if some of the traditionally accepted views about the authorship and date of its various books were found to be wrong, then the Bible would lose its authority. They were not content to be assured that though much of the Old Testament had to be considered to be folklore it was folklore with a moral.

It was in connection with the Old Testament that the battle was most fierce. As far as the New Testament was concerned English biblical scholarship was able to come to terms with German criticism and to show that the extreme positions sometimes advocated were not tenable.

German critical scholarship in the New Testament field was most clearly represented by the so-called 'Tübingen School' of F. C. *Baur* (1792–1860) and his followers. These scholars interpreted the New Testament in Hegelian terms as a conflict between Peter and Jewish Christianity on the one hand and Paul and Gentile Christianity on the other. They saw the early Catholic Church as a synthesis of the two. As this view was applied, the New Testament writings, and indeed Christian writings of the first two centuries, were assigned to one or the other side in the supposed conflict or were said to show signs of the later synthesis. For such a construction of early Christian history to be tenable much of the material had to be assigned to relatively late dates and the traditional views of authorship often had to be abandoned.

In a notable series of commentaries on the Pauline epistles – *Galatians* (1865), *Philippians* (1868) and *Colossians and Philemon* (1875) – the Cambridge New Testament scholar *J. B. Lightfoot* (1829–89), later Bishop of Durham, showed, by use of the strictest historical critical methods, that the Tübingen scheme was not tenable. With two friends, *B. F. Westcott* (1825–1901) and *F. J. A. Hort* (1828–92), making the so-called Cambridge triumvirate, Lightfoot planned a series of commentaries on the entire New Testament. The complete series did not appear. However, enough was produced to show that the strictest critical study did not support Baur's thesis but led to conclusions much closer to the traditional views on such matters as the date and authorship of the various New Testament books.

For many English Christians the works of such men as Lightfoot, Westcott and Hort provided an antidote to the excesses which were sometimes produced as the latest biblical scholarship. But such works did not reach a very wide public; they were concerned with one area of the debate only, that is the historical rather than the philosophical or doctrinal; and in any case for many readers even the works of such relatively conservative scholars were flawed because they did accept that the critical approach to Scripture was an appropriate one.

As far as the Old Testament was concerned there was nothing similar to the work of Lightfoot, Westcott and Hort, and the changes in traditional views which appeared to be demanded by the most recent criticism were considerable.

Reactions varied. Pusey, who in his youth had been acquainted with some of the German biblical scholars and had once come forward as an apologist for them, now presented himself as an opponent of biblical criticism. He turned his great learning to a commentary on the Book of Daniel in which he argued for the traditional sixth-century BC date for its composition, against the second century BC date which was coming to be accepted. *H. P. Liddon* (1829–90), a scholarly and devout Canon of St Paul's and generally recognized as Pusey's successor as leader of the High Church party, showed how near to the heart of the accepted Christian faith biblical criticism appeared to go. In his Bampton Lectures, *The Divinity of Our Lord* (1887), he drew attention to the number of occasions in the Gospels where Jesus had quoted the Old Testament and had apparently accepted the traditional views about it. It seemed, for instance, that Jesus had accepted that Moses wrote the Pentateuch (Mark 7.10), that David wrote the Psalms (Mark 12.35 f.), and that Jonah had spent three days and three nights in the belly of the whale (Matthew 12.39). Such passages, and more could be quoted, were very widely used to discredit biblical criticism. The implication was that for the critics to deny such ascriptions of authorship, or the historicity of such events, was the same as to question the divinity of Jesus. It was accepted that divinity implied omniscience and that therefore Jesus knew who the authors had been and whether or not the events recorded were historically correct.

Others tried to maintain an orthodox position while allowing that the practice of biblical criticism was, in principle at least, appropriate for Christians, and that what seemed to be the irrefutable findings of the natural sciences could be accommodated to an orthodox Christian outlook. The most influential and all-embracing attempt to come to terms with the criticisms of the age and to maintain the orthodox position came from the University of Oxford and from the successors of the Tractarians. It came in the collection of essays entitled *Lux Mundi* which was published in 1889 under the editorship of Charles Gore, at that time Principal of Pusey House, Oxford.

Just over sixty years after its publication, J. K. Mozley wrote of *Lux Mundi*, 'Few books in modern times have so clearly marked the presence of a new era and so deeply influenced its character.'[1] Critics at the time did not always see it in that light. It was natural that it should be compared with the previous collection of theological essays to come from the University of Oxford, *Essays and Reviews*. Some critics put the two together and dismissed them both as hostile to traditional Christian orthodoxy. However, a comparison of the two helps to show the more positive and constructive nature of *Lux Mundi*, at least in intention.

Unlike the earlier collection *Lux Mundi* was the product of a group of men who were well known to each other and who were conscious of sharing certain basic religious as well as philosophical convictions. It came from the same group of Anglican academics, known to themselves as the 'Holy Club', who were largely influential in the formation of the Christian Social Union in the very year in which *Lux Mundi* was published. They met regularly in the rectory at Longworth near Oxford where one of their number, J. R. Illingworth, was rector. There the papers which later appeared as chapters of the book had been read to the group and criticized by it. Thus there is a coherence about *Lux Mundi* which is lacking in *Essays and Reviews*.

There is also a difference in the intention and what might be called the tone or manner of the two works. Broadly speaking, *Essays and Reviews* was drawing attention to intellectual problems which the writers felt English Christianity, and particularly the Church of England, was not facing. They were trying to alert their readers to certain elements of modern thought and they did so in a somewhat aggressive manner. In contrast the intention of *Lux Mundi* was more constructive, even pastoral. Recognizing the problems of the age, the contributors to that volume nevertheless believed that it was possible to present Christian faith boldly but in a way which took account of those problems. Unfortunately, in the preface to the first edition, this intention was stated in a way which led to misunderstanding. The phrase used was, '. . . to attempt to put the Catholic faith into its right relation to modern intellectual and moral problems'.[2] This gave offence in that it looked as if the modern problems were given a priority and that the Catholic faith had to be adapted in order to fit in with modern thought. Men such as Liddon would have preferred to speak of the need to see the modern problems in the light of the Catholic faith. In the preface to the tenth edition (and such was the popularity of the book that this appeared in the year after the first edition), Gore had to explain that 'it was not by any means intended to suggest that the modern problems or the modern sciences were the things of first importance and the faith only secondary'.[3] He further explained, 'We were writing as for Christians, but as for Christians perplexed by new knowledge which they are required to assimilate and new problems with which they are required to deal.'[4]

Finally, the contributors to *Lux Mundi* were all High Church-men standing consciously in the tradition of the Tractarians. It was from that tradition that they took what was perhaps their most significant characteristic. They were all steeped in patristic theo-logy and seem instinctively to have looked to the writings of the Fathers for the tools with which to express their faith, and there they found what they considered to be some remarkably up-to-date and relevant ideas.

The main thrust of the book is expressed in its sub-title, 'A Series of Studies in the Religion of the Incarnation'. The doctrine of the incarnation, the coming of the Son of God into the world to live as man, had been the main focus of the thought, and of the worship, of the Greek Fathers of the Alexandrian school. They had expressed it in terms of the divine Logos, or reason, of St John's Gospel. In the incarnation, they argued, the divine reason which had always been present as an organizing and directing force in nature and history had assumed a human form. In one sense this was seen as a perfectly natural and reasonable thing to have happened. Since man had originally been created in the image of God and was recognized as the 'highest' of God's creatures, it could be seen as fitting for the 'Logos' to appear in human form. At the same time it was a new departure for humanity, since Adam had turned from God and lost his communion with him. Thus the coming of the 'Logos' in the person of Jesus could be seen as introducing a new humanity which was superior to what had gone before. The writers of *Lux Mundi* were able to adapt this approach to the nineteenth century. However, the tension between presenting the incarnation as something natural and reasonable on the one hand, and as something quite new on the other, was not easy to maintain.

To begin from the incarnation may have had another advantage for them. It set them apart from the more Evangelical wing of the Church which traditionally began its thinking from the cross of Christ as an act of atonement. That starting point tended to stress the distinction between God and man, seeing God as quite separate from the world. That distinction, or transcendence of God, was part of what was accepted as orthodox thinking and was assumed in the usual views of creation, sin and judgement. These were the kinds of views which now seemed to be under attack.

In contrast *Lux Mundi* stressed the immanence of God, the idea of God as always present to, and somehow working within, his creation. This approach fitted well with the fashionable stress on evolution. Writing on 'The Christian Doctrine of God', Aubrey Moore rejoiced that 'Evolution has restored to us the immanence of God which Deism denied'.[5] Writing on 'The Incarnation and Development', J. R. Illingworth accepted evolution as 'the category of the age', used it to support the argument from design, and also argued that religion is universal to man and that, 'In short, the history of the pre-Christian religion is like that of pre-Christian philosophy, a long preparation for the Gospel'.[6] Writing on 'The Sacraments', E. S. Talbot, having stressed the relationship of spiritual and material, and hence the appropriateness of the gospel sacraments as vehicles of divine grace, comments, 'We seem to see the material world rising from height to height; pierced, indeed, and, as it were, surprised at every stage by strange hints of a destiny beyond all likelihood; yet only gradually laying aside the inertness of its lower forms, gradually seeming to yield itself, not merely to the external fashioning of spirit, but also to its inner and transforming occupation: till in humanity it comes within sight of that which God has been preparing for it, even the reception of his own image and likeness.'[7]

These quotations, which are typical, show the pervasive influence of the ideas of divine immanence and of evolution in *Lux Mundi*. At the time they were also seen to fit in with the thinking of the Oxford philosopher T. H. Green. Though not an orthodox

Christian, Green insisted on the recognition of a spiritual force which in some way undergirded and flowed through the material and with which, ideally, the human spirit was in contact. For Green this was a development of Hegelianism, but it had similarities to the patristic thinking which so influenced the contributors to *Lux Mundi*. A number of them had also been pupils of Green.

However, the single essay which attracted most attention was that of the editor, Gore, who wrote on 'The Holy Spirit and Inspiration'. In the preface to the tenth edition Gore complained of 'the disproportionate attention which has been given to some twenty pages on the subject of the inspiration of the Holy Scripture'.[8] He should not have been surprised since this was the area in which the traditional position seemed to be most under attack from modern critics.

Gore's essay contained two shocks for the older Tractarians such as Liddon. In the first place it accepted that biblical criticism was appropriate for Christians and assumed that its methods would be used as an approach to Scripture. This was demonstrated with particular reference to the Old Testament. Gore began with a wide ranging survey of the work of the Holy Spirit in nature, man and the Church, and drew attention to what he called 'the gradualness of the Spirit's method', that is, revelation is progressive, believers have received what is appropriate for their own time. Applied to the Old Testament this means it is possible, with the critics, to speak of different types of literature, of the idealizing of history and of the need to correct early ideas by later ones. The Old Testament, he wrote, 'postulates a climax not yet reached, a redemption not yet given, a hope not yet satisfied'.[9] It points, in other words, to the incarnation where alone finality is found.

What then of the testimony of Jesus and his acceptance of traditional ideas concerning the Old Testament? This was the second shock. Jesus, said Gore, deliberately limited himself to the ordinary human knowledge of his time, 'He willed so to restrain the beams of Deity as to observe the limits of the science of his age, and he puts himself in the same relation to its historical knowledge'. In a footnote Gore referred to the New Testament passages which refer to Jesus' self-emptying (2 Corinthians 8.9; Philippians 2.7).[10] Later he developed this in a full scale treatment of the person of Christ. This met the immediate problem of modern scholars appearing to know more than Christ had done, but it was difficult for the older Tractarians to accept and Gore was severely criticized. It was said that disappointment with Gore in particular, and *Lux Mundi* in general, hastened the death of Liddon who died in 1890.

With *Lux Mundi* Gore was established as a major figure and he remained prominent in English religious life until his death in 1932. We have noted his work as a Christian Socialist. As a theologian he worked out in more detail the lines laid down in *Lux Mundi*, though he did not press the idea of immanence as far as some of his fellow contributors were to do. He had a strong sense of the sin and evil in the world, and consequently of the need for an action on the part of God to put it right or to redeem men from it. Thus he stressed the significance of the cross.

As Bishop in turn of Worcester (1902–5), Birmingham (1905–11) and Oxford (1911–19), he was heavily involved in the life of the Church of England, and he dismayed some of his former admirers by emerging as a champion of discipline. He expected those whom he ordained to accept the historical truth of the virgin birth and resurrection of Jesus, and he saw it as his role as bishop to maintain the common tradition of the Church of England. Thus he opposed both what he saw as excessive Catholicism and what he saw as excessive Protestantism.

As bishop he proved himself a good administrator, but his chief strength was as an expositor of the Bible and as a teacher. Remarkably it was during his retirement that these gifts really flourished, especially in a trilogy, *Belief in God* (1921), *Belief in Christ* (1922) and *The Holy Spirit and the Church* (1924), later republished together as *The Reconstruction of Belief* (1926). Equally impressive was his part in editing *A New Commentary on Holy Scripture* (1928). These works may be a better memorial to him than *Lux Mundi* and some of his more controversial actions as bishop.

Notes

1   J. K. Mozley, *Some Tendencies in British Theology* (SPCK 1951), p. 17.
2   C. Gore, ed., *Lux Mundi* (John Murray 1889), p. vi.

3   op. cit. (10th edn 1890), p. x(n).
4   ibid., p. x.
5   ibid., pp. 71–5.
6   ibid., p. 150.
7   ibid., p. 309.
8   ibid., p. x.
9   ibid., p. 254.
10   ibid., p. 265.

7
Liberalism, Modernism and Reaction

Lux Mundi was essentially an assertion of Catholic orthodoxy. The writers denied that they were 'guessers at truth'. Recognizing the impact of scientific thinking and biblical criticism they nevertheless believed that it was possible to state the traditional faith of the Catholic Church in a manner appropriate for modern man. Gore's use of the phrase 'Liberal Catholicism' to describe his own theological approach is significant. He sees himself as a teacher of the Catholic faith who accepts the validity of critical methods of study. In other words, he is a true descendant of the Tractarians who has taken account of the influences which produced the Broad Church.

This approach was helpful to many. However, there were others who felt that orthodoxy could not so easily be preserved. As far as they were concerned the acids of modern criticism had eaten more deeply into the fabric of orthodoxy than Gore had realized or would admit. It seemed to them that much which had once been accepted must be jettisoned or reinterpreted. In English religious thought much of the first forty years of the twentieth century was taken up with this debate. It was rarely so simple as a dispute between clearly defined schools of thought, though there were, as we shall see, movements which can be fairly clearly defined. It was more a matter of different responses to shared problems and influences.

We saw that the Broad Church was influenced by German thought. It is in Germany that the development of the movement, or mood, known as Liberal Protestantism can be most clearly charted.

Development of Liberal Protestantism
German theological thinking was some way ahead of that in

England. In the face of early scientific and moral criticism, *F. D. E. Schleiermacher* (1768–1834), sometimes referred to as 'the father of modern theology', set in train an approach to religion which, in spite of criticisms, has had followers ever since and which has even influenced its critics. He asserted a radical discontinuity between science and religion: 'Religion resigns at once all claim on anything that belongs to science or morality.' That is, religion is not a matter of ideas about the world or man which make their claim on the human intellect and may be verified there, that is the realm of science. Neither is it a matter of precepts for action which correspond to that which is 'right' for the actor or his society, that is the realm of morality. Instead, said Schleiermacher, the basis of religion is in feeling. It is not something objective and open to criticism, it is subjective and self-authenticating coming directly from God.[1]

Pursuing this theme Schleiermacher argues that all men at some time 'feel' that there is more to the world than is dealt with by science and morality. We might say they have an intuition of an area beyond explanation. He goes on to analyse this feeling as a sense of dependence on 'the whole'. This feeling, he believes, has always been fundamental to Christianity and the various doctrines of the creeds are ways of expressing it.

Schleiermacher's thinking is complex and wide ranging. For our present purpose it is sufficient to notice the impetus he gave to subjectivity and the correspondingly lesser importance he gave to the dogmatic elements in Christianity.

This movement was both extended and, in his view, corrected by the Lutheran scholar *Albrecht Ritschl* (1822–89). Ritschl was aware of the criticisms of Christianity. He too was critical of the old orthodoxy and the idea of an infallible Scripture. But he wanted a more positive stress. While agreeing with Schleiermacher that Christianity could not be reduced to science, philosophy or anything else, he argued against him that we should not begin our thinking from subjective experience. Rather, we should begin from the objective facts which give rise to those experiences. Chief of those objective facts for the Christian Church is the person of the historical Jesus. Christianity, for Ritschl, is basically a personal and moral response to the person of Jesus. In this response the believer makes what Ritschl called a 'value judgement' about

Jesus. He acknowledges that Jesus has the 'value of God' for himself.

Ritschl goes on to argue that men and women are made aware of the person of Jesus through the Christian Church and that the 'value judgement' commits them to the Church. He did not intend to promote individualism. But, while the Church as the bearer of the tradition about Jesus is important for Ritschl, he is very critical of the dogmas which had developed to explain the person of Jesus. In place of the dogmas he wanted to get back to the Jesus of history.

This historical digression helps us to understand Liberal Protestantism. Broadly speaking it is the followers of Ritschl, exposed to the criticisms of Christianity current at the end of the nineteenth and beginning of the twentieth centuries, who were the Liberal Protestants. They represented a mood rather than a school. Aware of the problems, and apparently fearful of appearing obscurantist, they were concerned to present Christianity in a positive light to their contemporaries. There were variations in emphasis but their chief themes, most of which have already been mentioned, may be summarized.

First, though not always recognized, there was an underlying rationalism. This appears in their opposition to the classical dogmas about Jesus and his work. They were embarrassed by the supernatural elements in the Gospels. This appears more as a tacit assumption than something which is argued. It is simply assumed that Jesus is a man, though clearly an exceptional one. Men do not perform miracles, neither are they generally held to be agents in an eschatological judgement of the world. These elements in the Gospels were therefore usually ignored or explained away. Sometimes an exception was made for the healing miracles which could be seen as the application of psychological principles and thus an illustration of how far Jesus was advanced beyond his contemporaries.

Secondly, they were optimistic about the progress of humanity. We noted this also as a characteristic of the Broad Church. With Liberal Protestantism it came from observation of the real improvements which the application of science was indeed bringing about in human life, and from an extension of the theory of evolution. It was also undergirded by the idealism of Hegel.

Thirdly, and closely related to the idea of progress, they had a very high view of man. Man was seen as the peak of creation and there was a stress on his moral perfectibility. This was accompanied by a virtual dismissing of the concept of sin. In most Liberal Protestant writings there is an appeal to man's 'higher aspirations', and a tendency to make modern man, modern criticism or modern civilization the final court of appeal concerning what can be true or possible.

Fourthly, there was a desire to separate the 'husk' from the 'kernel' of Christianity. They believed that there is some basic irreducible essence (or 'kernel') of Christianity which is always true, but that this is distinguishable from the form (or 'husk') in which it may be presented at any particular time. This essence they identify as the religion of Jesus. It is important to notice that it is the religion *of* Jesus, that is the religion which he practised, and, by implication, taught, for which they are looking. They are not looking for the religion *about* Jesus, that is the religion of which he is the centre as the object of worship.

Finally, quite naturally following the last point, there was a stress on discovering the 'Jesus of history'. The phrase 'Jesus of history' became almost a slogan for the movement. There was an assumption that a basically simple, straightforward and understandable Jesus has been overlaid by later dogmatic accretions – such ideas as his deity and his death as an act of atonement as they are expressed in the creeds. These accretions were attributed by some to St Paul and by others to the early Church, but it was agreed that they had to be stripped away so that the real Jesus could be revealed and encountered once more. In terms of later New Testament scholarship they had a remarkable confidence in the ability of historical methods of criticism to find the 'Jesus of history', but there is no denying the enthusiasm and the real scholarship with which they set about the task.

The classic exponent of Liberal Protestantism is usually held to be *Adolf von Harnack* (1851–1930). Harnack, a professor at Berlin, was basically a church historian. His *History of Dogma* (1886–9) was used by students well into the twentieth century. But his best known work was a series of lectures *The Essence of Christianity* (1901), translated into English as *What is Christianity?*

Harnack believed that the Synoptic Gospels could be treated as basically historical accounts of the life of Jesus but that the supernatural elements had to be stripped away. Thus he is left with the teaching of Jesus. In his exposition of this teaching in *What is Christianity?* he identifies three elements. The first is the Kingdom of God seen as an inward spiritual rule, 'the rule of the holy God in the hearts of individuals'. To experience this rule is to experience victory over evil. This is expressed by the synoptic writers in terms of healing miracles and the offer of forgiveness. It is a quality of life which is eternal: Harnack is clear that death is not the end. The second element is the fatherhood of God and the infinite value of the human soul. The believer is invited to share Jesus' experience that God is Father and so to live confidently in the Father's world. Because all others are equally God's children they must be highly valued and treated accordingly. Finally, he finds in Jesus' teaching what he refers to as the higher righteousness and the command-ment of love. In contrast to other religions and religious leaders, Jesus goes to the heart as the motive force of ethics; he does not leave men with a collection of external rules. Man is called upon to cultivate love for God and for others, thus copying Jesus. The more he does so the less will he need external rules.

The essential feature of all this is an inward relation to God conceived individualistically. It can be summed up as the Father-hood of God and the Brotherhood of man. The Church's later dogmatic teaching is seen as unhappy elaboration brought about by Hellenistic thinking, it is an addition to the essentially simple gospel and should be discarded.

An influential contemporary of Harnack's was *J. W. Herrmann* (1846–1922). Herrmann's influence came through his stress on the importance of the inner life of Jesus. He argued that while criticism might make men doubt the biblical records of Jesus' life, and while dogmas are merely historical expressions of the Church's faith at certain points in history and are not permanently valid, nothing can blot out the impact of the inner life of Jesus. This, he argued, has a power to transform those who meditate upon it and to bring them into communion with God. Thus he presented both a remarkable historical scepticism and a most attractive adherence to the Jesus of history.

Modernism

Though Liberal Protestantism may be seen as the continental movement which most influenced English religious thought during this period, it was not the only one. In conscious opposition to it, though sharing some of its basic assumptions, was the movement which came to be known as Modernism.

In its best known form Modernism was a movement within the Roman Catholic Church which can roughly be defined as an attempt to find a synthesis between accepted Roman Catholic positions and the new learning represented by scientific advances and biblical criticism. Its chief exponent was the French scholar *Alfred Loisy* (1857–1940). We shall consider the movement's considerable impact on the Roman Catholic Church later. Here it will suffice to say that the title 'Modernism' was not one which Loisy and his sympathizers chose for themselves. It was given to their approach by their opponents, but it has been widely used and was later accepted with more enthusiasm by some of its English exponents.

Loisy was writing in conscious opposition to Harnack's *What is Christianity?* He recognized that Harnack's approach was a way of coming to terms with biblical criticism and with the current criticisms of traditional orthodoxy. However, for Loisy, Harnack was wrong in his treatment of the 'Jesus of history' and also in the very nature of his appeal to history. The result was that, as far as Loisy was concerned, Harnack, and here he stood for the Liberal Protestants in general, was left with a false individualism which overlooked the place of the Church in Christianity.

As far as the 'Jesus of history' was concerned, Loisy argued that it was quite wrong to concentrate on his ethical teaching and to dismiss the supernatural elements and the eschatological teaching of the Gospels out of hand. His own portrait of Jesus, in *The Gospel and the Church* (1903), largely anticipated the one which would later be given at greater length and more powerfully by Albert Schweitzer. He saw Jesus not chiefly as an ethical teacher but as one who saw himself as the Messiah of Israel about to bring in the Kingdom of God, a supernatural incursion of the divine into history. The ethical teaching which Jesus did give was intended only for the short time which would elapse between his death and his return in glory which would be accompanied by the setting up of that Kingdom which should be understood in Jewish terms as a messianic community. In fact Jesus had been mistaken, at least in so far as he had used the categories of his own time. The Kingdom had not come. What had come was the Catholic Church. For Loisy, this did not mean that the whole of later Catholicism should be accepted without criticism, but it did, against Liberal Protestantism, establish the importance of the Church.

More interesting is his treatment of the appeal to history. For the Liberal Protestants to describe Christianity as an 'historic religion', or to appeal to history, meant to uncover the original historical events and teaching which had established Christianity, with the assumption that these events and teaching should have a normative role for later Christians. In other words, to find out what Christianity is one must go to its origins. Loisy, and other Modernists, suggest a different kind of appeal to history. With an eye on the Liberal Protestant illustration of the husk and the kernel, they argue that to find the essence of anything one does not go back to its origin but considers its whole development. The essence of an oak tree is not an acorn; one must consider the entire development from the acorn to the full grown tree. Thus, to find the essence of Christianity one does not go back to its beginnings but considers its whole history. By that he means the history of the Catholic Church.

If this approach is accepted it is possible to argue that the essence of Christianity is found in those basic ideas of the relationship between God and man which are found in the Church at all times in its development, with the recognition that those ideas themselves may develop. At heart this is the theory put forward by Newman in his *Essay on the Development of Doctrine* (1845). The stress is moved from facts to ideas. The very elements which Liberal Protestantism found most important, the historical facts, are downgraded, and those which Liberal Protestantism tended to dismiss, the doctrines of the later Church, are stressed. For Modernism it is a most important advantage that the doctrine need not always be expressed in the same way, it may develop, and it has a significance and a life which need not be dependent on historical facts. Even a statement of doctrine which appears to state an historical fact, the virgin birth is a good example, may be criticized, or even denied, on an historical level, while the essential teaching which it is believed to preserve may be affirmed.

The apparent benefits of such an approach are clear. It was possible to accept a critical attitude to Scripture while claiming to affirm what Scripture was *really* saying. It also meant that Christian theology could be understood in an evolutionary form, both in the sense that Christian teachers could understand the process of evolution as an expression of the immanence of God, and also in the sense that theology itself could be seen to be in a state of evolution. It could leave behind those statements of faith which had come to appear old-fashioned or inadequate and press on to possible new concepts. The problem which was to prove the Achilles' heel of Modernism was the question of who was to decide which statements should be left behind and which possible developments were the right ones. Loisy had cast the pope in this role, but the pope declined it!

Developments in England

Liberal Protestantism and Modernism were both responses to changes in the mood of the age brought about largely by advances in science and by biblical criticism. The Anglican theologian *Oliver Quick* (1885–1944) writing in 1922 suggested three contrasts between the two movements which we have mentioned above. Liberal Protestants found the basis of Christianity in historical facts, Modernists in ideas; Liberal Protestants looked for the essence of Christianity in its origin, Modernists in its development; Liberal Protestants stressed the individual as the organ of Christianity, Modernists the community.[2] But such distinctions, useful though they are, are best made from a distance. As we consider the impact of new thinking on English religious thought, especially among those who could not be satisfied with the restated orthodoxy of Gore and the *Lux Mundi* group, the labels are less helpful. Ideas from Liberal Protestantism and from Modernism are often found side by side or combined. Within the Church of England this combination is found in the approach of the self-consciously modern Churchmen's Union for the Advancement of Modern Thought, founded in 1898, which became the Modern Churchman's Union in 1928. Under each of its names the Churchmen's Union was responsible for a number of conferences in which its approach to the faith was expounded and which often attracted the attention of the secular as well as the religious press – attention which was sometimes hostile and, according to supporters of the Union, misleading. The Churchmen's Union was also responsible for the magazine *The Modern Churchman*, which was founded in 1911, and was for a long time the organ of its views. Nevertheless, Modernism in England, perhaps particularly in the Church of England, never meant quite the same as it did in French Roman Catholicism.

In England those who felt that a modern scientific outlook and a critical approach to the New Testament made some traditional elements of the faith difficult to hold, tended to combine a Liberal Protestant appeal to a basically simple, and easily understandable, Jesus of history with a Modernist stress on capturing the essential meaning of a traditional dogma rather than insisting on the literal accuracy of statements of the creeds. They expressed a desire to shake off the bonds of tradition and to state the faith in modern terms. Furthermore, they expressed this desire with what their opponents considered to be a naïve confidence in the inevitable correctness of modern thought and its supremacy over anything which had gone before. This tendency lent a certain pugnacity, even arrogance, to some of their writing and speaking which brought them into more conflict than they probably intended.

A particular source of concern was the question of clerical subscription to the creeds. The Churchmen's Union, and its supporters, felt that it was unreasonable to demand that Anglican clergymen and those wishing to be ordained should be called upon to profess their acceptance of the creeds as being literally true. In contrast, Gore, now a bishop, refused to ordain any who could not make such a subscription wholeheartedly. He made his views public in an Open Letter to the clergy of his diocese, Oxford, under the title *The Basis of Anglican Fellowship in Faith and Organisation* (1914). The result was a number of pamphlets or Open Letters in which several leading Anglicans set out their opinions on the question of subscription to the creeds. The usual position was that some general assent to their essential meaning should be accepted rather than a total belief in their historical accuracy.

A notable contribution to this debate came from *William Sanday* (1843–1920). Sanday, who from 1895 was Lady Margaret Professor at Oxford, was one who had come slowly to accept broadly Modernist views. In 1912 he let it be known that he could no longer accept the miraculous elements in the Gospels. Like many others, Sanday appears to have been willing to keep his views within the academic community. However, Gore was his diocesan bishop and an old friend, so he felt compelled to make some comment on the position which Gore had taken. He did so in an Open Letter, addressed to Archbishop Randall Davidson with the title *Bishop Gore's Challenge to Criticism* (1914). In the course of this letter he set out briefly what Roger Lloyd was to call the 'essential purpose of Anglican modernism'. Having argued that the cultivated modern man should have a place in the Christian Church as well as the simple believer, he went on, 'I believe that the cultivated modern man may enter the Church of Christ with his head erect – with some change of language due to differences of time, but all of the nature of reinterpretation of old truths, and without any real equivocation at his heart. I believe he can afford to say what he really thinks – provided only that his fellow Christians of more traditional types are willing to greet him with the sympathetic intelligence which he deserves.'[3]

Sanday spoke for many. Some of the most significant Anglican divines of the day would broadly have agreed with him. Among others, *B. H. Streeter* (1874–1937) the eminent Oxford New Testament Scholar; *J. F. Bethune Baker* (1861–1951) the patristics scholar; *H. M. Gwatkin* (1844–1916) the early church historian; and *W. R. Inge* (1860–1954) the authority on Platonism and Dean of St Paul's, all argued against Gore and were, to a greater or lesser extent, in sympathy with the Churchmen's Union. One of the most influential figures in the movement, though not himself an outstanding scholar, was *H. D. A. Major* (1871–1961). Born in New Zealand, Major later studied at Oxford and became Principal of Ripon Hall, a college set up to train Anglican ordinands according to Modernist principles. In addition he was for many years President of the Modern Churchmen's Union and editor of the *Modern Churchman*. He wrote widely in defence and explanation of the movement's aims and was its major apologist.

Among Nonconformists Liberal Protestant ideas were generally stronger than Modernist ones. But Sanday's comments, and much of Major's advocacy, would be congenial to men such as *T. R. Glover* (1869–1943), whose *Jesus of History* (1917) was a model of its type, and the eminent Congregationalist *C. J. Cadoux* (1883–1947) whose *The Case for Evangelical Modernism* (1938) was in part an attempt to commend Modernist thinking to his own constituency.

Sanday's letter sets the tone of much Modernist writing. There is the underlying assumption that 'modern cultivated man' is a peculiar type and that adjustments of the faith have to be made for his benefit. There is also the assumption that such adjustments are inevitable, but that they really amount to no more than a reinterpretation of the old language. Those who followed this line saw themselves partly as apologists, presenting the essence of old truth in a new situation, and partly as leaders in a movement of liberation and renewal, sweeping aside the traditional orthodoxy of the past and setting men free for a more confident, exciting and adventurous discipleship, more fitting for a more enlightened age.

When we ask how they understood the faith, their criticisms and denials are more prominent than their positive assertions. In general they were unhappy with the idea of the transcendence of God, preferring to think of an immanent life-force working through the process of evolution. Jesus was seen as exhibiting in a unique way the experience of divinity which was common to all men. Sin was part of man's lower nature but something to be outgrown rather than judged, thus Jesus' work of atonement was seen in exemplarist terms – he was the prophet showing a new and better way rather than the sin-bearer taking upon himself the judgement of God. Miracles were ruled out by modern science and the idea of an authoritative Scripture was considered to have been demolished by biblical criticism. On the whole they were embarrassed by religious enthusiasm whether of a Catholic or Protestant form. However, they were anti-materialists and believed it was possible to appeal to an inner spirituality in every man which represented his true self.

Some interesting, fairly cautious attempts to apply this type of thinking to major Christian doctrines appeared in the collection of essays entitled *Foundations* (1912), edited by B. H. Streeter. It would be a long task to set out all the variations offered, but two representative figures may give a flavour of the time and the movement.

R. J. Campbell (1867–1956) is interesting as a Nonconformist who advocated a fairly extreme Modernism and who found his home in a sacramental Anglicanism as his Modernism abated. His father had been an Irish Presbyterian who emigrated to England and entered the Methodist rather than Presbyterian ministry because he refused to subscribe to the Westminster Confession. Campbell himself claimed to have a naturally religious temperament, but to be repelled by any talk of conversion or personal religion. He became a Congregationalist because of what he saw as that denomination's lack of dogmatism.

From 1903 to 1915 Campbell was minister of the City Temple in London and thus occupied one of the most influential pulpits in the English speaking world at a time when great influence was exercised from pulpits. He was not trained in theology but read widely in the area. Years later, in his autobiography, *A Spiritual Pilgrimage* (1916), he recorded with naïve and touching pride the books he read in the early days of that ministry, mainly translations of German works of biblical criticism and philosophy. It was a heady mixture for which he was perhaps not adequately equipped, but which he sought to distil and pass on to others.

In the autumn of 1906 Campbell addressed the London Board of Congregational Ministers on 'The Changing Sanctions of Popular Theology', a paper later published in *The Christian World*, which gave an interpretation of God's dealings with man almost exclusively in terms of divine immanence. The result was a controversy within Congregationalism in which Campbell was accused of departing from the Evangelical faith. In fact Campbell knew, and rejoiced in the fact, that his teaching was hostile to Evangelical Nonconformity. Soon after the controversy broke he outlined his position in a hastily written and somewhat disputatious book, *The New Theology* (1907). He defined the New Theology as 'the attitude of those who believe that the fundamentals of the Christian faith need to be rearticulated in terms of the immanence of God', and went on to explain, 'Those who take this view do not hold that there is any need for a new religion, but that the forms in which the religion of Jesus is commonly presented are inadequate and misleading.'[4] One result was that he was invited to give a number of interviews to the *Daily Mail*, and that that newspaper set aside a column a day for correspondence on the issue during the spring of 1907.

As he worked out his rearticulation of the faith, it was clear that Campbell insisted on a living devotion to Jesus as the irreducible minimum for Christianity. However, the precise status of Jesus is not clear. He is described as 'divine' because he is in tune with the evolving process of the universe. 'Granted', Campbell wrote, 'that the devotion of Christians has been right in recognising in him the one perfect human life, that is the one life which consistently and from first to last was lived in terms of the whole, what are we to call it except Divine?'[5] Campbell argues that this does not deny the uniqueness of Jesus since no other man has reached this level; 'But this is not to say that we shall never reach this standard too; quite the contrary. We must reach it in order to fulfil out destiny and to crown and complete his work.'[6] Clearly the gulf between godhead and manhood reflected in the creeds has gone. Campbell said as much in an interview in the *Daily Mail*, 'We believe that there is no real distinction between humanity and Deity. Our being is the same as God's though our consciousness of it is limited.'[7]

Ideas of sin and atonement were also set aside. Sin is seen as a relic of man's animal nature exhibited in selfishness, and it is gradually being outgrown. On one occasion he challenged his hearers to observe the work of Keir Hardie and the Independent Labour Party, and to appreciate what he saw as their struggle to overcome human selfishness in society as an exhibition of the ongoing work of atonement. The death of Jesus on the cross becomes a supreme example of the self-sacrifice needed to overcome selfishness.

Within Nonconformity the reaction was mixed. That Campbell did not have wide support within Congregationalism can be seen by the names of those who wrote against the movement in the volume *The Old Faith and the New Theology* (1907) edited by C. H. Vine. Most reviewers or commentators criticized the blurring of distinctions between God and man and the tendency to pantheism. Some drew attention to Campbell's poor academic background and suggested he was not intellectually competent for the role of educator of the Church in which he seemed to have cast himself.

Perhaps the shrewdest comments came from the Congregationalist theologian *P. T. Forsyth* (1848–1921), an exponent of orthodoxy who had once been attracted by Liberalism. At first somewhat dismissive, '. . . some popular attempts at theology are like a bad photograph – under developed and over exposed',[8] he later, almost alone among Nonconformist critics, drew attention to Campbell's devotion to Jesus and commented, 'One or other must go, by a spiritual logic in the course of time – his prayers to Christ or his view of Christ and the cross.'[9] That was well said and typical of Forsyth. A weak theology, and especially a weak Christology, can never sustain a rich devotion to the person of Jesus.

Interestingly the most sympathetic criticism, and the most effective, did not come from the evangelical Nonconformist orthodoxy which Campbell saw as his chief enemy. It came from Gore in his book *The New Theology and the Old Religion* (1907). Gore knew the attractiveness and the religious value of an immanentist view of God, but he was also aware of its dangers. He had known Campbell when the latter was a student at Oxford. In Gore's blend of prophetic biblical religion and Anglo-Catholic sacramentalism Campbell seemed to have found what he needed. In 1915 he bought the publishing rights of *The New Theology* to prevent it being reissued, and in the following year he was re-ordained as an Anglican. He died as Canon and Chancellor of the Diocese of Chichester.

The furore over *The New Theology* lasted little more than a year, but it showed the trend which popular theology was taking. As Sir J. C. Compton Ricket told the Congregational Union in 1908, 'No recent utterance would have set the heather on fire if that heather had not been already dry as tinder.'

Hastings Rashdall (1858–1924) was as near as anybody to being the acknowledged leader of Anglican Modernists. He spent most of his life as student and teacher at New College, Oxford. From 1885 he was Dean of Divinity there, combining his academic work from 1910 with a canonry at Hereford. In 1917 he became Dean of Carlisle . At that point he left academic life but did not change his academic interests. His gifts and temperament fitted him for academic life, and perhaps made him less suitable as a leader of a popular movement within the Church. His genuine sympathies with Modernism are plain. He was a Vice-President of the

Churchmen's Union for the Advancement of Modern Thought from its inauguration in 1898, and became President of the Modern Churchmen's Union in 1923. It may be that his association with the movement led to his being associated in the popular mind, and in the minds of some theological opponents, with ideas that were more extreme and unorthodox than any that he held himself.

The basis of Rashdall's thinking was the individual moral consciousness. He believed that modern cultivated man turned from the Christian Church because he could no longer accept the supernaturalist framework in which Christian theology and ethics had traditionally been presented. However, as far as he was concerned, that framework was not essential to Christianity and should itself be discarded. He was convinced that God made himself known to all men through moral consciousness, and that Jesus differed from others because of his greater moral sensitivity and commitment to the moral way. In other words Jesus was different from other men in degree rather than kind, though Rashdall accepted that this difference was sufficient to make Jesus unique and to justify describing him as divine.

Rashdall believed that his position was orthodox. He recognized that it might, theoretically, be difficult to make a distinction between Jesus and any other ethical teacher, but he insisted that the important feature of Christianity was the teaching, not the one who gave it: 'I think it should be very distinctly realised that the truth and value of the Christian Ethic does not depend on the fact of its having been taught by Jesus himself . . . If it could be shown that the sayings which we have been in the habit of regarding as most characteristic of the historical Jesus were in reality none of his, if it could be shown that there never was an historical Jesus, or that we know nothing to speak of about his teaching, the truth and value of the teaching attributed to our Lord in the Gospels would not be one whit diminished.'[10] He was not himself so sceptical of the historical evidence but was quite sure that Jesus never made any claim to uniqueness or divinity.

His stress on ethics and the potential of all men to respond if they so desired dictated his views on sin and atonement. In a classic treatment of the subject, *The Idea of Atonement in Christian Theology* (1919), he argued that sin is a refusal to recognize and obey the voice of God in moral consciousness. Therefore, what is required to bring man back to God's way is that he should repent and commit himself to listen for that voice and to obey its commands. In this view of atonement, which is based on the teaching of the medieval teacher Peter Abelard, Jesus is presented as the great teacher and example who is willing to go to his death in pursuit of his ideal. The key thing is his teaching, not his death. The tradition in Christian theology which links forgiveness and atonement with God to the death of Jesus came about, Rashdall believes, by a false reliance on the Old Testament and a wrong emphasis on Paul rather than on Jesus himself.

It was his Christology which led to the great controversy of his career. In 1921 the conference of the Modern Churchmen's Union met at Girton College, Cambridge, and took as its theme 'Christ and the Creeds'. Rashdall's paper, 'Christ as Logos and Son of God', does not seem exceptional among the others. He denied that Jesus claimed to be divine: 'Jesus did not claim divinity for himself ... Never in any critically well-attested sayings is there anything which suggests that his conscious relation to God was other than that of a man towards God – the attitude which he wished that all men should adopt towards God.'[11] As he later said, this was the sort of thing he had been teaching for years and he considered it quite conservative. However, the paper was widely reported as denying the divinity of Christ. Chief among his theological critics was Gore, an opponent since Rashdall had spoken against subscription many years earlier. The press also took up the matter and with such virulence and lack of knowledge of the issues involved or the actual contents of the paper that Rashdall was able to sue one national newspaper for damages.

An interesting feature is Rashdall's assumption that he is saying nothing unusual. The supernaturalist framework, the creeds, even the traditional view of Jesus can all be put aside in favour of ethical idealism, and presumably for no other reason than to appeal to cultivated modern man. In the last pages of his work on atonement he suggests that the dividing line between men will be between those who accept and those who reject Christ's ideal: '... the meaning of the Church's early creed, "There is none other name given among men by which we may be saved", will be something of this kind: "There is none other ideal given among men by which we may be saved except the moral ideal which Christ taught by his words, and illustrated by his life and death of love; and there is none other help so great in the attainment of that ideal as the belief in God as he has been supremely revealed in him who so taught and lived and died".'[12]

Reactions

The approaches we have described as Liberal Protestant or Modernist, and the amalgam of them frequently found in England, frequently recur in the history of theology. The exponents of them whom we have mentioned were responding to real problems. Furthermore it is reasonable that those who attempt to present the Christian gospel should take account of any subjective spiritual awareness or innate moral sense in those to whom they are speaking. Nevertheless, even when this approach was at its height it had critics and a number of considerations conspired to weaken its influence, at least for a time.

Many felt that it had moved too far away from traditional Christian orthodoxy towards stressing the simple moral goodness in all men. Instead of being a gospel of judgement and grace to the world, Christianity was identified as the spiritual expression of the best in European, or British, culture. Teachers as different as the Anglo-Catholic *J. N. Figgis* (1866–1919) and the Congregationalist P. T. Forsyth warned their contemporaries against the complacency thus engendered.

In the realm of biblical criticism *Albert Schweitzer* (1875–1965) shook the Liberals' confidence in their picture of the Jesus of history. His book *The Quest of the Historical Jesus* was translated into English in 1910. It is a survey of attempts to write a life of Jesus. The conclusion is twofold. In the first place, those who have attempted the task have approached it with certain presuppositions and have produced a picture of Jesus which is congenial to themselves but which normally goes beyond the available evidence. Secondly, and more sensationally, Schweitzer argued that as far as the available evidence goes it presents a picture of Jesus who was an apocalyptic visionary, who thought in the terms of the Judaism of his own day and who expected God to intervene dramatically in world history to set up his Kingdom during his own lifetime. In that case Jesus died as a disappointed visionary.

As far as his ethical teaching is concerned, Schweitzer argued that it was by no means central to his message and was in any case impossible to live by for any length of time. In his words it was an interim ethic, demanding a life-style which could only be sustained for the short period until the expected Kingdom was established.

Subsequent New Testament scholarship has agreed that Schweitzer's conclusions were extreme, but that he had drawn attention to important themes which were being overlooked. After Schweitzer the supernatural element in the Gospels, and especially in the thinking of Jesus himself as it is presented there, had to be taken more seriously. Jesus could not be seen simply as a teacher of ethics, nor could Christianity be reduced to a moral system. In terms of New Testament criticism Rashdall had been out of date even as he wrote.

A much more serious blow to Liberal confidence came with the outbreak of war in 1914, a war between nominally Christian nations. During the next four years cultivated modern man showed just how far he had developed, and serious thinkers began to ask again whether the old Christian doctrines of sin, judgement, grace and redemption might not have more to say to the moral condition of modern man than had recently been supposed. A number of formerly confident Liberals have written of their rediscovery of the depth and spiritual reality of such doctrines. In addition to Campbell's *A Spiritual Pilgrimage* (1916), the autobiography *On to Orthodoxy* (1929) by D. R. Davies expressed the views of many.

Finally all forms of Liberalism in theology suffered from the criticisms of *Karl Barth* (1886–1968). In 1914 Barth was a Swiss pastor already questioning the methods and conclusions of his Liberal Protestant teachers. He has described eloquently his own breach with Liberal Protestantism when he found that most of those teachers had pledged support for Kaiser Wilhelm II and the German war policy. His response appeared first in his commentary on *The Epistle to the Romans* (1918) which, in the words of Karl Adam, 'fell like a bomb on the playground of the theologians'. As his theology developed it was concerned with the initiative and the grace of God. His starting point can be broadly summed up as an attempt to answer the question, 'What has the Christian Church to say to modern man that modern man cannot say to himself?' There could scarcely be a more radically different starting point from the wooing of cultivated modern man, and this was to be the dominant theology of the next forty years. But that must wait for a subsequent chapter.

Notes

1 F. D. E. Schleiermacher, *On Religion: Speeches to its Cultured Despisers*, tr. J. Oman (New York, Harper & Row 1958 edn), pp. 27 ff.
2 O. C. Quick, *Liberalism, Modernism and Tradition* (Longman and Co. 1922), chs 1–2.
3 G. K. A. Bell, *Randall Davidson, Archbishop of Canterbury* (Oxford University Press 1935), vol. i, p. 678.
4 R. J. Campbell, *The New Theology* (Chapman and Hall 1907), p. 3.
5 ibid., p. 75.
6 ibid., p. 76.
7. *Daily Mail*, 12 January 1907.
8 *The Tribune*, January 1907.
9 *Daily Chronicle*, 4 February 1907.
10 H. Rashdall, *Conscience and Christ* (Longmans 1916), pp. 274 f.
11 H. D. A. Major, ed., *The Modern Churchman*, vol XI, No. 6, p. 278 (this edition of the journal included all the papers delivered at the Girton Conference).
12 H. Rashdall, *The Idea of Atonement in Christian Theology* (Macmillan 1925), p. 463.

8

The Free Churches

The nineteenth century saw a remarkable growth in the numbers, confidence and .influence of what later became known as the English Free Churches. At the beginning of the century Old Dissent, consisting chiefly of Baptists, Congregationalists and Presbyterians had seemed on the defensive. As the century proceeded large numbers of traditional English Presbyterian ministers abandoned the orthodox belief in the divinity of Jesus and became Unitarians, often taking their congregations with them. For a time Unitarianism flourished and made some contribution to intellectual and social life. Joseph Chamberlain, who once appeared a possible successor to Gladstone as leader of the Liberal Party, and C. P. Scott, editor of the Liberal *Manchester Guardian* newspaper, were both Unitarians. But later the influence of the movement declined.

For Baptists, Congregationalists and the smaller but influential Society of Friends (Quakers) there was a new surge of life. They had received a fresh impetus from the New Dissent represented by Methodism in its various forms. For their part Methodists, though generally maintaining a certain distance from the others, increasingly accepted their own separation from the Church of England and their role as the largest of the non-Anglican Churches. Later in the century other groups, such as the Brethren, the Churches of Christ and the Salvation Army appeared and shared the time of growth.

The description 'Free Church', which we shall use in this chapter in spite of some anachronism, first became common towards the end of the century. It came from a desire to affirm what the non-Anglican Protestant bodies have in common and to assert their essential churchliness. They were no longer happy to be characterized by their differences from the Church of England, and by what, in Anglican eyes, were negative features, as in the titles Dissent and Nonconformity. With renewed confidence they proclaimed their positive views on churchmanship and on the nature, privileges and responsibilities of the Christian life. During the last quarter of the century they were on the crest of a wave. It carried them to the First World War and then, in the space of little more than a generation, it ebbed and has never since flowed again with such vigour.

The repeal of the Test and Corporation Acts in 1828 made it formally possible for men to take public office without the necessity of receiving the sacrament of the Lord's Supper according to the rite of the Church of England. Those who had wished to do so had sometimes evaded the force of that law by a token reception, the practice of occasional conformity. In addition, since the early eighteenth century a Bill of Indemnity had been passed annually to protect those who infringed the law. But for conscientious men the situation was unsatisfactory.

In proposing the repeal in the House of Commons Lord John Russell argued that religious divisions in England were not as serious as they had been, and that they had given way to political ones. Furthermore, he argued, the mood of the day was strongly in favour of liberty of conscience and freedom of worship, an argument which had long been dear to Free Churchmen. No doubt with memories of the American War of Independence and the French Revolution in mind, there were those who opposed the repeal on the grounds that it would weaken the Church of England and, by destroying the unity of Church and state, be injurious to the constitution. To meet these objections a clause was inserted demanding that candidates for public office should make a declaration promising to do nothing to injure the Church of England, a practice abolished in 1866. In fact, as we have seen, the greater freedom offered to Free Churchmen, together with the provisions of the Reform Act of 1832, influenced the leaders of the Oxford Movement and brought to light again some of those divisions which Russell felt had lost their power.

Life and organization

Descriptions of Free Churchmen which come to us from the nineteenth century do not usually flatter them. With a grudging acknowledgement of the sterner virtues, the chief impression is one of narrowness. Hazlitt, in 1819, while praising their support of liberty, wrote, 'The Dissenter does not change his sentiments with the seasons; he does not suit his conscience to his convenience . . . He will not give up his principles because they are unfashionable . . . He speaks his mind bluntly and honestly'.[1] Both Thomas and Matthew Arnold associated them with narrowness and smallness of mind. Taking up the motto of the newspaper *The Nonconformist*, 'The Dissidence of Dissent and the Protestantism of the Protestant Religion', Matthew, in 1869, wrote with patronizing superiority; 'Do not let us deny the good and the happiness which they have accomplished; but do not let us fail to see clearly that their idea of human perfection is narrow and inadequate and that the Dissidence of Dissent and the Protestantism of the Protestant religion will never bring humanity to its true goal . . . Look at the life imaged in such a newspaper as the *Nonconformist* – a life of jealousy of the Establishment, disputes, tea-meetings, openings of chapels, sermons; and then think of it as an ideal of a human life completing itself on all sides, and aspiring with all its organs after sweetness, light and perfection!'[2]

In fiction a similar view is found. Dickens in *Pickwick Papers* (1837) and *Bleak House* (1853) treats the Free Church preacher as a figure of fun. Charles Kingsley's picture of his hero's pious Baptist mother in *Alton Locke* (1850) is condescending, though not without respect. George Eliot and Mark Rutherford both knew the subject at first hand and are not unsympathetic, but the pictures they give in *Felix Holt* (1866) and *The Revolution in Tanner's Lane* (1877) conform to the notion of narrowness. Mrs Oliphant also wrote from experience and her *Salem Chapel* (1863) probably portrays some aspects of the life of such a chapel, but the whole is melodramatic and overdrawn.

A more sympathetic picture, and one which probably catches the plain man's views better than any other, comes almost incidentally in Thomas Hardy's *Far from the Madding Crowd* (1874). A group of working men are drinking in an inn and talk, as Hardy's minor characters often do, of religion. Agreeing that they all belong to the Church of England they contrast the demands and life-style of Church and Chapel: 'There's this to be said for the Church, a man can belong to the Church and bide in his cheerful old inn, and never trouble or worry his mind about doctrines at all. But to be a meetinger, you must go to chapel in all winds and weathers, and make yourself as frantic as a skit. Not but that chapel members be clever chaps enough in their way. They can lift up beautiful prayers out of their own heads, all about their families and shipwracks in the newspapers.' 'Chapel-folk be more hand-in-glove with them above than we', says another, and the first agrees, 'Yes . . . We know very well that if anybody do go to heaven, they will. They've worked hard for it, and they deserve to have it, such as 'tis.'[3]

Those who claimed to be heirs of the Reformation and guardians of the doctrine of justification by faith alone might not have been pleased to hear that they had worked for a place in heaven. But the implication that they were the ones who took their religion seriously, that more than the average member of the Church of England they exhibited that 'seriousness' which the Evangelical Anglican Wilberforce had given as the mark of 'real Christianity', was true enough. The abundance of meetings and the fact that they practised extempore prayer in which they prayed about their family concerns and the affairs of the day were also life-like touches.

For the Free Churchmen themselves, particularly in the early part of the century, the most appropriate picture from literature came from an earlier age, from Bunyan's *Pilgrim's Progress*. Here, if anywhere outside Scripture, was their model. The individual pilgrim, aware of his burden of sin until it is deliberately and consciously laid at the foot of the cross, who is then committed to the journey from the City of Destruction to the Celestial City, that was their pattern. The way is difficult. The pilgrim meets stiff opposition and is hindered by weakness, temptations and false friends. But, Bible in hand, and supported by true friends, constantly reminded of his own inadequacy and dependence on the grace of God, his journey is crowned with success. The combination of heroic personal commitment and struggle, with an acknowledgement of unworthiness and a humble submission to God, mirrors the lives of many. That such saints could be found in the Church of England is not in question. The peculiar history, disabilities and privations of the Free Churches made the picture peculiarly appropriate to them.

Such people would not have been conscious of narrowness in their lives or their outlook. They lived in the light of eternity. They had a world view which stretched from before the creation of the world to the final judgement and the consummation of all things in Christ. It took in God and his angels, Satan and his demons. In the middle, in the life of man, a drama of eternal significance was played out. Nothing could be more vital than that the individual had made his or her own peace with God, was assured that his sins had been paid for on the cross at Calvary and that every thought and action should be such as could await the final judgement of all things with confidence. Whatever critical descriptions may be appropriate to such an outlook, narrowness hardly seems to be one of them.

Yet that there should appear to be a negative streak and, at least from outside, an impression of narrowness is understandable. Free Churchmen generally stood for the principle of voluntaryism in religion. They believed that each man should be free to choose and practise his own religion (though in fact this meant his own form of Christianity), and that the state should not support any to the detriment of others. This led to opposition to the establishment of the Church of England and hence to a negative tone.

Then the life of the chapel could be all consuming and demanding. Sunday worship, though in most cases the highlight of the week, was a relatively small part of the whole. There would also be a round of Bible studies, prayer meetings, choir practices, fellowship meetings for men, women, young people and children, committees of various sorts, organized charity groups and social events. Throughout the year there would be a succession of annual events to be organized: not only the main festivals of Christmas, Easter and Whitsun, but also Harvest, Chapel and Sunday School anniversaries, visiting preachers from overseas missionary societies and probably a local evangelistic mission or revival. As the century progressed, provision for social and cultural activities increased so that many chapels had musical events, sporting activities, lectures and bazaars. It added up to a full life. Chapel could absorb the whole non-working life of a family, effectively cutting them off from any other activity and giving an impression of narrowness.

The same impression was fostered by their strict moral outlook. The importance of Christian witness was emphasized. At its best this was shown in commitment to evangelism and service to others, but there was always a stress on the saint being 'unspotted from the world'. It has always been easier for the Christian to measure his witness by the things which he does not do rather than those which he does do. Thus Free Churchmen were often known by their opposition to, or at least their abstaining from, the pleasures of others.

The life of the Free Churchman was centred on the local chapel. In contrast to the Church of England lay people took a large part in its leadership. As well as the minister, laymen (less often laywomen) would conduct worship, lead groups and take responsibility for pastoral care. Membership was not automatic, even for children of members. A definite decision was involved and it carried with it the acceptance of responsibility not only to attend and support Chapel activities but also to lead a worthy life. Minute books show that those suspected of failing in their discipleship were first encouraged, then admonished and finally, in extreme cases, excommunicated.

For Baptists entry into church membership was accompanied by baptism, which was only administered to believers who had made a conscious decision of faith. The others practised infant baptism which was followed by a rite of admission to full church membership normally for young adults.

Both Baptists and Congregationalists were Independents in church organization. That is they insisted that the local church is independent and complete in itself. It is not subordinate to something larger, the universal or Catholic Church. In its own setting it *is* the Catholic Church. Its seat of authority is the Church Meeting, the gathering of all members, and it is this body which, under the guidance of God, sets aside members as officers and 'calls' the minister. Ideally this is not an exercise in democracy, with each member having a vote. It is rather a theocracy as the entire body seeks the guidance of God through Scripture and prayer. The wonder is not that those professing it so often failed to reach this high ideal of the Church, but that they so often came near to it.

Presbyterianism and Methodism were both more centralized in their organization. For Presbyterianism each local church is related to, and to some extent under the authority of, a local synod composed of ministers and elders. The local synod is similarly related to the national assembly. In the early part of the nineteenth century the decline of Presbyterianism and its uneven geographical spread made this a difficult system to operate for most of England.

Methodism was the most highly organized, keeping many of the features it had developed as a society within the Church of England. Ministers were known officially as travelling preachers and were under the control of Conference which appointed them to groups of churches known as circuits. The appointment was normally for three years. There would be a number of ministers to each circuit and they would travel around the churches in the circuit, which could cover quite a wide area. Ministers were assisted by a body of Local Preachers who in fact conducted most of the services. For the individual Methodist the basic unit of organization was the Class Meeting. Each member was put into a class of twelve or so members which met under a leader, normally a lay person, for mutual help and instruction. Originally this had also involved payment of one penny per week which was used to support the work locally and to help members in need, but this custom was not always continued.

This strong central control and organization had been a major factor in the early growth of Methodism but by the beginning of the nineteenth century the conservatism of Conference, under the autocratic control of *Jabez Bunting* (1779–1858), and the unsettling effect of the constant movement of ministers, together with demands for local autonomy and greater participation of lay men in Conference had combined to produce strains and had led to the formation of independent Methodist connections. The most important were the Methodist New Connexion, which broke away from the original Wesleyan Methodist Connexion in 1797 on the issue of lay participation in Conference; and the Primitive Methodist Connexion which stemmed from the expulsion from the Wesleyan Methodist Connexion in 1808 and 1810 of two ministers, Hugh Bourne and William Clowes, who held open air meetings in defiance of Conference decisions. There were also a number of other smaller breakaway groups.

A Period of Expansion

Most of the Free Churches experienced growth in the nineteenth century. The removal of laws against them made their lives easier and some who had admired them from afar but had been unwilling to take the decisive step of joining were now emboldened to do so. At the same time those Free Churchmen who were successful in business, and there were quite a large number of them, were less likely to leave and join the Church of England for social reasons. But the major reasons for the steady growth in numbers and influence were more positive.

Their strength was in the middle classes. Their peculiar virtues of sobriety, thrift and hard work were attractive to such people. Furthermore their form of church government both demanded laymen of some education and also offered a channel of local influence to those who were looking for it.

However they did not neglect the poor. In many cases they had vigorous evangelistic drives which did reach the poor and those not immediately attracted to organized religion. The Primitive Methodists especially continued to work among the most deprived, such as the pit men of County Durham, and did attract such people into their churches. They also offered pastoral care to depressed agricultural workers and the new poor in the industrial towns. The Nonconformist minister, as much as the Anglo-Catholic priest, was no stranger to the need and depravity of the period. However, those who responded tended to adopt the Free Church life-style and move into the middle classes. Thus it would be true to say that the Free Churches not only attracted the middle classes, but helped to create them. At the same time there began a drift, never subsequently reversed, of Free Church life and witness away from the inner cities and the villages to the suburbs and country towns. In this way they became more attached to the middle classes and more removed from the poor.

Free Church worship emphasized the sermon and during the century they produced a remarkable collection of outstanding preachers each with his own particular emphases and each drawing a slightly different type of congregation. The Congregationalist *R. W. Dale* (1829–95) was at Carr's Lane Church in Birmingham for over forty years and exercised a remarkable influence on the life of that city. Through his friendship with Joseph Chamberlain, and somewhat less with Gladstone, he also exercised a major influence on the Liberal party and thus on national politics. The Methodist *Hugh Price Hughes* (1847–1902), who founded the *Methodist Times* in 1885 and who was in charge of the Methodist West London Mission from 1887, did much to convince his fellow Methodists of the importance of social issues. We shall note later his influence on political life. Perhaps the outstanding preacher was the Baptist *C. H. Spurgeon* (1834–92). During the 1850s his preaching in London attracted such crowds that he had to hire theatres and music halls to contain them. Eventually the Metropolitan Tabernacle with seating for over 5,000 was built for him in 1861. A conservative Evangelical, he reached thousands through his preaching and writing and was perhaps more influential through the ministers trained at the College he founded and which bears his name.

Men such as these, and there were many others, attracted many to the Free Churches. New chapels were built and were often full, but the move to the suburbs continued. The drift was not at first noticed. It was simply that chapels were built where people wanted them. But that also meant they were built where there were people who could afford them, and influence among the poor and the working classes continued to decline.

A result of growth was a concern among Baptists and Congregationalists for closer links between the chapels. At first this was on a local, then a county, basis. The Baptists formed a General Union in 1812 which was reorganized in 1832. Also in 1832 most Congregationalists came together in the Congregational Union of England and Wales. In both cases the autonomy of the local church was affirmed and neither Union claimed the power to legislate. Nevertheless both were regarded with some suspicion and it was a generation before they were more or less totally accepted.

Once accepted the advantages of such Unions were clear. There was a sharing of resources in terms of training ministers, in the support which could be offered to weaker churches and in evangelistic efforts. The annual meetings of the Unions were important as rallying points, as centres of theological debate and, perhaps most of all, as channels by which the government, and society at large, could be made aware of the views of an increasingly influential section of the population.

In 1876 the Presbyterian Church of England was constituted with close links with the Church of Scotland. It was never very large, nor very evenly spread thoughout the country, but its influence was out of proportion to its size.

Another Free Church group whose influence was far greater than its size appeared to warrant was the Society of Friends, or Quakers. They have been described as 'the aristocrats of Dissent'. Among their influential members were the families of Cadbury, Rowntree and Fry. More than the others they attracted the wealthy and influential members of society. Without formally abandoning the theological principles of their founder *George Fox* (1621–91), who had roundly condemned the church life of his day and had encouraged his followers to expect immediate and dramatic experiences of the Holy Spirit, they had developed a quietist and contemplative outlook. They continued to be active campaigners on social issues in which they frequently took the lead.

A number of other groups sprang up, usually in protest against denominationalism and seeking to return to the simplicity of the New Testament. Two are worthy of note. A former Anglican priest, *J. N. Darby*, became leader of a movement which began in Dublin and at first consisted of prayer meetings and Bible studies attended by members of various churches. This developed into the Brethren, a group committed to a simple New Testament Christianity. Sometimes known as the Plymouth Brethren because they developed strongly in that city, they practise believer's baptism and have no ordained ministry. Since their foundation they have experienced a number of divisions. The other group is the Churches of Christ, sometimes known as the Campbellites after their founder. This group too was an attempt, beginning in the 1830s, to overcome denominational divisions by a return to the New Testament. They grew in this country but were more successful in the United States where they are known as the Disciples of Christ.

It is not easy to express this growth in terms of numbers. In the early period only Methodists kept numbers. But even for them, and for the others when they began the practice, numbers were expressed in terms of membership. Since all Free Churches have always had a large number of adherents, people who often take a full part in the life of the Chapel without taking the step of becoming full members, this does not give an accurate indication of their strength. A national census of worshippers was taken in 1851, and a London one in 1904. The methods of counting are generally agreed to have been suspect, but the results indicated first that Free Churchmen had increased relative to the Church of England, and then that they maintained their numbers better.

From the evidence available it is reasonable to suggest that the actual numbers of Free Churchmen increased steadily from the beginning of the nineteenth century into the early years of the twentieth. Until the 1840s the increase more than kept pace with the increase in the population. There was then a period of levelling and by the beginning of the twentieth century while the actual figures were still rising the increase was not keeping pace with population growth. During the twentieth century there has been a steady decline, at least until the 1970s.

Removal of Disabilities

The repeal of the Test and Corporation Acts (1828) was seen by many Free Churchmen at the time as a decisive step towards the disestablishment of the Church of England, a view they shared with some leaders of the Oxford Movement. Two types of question were involved. The first was what might be called the pure argument, which could be advanced on theological, philosophical or political grounds, that it was wrong for Church and state to be so closely bound together. It was an offence against the Free Churchmen's belief in voluntaryism and religious equality, and it had within it the danger of state control over religion. But there was also a second, more pragmatic, type of argument based on Free Church grievances at their 'disabilities'. The Church of England was in a favoured position. It received benefits from the state, financial and in terms of prestige, which were denied to the Free Churches. In addition Free Churchmen were obliged to accept the ministrations of the Church of England for the registration of births, since only the baptismal registers of the parish church were recognized for such registration, for marriages and for burials in parish graveyards; they also had to pay rates for the maintenance of the parish church; and they could not graduate from the universities of Oxford, Cambridge or Durham.

Not all Free Churchmen were committed to the complete separation of Church and state. Methodists particularly were very slow to shake off their connection with the Church of England and even slower to commit themselves to anything which looked like involvement in politics. But all were concerned about the removal of grievances. In fact the two causes became confused.

The chief spokesman for disestablishment was *Edward Miall* (1809–91), a Congregationalist minister who resigned his pastorate in order to give his entire time and energy to the cause. In 1841 he established a newspaper, *The Nonconformist*, to propagate his views. Miall argued that all Free Church grievances stemmed from the failure to deal with this central issue. He tried to convince his co-religionists that they were responsible for their own problems in that they were content to be tolerated when they should be demanding equality. For him that meant disestablishment. To forward the cause he founded, with a number of supporters, the Anti-State Church Association in 1844, which in 1852 became The Society for the Liberation of Religion from State Patronage and Control, or the Liberation Society. When, in 1843, there was a division in the Church of Scotland largely over the relations of Church and state, and again when, in 1869, the Liberal government disestablished the Anglican Church in Ireland, the disestablishment of the Church of England seemed a real possibility. Miall himself became a Member of Parliament and on several occasions proposed the disestablishment in the House of Commons. However interest in the question passed and from the mid 1870s it dropped from public concern.

One reason for the decline in the appeal of the Liberation Society was that it adopted an increasingly secular line of argument. Men such as Dale believed passionately that the Christian Church should be free of state control, but his reason was that the Church was subject to the control of Christ. In other words it was a theological argument. When he found that other supporters of the Liberation Society were primarily concerned with the amount of money which the Church of England might get from the state, and that his theological argument was not congenial to them, he withdrew his support. Another who feared that the society's arguments were becoming less specifically religious was Spurgeon, and his dissatisfaction led to the Society's not being allowed to use the Metropolitan Tabernacle for its meetings.

A more important reason was that the genuine grievances of the Free Churches were in fact being removed. In 1836 they secured the right to solemnize marriages in their own licensed chapels and, in the same year, a general registration of births, marriages and deaths was established. After much dispute, including occasional campaigns of non-payment, the compulsory church rate was abolished in 1868. Entry to the ancient universities was secured in 1854, though Free Churchmen could not hold Fellowships until 1870 and could not proceed to the higher theological degrees of Bachelor and Doctor of Divinity until 1918. The last of the grievances to be removed was that concerning burials. From 1852 it was possible for large towns to establish municipal cemeteries, but for most people it was still necessary to use the parish churchyard and it was not until 1880 that a Bill was passed which allowed a non-Anglican service at the graveside. Even then the vicar could claim a fee and some clergymen were reluctant to permit what they felt were basically non-Christian ceremonies in their churchyards.

At the same time it gradually became more common for Free Church ministers to seek and obtain positions as chaplains to workhouses and hospitals. This could be seen as providing pastoral care for members of their own denominations, or even as evangelism, but it meant also receiving money from the state or the local authority. In such cases rather than campaigning against the establishment of the Church of England the Free Churches could be seen as sharing in the advantages of establishment.

'The Nonconformist Conscience'

Charles Stewart Parnell was leader of the Irish Party in Parliament, a campaigner for Home Rule for Ireland and an ally of W. E. Gladstone. In a widely publicized divorce case in November 1890, he was found guilty of adultery. For a short time it seemed likely that Gladstone would continue to support him. A number of influential Free Church leaders demanded that Parnell should go. The Baptist John Clifford wrote in the *Pall Mall Gazette* that English radicals 'must insist on Mr. Parnell's immediate retirement . . . Men legally convicted of immorality will not be permitted to lead in the legislature.'[4] At his afternoon service on the Sunday following the verdict the Methodist Hugh Price Hughes, while professing his support for the cause of Home Rule, stated categorically, 'we stand immovably on this eternal rock; what is morally wrong can never be politically right.'[5] Soon after, having consulted other Free Church leaders, Gladstone published a letter in which he agreed that Parnell should resign his leadership of the Irish Party.

It was in response to the campaign against Parnell that *The Times* first used the phrase 'The Nonconformist Conscience'. It was not meant as a compliment but rather to embarrass both Gladstone and his Free Church supporters. Most, though not all, Free Church opinion was in favour of Home Rule, but it was already acutely embarrassed by some of the tactics of some of the Irish Party which included civil disobedience and even murder. There was something decidedly inconsistent, *The Times* suggested, in a conscience which could tolerate such behaviour and yet be so affronted by adultery.

The episode is illuminating in a number of ways. It shows something of the nature of Free Church thought in relation to politics and social life; it shows its involvement with Gladstone; it shows the confidence of Free Churchmen in their influence, and their ways of using it; and it shows the increasing difficulties which their moralistic approach to life produced. High moral principles, however apparently straightforward and sincerely held, were not easily applied to complex issues, and men who believed they were acting from the highest and clearest motives could be accused of duplicity and hypocrisy.

In a full study of the Nonconformist Conscience, D. W. Bebbington has drawn attention to some basic convictions underlying it and to some features of the 'crusades' which sprang from it. The convictions were three, that there should be no boundary between religion and politics, that men in public office should be of the highest character, and that the state had a responsibility to promote the moral welfare of its citizens. From the inside this was no doubt unexceptionable, but from the outside there is at once the suspicion of a pressure group attempting to impose its will. In practical terms it led to the condemnation of what opposed biblical teaching or of what hindered the spread of the gospel. It is worth recalling that in much of their agitation the Free Churchmen were simply expressing the common Christian conscience of the time and that even those who professed no religious belief often accepted the moral arguments. There is nothing particularly odd in men and women accepting the arguments against the very sins in which they themselves indulge! The peculiar features were the harnessing of the chapel methods and mentality – the oratory, the passion, the emotionalism and threat of divine judgement – and the unfortunately negative tone of much of the agitation. It was easier to identify and campaign against certain evils than to combine to build up a better society.

It could be argued that motives similar to those involved in the Nonconformist Conscience had prompted opposition first to the slave trade and then to the institution of slavery. As early as 1743 the Quaker John Woolman had begun the protest and in the subsequent agitation Quakers and Free Churchmen generally had played a part beside Evangelical Anglicans. To a lesser extent they were involved in the agitation to reduce working hours and to improve conditions in factories. However, it was in the second half of the century, and through their influence in the Liberal party, that their particular type of agitation was more prominent and effective.

Their oratory spoke of the damaging effects of certain ills on the nation and they aimed at and achieved legislation on a national scale. But, at least during their period of greatest strength, they did not tackle the underlying causes of those ills in a systematic way, as the Christian Social Union attempted to do. They did not speak, as the late twentieth century came to do, of structural sin. They were more concerned with personal sins.

A particular cause of concern was sexual purity and the exploitation of women. During the 1870s, with Quakers and Methodists taking the lead, they campaigned for the repeal of the Contagious Diseases Acts. These acts, passed in 1864, 1866 and 1869, stipulated that women working as prostitutes within fifteen miles of certain military and naval towns should have medical examinations every three months. Their purpose was to check the spread of venereal disease. To the campaigners they appeared to condone prostitution and, incidentally, a certain attitude towards women. The argument was that fornication is sinful and that what is wrong in individuals should not be condoned, or even encouraged, by the state. By petitions to Parliament, letters to MPs, letters to the press, the use of their own press and large public meetings they stirred such indignation against the Acts that they were suspended in 1883 and repealed in 1886. The Free Churchmen were the most prominent activists in this agitation, for Anglicans generally favoured the retention of the Acts, but the single most influential individual was *Josephine Butler*, the wife of an Anglican clergyman. It was Josephine Butler who won Hugh Price Hughes to the movement at a campaign in Dover in 1872 where Hughes was in his first pastorate; he never forgot it. It is an interesting comment on the conventions of the time that the Congregational Union refused to allow discussions on the topic at its annual meetings because ladies were present.

Mearns' *Bitter Cry of Outcast London* (1883) was chiefly concerned with housing conditions. Though agitation and a little practical work began at once on the underlying problem of housing conditions, it was the revelations of sexual impurity which most stirred the Free Churches. The most sensational response came from *W. T. Stead*, editor of the *Pall Mall Gazette*, who, in 1885, drew attention to the problem of juvenile prostitution by actually buying a child, ostensibly for immoral purposes, and telling the story in his newspaper. Stead served a short prison sentence and the age of consent was raised from thirteen to sixteen. An incidental victim of the increased concern for sexual purity was the politician Sir Charles Dilke, whose career was ruined when his adultery was discovered in 1886.

Other areas of personal morality in which campaigns occurred were drinking and gambling. Contrary to public opinion the Free Churches were not always committed to total abstinence. There was strong feeling against spirits, regarded as aristocratic and effete, but much less against beer. The prominent Congregationalist *J. Guinness Rogers* (1822–1911), whose name betrays his connection with the famous brewing firm, spoke of the time when a barrel of beer was provided for delegates at meetings of the Congregational Union. He, and others, complained that the total abstinence movement, which is normally dated from 1 September 1832, when the 'seven men of Preston' committed themselves by oath to refrain from *all* intoxicating liquor, was pursued in such an emotional manner that it became a substitute religion. Until about half way through the century Methodists, though urging temperance, refused to allow their buildings to be used for meetings campaigning on behalf of teetotalism, on the grounds that they were too extreme and emotional. However the movement gained strength after the foundation of the United Kingdom Alliance in 1853, which aimed at prohibition.

Rather than advocating prohibition or total abstinence, Free Churchmen were more likely to attempt to control the social harm which they saw to come from excess drinking by restricting licensing laws. Thus they generally supported 'local option', the suggestion that local authorities should have power to regulate the opening hours of public houses and the general availability of alcohol in their own areas. There was a great deal of agitation with the underlying assumption that here was a social problem for which the state had a responsibility. But there was an awareness that opinion in the Free Churches was divided and also an instinctive suspicion of extremism.

The campaign against gambling had more general support. Here there seemed to be clearer moral issues. It was opposed because it promotes gain without merit, and so undermines work and thrift, and because it promotes gain through another's loss, and so is anti-social. Furthermore its results in the lives of gamblers and their families were seen to be evil. However, there was no obvious way of legislating against it. Moves to prohibit the publication of information about horse racing in national newspapers were unsuccessful. The stress moved, therefore, to personal influence and both the Prince of Wales and Lord Rosebery were publicly criticized for their involvement with gambling. The Free Churchmen were no respecters of social status and they expected their views to carry weight.

Political Involvement

Agitation on social and moral issues necessarily brought Free Churchmen to the brink of political life. It was not a movement which they all liked and it increasingly revealed differences between them. Nevertheless the privilege of the vote carried inevitable responsibilities in the use of it, and the conviction that the state could and should be used for moral ends made greater political involvement inevitable.

The Free Church attitude to politics drew on different strands within their tradition. A prominent one favoured quietism and a separation at least from the practicalities of politics. Long into the nineteenth century Wesleyan preachers were forbidden to speak at political meetings or to introduce politics into sermons, and their chapels could not be used for political meetings. Gradually this came to be understood to mean that they were not to support any party, though they were free to be involved in moral causes. Another strand, because of their history as well as their convictions, drew them to a general support of anything which could be seen as a movement towards freedom and equality; hence the emotional appeal of Chartism and the Anti-Corn Law League, though there was little practical involvement with either. Against this was the fact that their peculiar virtues flourished in an ordered society and, as they were increasingly successful in business, there was a distinct tendency to favour order and to look askance at what threatened it. Finally, it was a long time before Baptists and Congregationalists shook off their antagonism to the Church of England. In many districts, especially rural ones, Church and Chapel represented different societies so there was a distinct tendency to oppose the Church. Since the Church of England was considered to be Tory it was natural for the Old Dissent to be Whig at the beginning of the century and Liberal at the end of it, after all these parties had proved to be their friends. The Methodists, especially the Wesleyans, were more inclined to support the Tories.

A major reason for their later adhesion to Liberalism was the personality of Gladstone. Himself an Anglican High Churchman with Tractarian sympathies, he forged a remarkable link with the Free Churches. He recognized not only the significance of their numbers at the polls, but their genuine concern on moral issues and the strength of the Nonconformist Conscience. He consulted their leaders and was largely responsible for the removal of their disabilities. On their side they saw in him a man of principle broadly committed to the same concerns as themselves. Some Free Churchmen just did not bother with the details of politics but were simply content to accept that Gladstone would do the right thing. Such was his hold on them that two years after his death the mention of his name at the annual meeting of the Congregational Union was greeted with applause. It is to the credit of both Gladstone and his Free Church supporters that they were able to criticize his education policy and he was able to change his mind on the question of Home Rule without destroying the trust between them. Yet there were a number of political issues which divided or distracted the Free Churches and thus contributed to their decline. The question of Home Rule for Ireland was particularly divisive, the more so because it was complicated by the Parnell case. Ireland was broadly Roman Catholic. Most Free Churchmen had some ingrained anti-Catholicism and they had some genuine fears for their fellow Protestants in Ireland. Nevertheless, when Gladstone espoused the cause of Home Rule in 1886 most Free Churchmen followed him. Various reasons have been suggested: that they hoped to be rewarded by moves towards the disestablishment of the Church of England; that they saw the Irish question as standing in the way of other legislation and wanted it settled at almost any cost; that their traditional commitment to freedom and their anti-imperialism made their support inevitable; or that they simply followed Gladstone.

However many were unhappy and some division and much uncertainty followed. Joseph Chamberlain emerged as leader of those Liberals committed to retaining the Union, partly because he feared that Home Rule would be the beginning of the disintegration of the Empire and partly because he feared for the safety of Protestants in Ireland. Spurgeon, perhaps predictably, was hostile to any sell-out to the Catholics. More significant was the opposition of a man such as Dale. He continued to urge support for Liberal parliamentary candidates and to enjoy the confidence of Liberal leaders but he could not support Home Rule.

There was heart searching too on questions of foreign policy and the role of the Empire. There was always a strong peace movement and a feeling that Britain should not interfere in the affairs of other nations. But the Empire was a fact, and the growth of missionary activity was another. For those who accepted that British influence must be essentially good, and who were moved by humanitarian and missionary motives, problems were bound to arise. Hence there were quite emotional appeals for British action in favour of Bulgarians and Armenians who suffered quite appalling atrocities at the hands of the Turks during the 1890s. The most serious crisis was the Boer War of 1899. Some were critical of any kind of military action but others, the majority, saw British rule as essential. Hugh Price Hughes' change of mind highlights the problems. For years he had spoken disparagingly of military strength but he was committed to the need for British victory. In the event, not without problems and hesitations, his pacifism gave way to his patriotism. In that he prefigured the general Free Church response to the war of 1914–18. By that time the influence of the Free Churches was in decline but they used it to urge moves for peace until the war began and turned it into a moral crusade once it had begun.

The question of elementary education touched a number of Free Church nerves, their voluntaryism, their conviction that the state had a responsibility for the moral good of the people and their animosity to the Church of England. They could not all be held.

Even after 1870 Anglicans retained the greatest influence in the universities, though Free Church colleges were often established in university cities and gradually achieved the status of university colleges. Most of the public schools and the old grammar schools were Anglican foundations, though the Free Churches, especially the Methodists, had begun to move into that field. Elementary education, where it existed, was also offered by the Churches with the Church of England playing the major role. The principle of voluntaryism led most Free Churchmen to accept that situation and to urge that the Free Churches should establish similar schools for their own children. Certainly early in the century they did not look for state intervention, much less the aggrandizement of the Church of England. Thus when, in 1833, the government made a grant of £20,000, with £11,000 going to the Anglican National Society and £9,000 to the non-denominational British and Foreign Society, Free Church opinion was suspicious. In 1843 they campaigned against a clause in the Factory Act which would have provided some education, including religious education, to children working in factories, fearing that it would fall into the hands of the Church of England.

It was in 1870 that the Education Bill introduced by W. E. Forster, a Quaker, brought elementary education within the reach of all. In 1876 local authorities were able to make it compulsory in their own areas, and in 1891 it was made free.

This raised two sorts of problems. Because it was generally accepted that education would include religious education there was a clear case of the state supporting religion. Methodists had already accepted this position but the Old Dissent only did so reluctantly. More important was the question of the religion to be taught. Forster's Act provided for the support of the Church school where there was one and the provision of a Board School – a school responsible to a local Board – where there was not. It was envisaged that the local vicar would be on the Board and that denominational teaching could be given. This meant that Free Churchmen would support Anglican teaching through the rates and that, when education became compulsory, they would have to send their children to an Anglican school. After considerable agitation a clause, proposed by William Cowper-Temple, was introduced excluding the use of catechisms peculiar to any denomination, but still the Free Churchmen were not satisfied. For a time they even argued that there should be no religious teaching in schools. It is a sign of Gladstone's independence from his closest supporters that he stuck with Forster and the Bill was carried.

Subsequently, in London and some other areas, there were disputes on the School Boards. Some Anglo-Catholics in London wanted a more dogmatic presentation of their own position while Free Churchmen became more committed to the position of Bible teaching without comment.

More serious controversy arose over the 1902 Bill introduced by a Conservative administration. This abolished the Board schools and brought all elementary education, including Church schools, under the control of Local Education Authorities. The Church schools would remain self-governing and receive support from the rates. In face of Free Church opposition the Bill was carried. Committees of protest were set up in various parts of the country and some individuals refused to pay the rates, preferring fines or imprisonment. The hostility to the Bill united Free Churchmen for their last great crusade. It was largely responsible for the fall of the Conservative government and the sweeping victory of the Liberals in 1906. Sadly, though the question of education was debated throughout the life of the next administration, no satisfactory compromise was reached. The practice of issuing local syllabuses of religious education was introduced after the 1914–18 war, but the 1902 Education Act remained substantially intact until the Act of 1944.

The Parliament of 1906–13 included 181 Free Churchmen. It was the peak of Free Church involvement in politics and measures were carried which can now be seen as laying the foundations of the Welfare State, for instance the Old Age Pensions Act (1908) and the National Insurance Act (1911). But, strangely, the distinctiveness of the Free Church involvement was already in decline. Subsequent years have witnessed numerous individual members of the Free Churches who have been active politically but any significance which the actual denominations may have is quite different.

A Period of Decline

The life of the Free Churches in the twentieth century has involved notable contributions to theology, especially biblical studies, and to national life. Nevertheless it has generally been a period of decline. Changes in four closely interlocking areas help to explain this.

First there have been changes in the theological and spiritual area. The Free Church tradition was hit very hard by the criticisms of science and the advances in biblical criticism. Their traditional appeal was to the Bible. From it they had developed their form of church organization and their understanding of the Christian life. In addition they had developed a coherent theological system. It was the glory of the Free Churches that a far greater proportion of their lay people were able to express themselves theologically than was the case with the Church of England. The extensive use of lay leadership depended on it. Thus it could seem that the very foundations of their faith and life were under attack.

While Spurgeon never really came to terms with biblical criticism, men such as Dale and *A. M. Fairbairn* (1838–1912), first Principal of Mansfield College, Oxford, attempted to mediate the new thinking to their generation. Nevertheless, there has been a lack of confidence in this area among the rank and file.

This has both contributed to and been accompanied by a more disastrous loss of confidence in what might be called the spiritual realm. Christian life is never simply cerebral, it involves too the life of prayer, worship and experience of God, the knowledge of the heart as well as the head. This heart knowledge had been emphasized by the Free Churches. They had nurtured it through their prayer meetings, it had informed their worship and they had been able to speak of it in a simple unembarrassed way. They had stressed the significance of conversion, the conscious movement of the individual into an experience of God.

Such things did not suddenly vanish from Free Church life in the twentieth century but they certainly became less prominent. They were affected by the immanentalist view of God, and their traditional stress on religious experience became a stress on the experiences common to all men. It lost contact with the doctrines of the creeds and a vague religiousness took the place of a felt confidence in God as Father, in Jesus as redeemer from sin and in the transforming power of the Holy Spirit.

This trend was recognized before the turn of the century. One response was the Forward Movement in Methodism, a rather vague attempt to re-establish spiritual priorities against political or social ones. In 1907 an influential book *Nonconformity and Politics*, published anonymously but generally reckoned to be the work of H. W. Clark, a Congregationalist, argued that the Free Churches had given too much time and effort to political questions. By then it was too late. Debates on Clark's book generally took the line that there should be more stress on spiritual experience; however the theological heart had gone. In 1915 P. T. Forsyth wrote: 'For a generation now we have been preaching that experience is the great thing, and not creed; till we are losing the creed that alone can produce an experience higher than the vagaries of idiosyncrasy, or the nuances of temperament, or the tradition of a group, or the spirit of the age.'[6]

A more obvious change was social. With certain honourable exceptions they had lost contact with the working classes, those who received the vote in 1918. More seriously they had begun to lose their hold on what might be called their own constituency in the middle classes. Political meetings drew men from prayer meetings, mass entertainment made inroads into any kind of church attendance, even encroaching on the Sabbath. In response Home Mission Committees were set up, but were generally not well funded. Methodists established Central Missions in working-class areas which combined evangelism and social work. In addition chapels provided cultural and sporting activities, many also supporting the 'Pleasant Sunday Afternoon' movement which provided music and lectures on Sunday afternoons. These were valuable ventures in their own right, but they did not stop the drift. Agitation for legislation to defend the Sabbath was counter-productive, giving its supporters the reputation for trying to interfere with the working man's freedom to use his one free day in his own way.

There were changes in the political sphere too. The Liberal party declined rapidly. In its place came the Labour Party and the Trades Union movement with a different relation to the Free Churches. Few of the politically active Free Church leaders were socialists in a theoretical sense. They were committed to the cause of the poor but not to the restructuring of society. Furthermore they were inclined to judge the new movement as a criticism of the Liberal party which they knew rather than to consider it in its own right.

This is not to say that the Free Church commitment to the Labour movement has been negligible. Many of that movement's leaders came from a chapel background, and the influence of Methodism on the Trades Union movement has often been documented. But this has to be judged cautiously. It may be that the chief contribution of the chapels was organizational and practical skills. Men who had served in chapels as chairmen, secretaries and treasurers of committees; who had exercised responsibility as Deacons and Class leaders; who had learned public speaking as Local Preachers; such men had a lot to give and they gave it unstintingly. They also brought a large measure of idealism, but it was more often the idealism of Liberal Protestantism than that of the Puritanism which had nurtured the Free Churches in earlier days. Dreams of an earthly Jerusalem had often replaced Bunyan's vision of the Celestial City.

Finally there have been ecclesiastical changes, some of which will concern us in subsequent chapters. There has been a moving together of the Churches. This has been reflected within denominations. Most of the divisions of Methodism were united in 1932. In 1966 most of the independent Congregationalist churches which had been in the Congregational Union of England and Wales combined to form the Congregational Church. In 1972 they combined with the Presbyterian Church of England to form the United Reformed Church to which, in 1981, was added most of the Churches of Christ. The United Reformed Church continues to stress the independence of the local congregation, but it accepts a greater degree of centralization through provincial synods. Baptists have continued to maintain the principle of Independency, but they give a greater influence to their regional associations and have also been involved in unity debates. Concentration on the issues of church unity, while good in themselves, may have distracted the Free Churches from evangelism and contributed to their decline.

Two other developments call for brief mention. The twentieth century has seen the growth of two other denominational groupings. The various Pentecostalist churches have been present in England since early in the century. More recently there has been a remarkable growth in the Black-led churches which are usually also Pentecostalist in theology. Additionally there has been growth among independent churches which have no denominational allegiance and amongst House Churches. These movements, which we will discuss in slightly greater detail later, represent a significant growth point broadly in the Free Church tradition. It remains to be seen whether they will, as some of their leaders suggest, replace the older Free Churches, but certainly they add life to them.

Notes

1 W. Hazlitt, *Complete Works* (1932), p. 241, cited J. Briggs and Ian Sellers, ed., *Victorian Nonconformity* (Edward Arnold 1973), p. 101.
2 M. Arnold, *Culture and Anarchy* (Cambridge University Press 1869), p. 30.
3 T. Hardy, *Far from the Madding Crowd* (Macmillan edn 1974), pp. 313 f.
4 J. Clifford, *The Times*, 20 November 1890, cited D. W. Bebbington, *The Nonconformist Conscience* (Allen and Unwin 1982), p. 100.
5 D. P. Hughes, *The Life of Hugh Price Hughes* (Hodder and Stoughton 1903), p. 353.
6 P. T. Forsyth, *London Quarterly Review*, vol. CXXIII, pp. 193 f.

9
Roman Catholicism

Insofar as its members did not conform to the established religion of the state Church, the Roman Catholic Church was similar to the English Free Churches. Like them it enjoyed a considerable growth in numbers and spiritual vigour during the nineteenth century. But at the beginning of the century there was little indication of the growth that was to come. Numbers were small and Roman Catholics were generally regarded with suspicion, if not with outright hostility, by most English people.

Popular views

Much later, in 1852, when a Roman Catholic hierarchy had been re-established in England and Wales, John Henry Newman preached one of his most famous sermons, 'The Second Spring'. In it he looked back and described the condition of Roman Catholics in England early in the century: 'here a set of poor Irishmen ... there, perhaps, an elderly person, seen walking in the streets, grave and solitary ... An old-fashioned house of gloomy appearance, closed in with high walls, with an iron gate, and yews, and the report attaching to it that "Roman Catholics" lived there; but who they were, or what they did, or what was meant by calling them "Roman Catholics" no one can tell – though it had an unpleasant sound, and told of form and superstition.'[1]

Newman is exaggerating to make his point – the contrast between the insignificance of English Roman Catholicism in the recent past and what he confidently believes will be its glorious future. Yet he captured something of the feelings of most of his fellow countrymen. Englishmen early in the nineteenth century did not know much about Roman Catholicism, but the words conjured up ideas of something mysterious and sinister, a form of religion which shrank from the light, which was at best superstitious and at worst evil.

This popular view was based on ignorance and misunderstanding, fostered by ultra-Protestant anti-Catholic propaganda. But quite well-educated English Protestants accepted a lot of it. It was assumed that Roman Catholics were ignorant of Scripture, and that such ignorance was fomented by their priests, and by the higher clergy most of all. It was assumed too that, in place of the clear light of Scripture, Roman Catholic devotion fed on superstitious stories of saints and sacred relics with miraculous powers. Worst of all, it was assumed that the saving work of Christ at Calvary was obscured by false teaching on the role of the Virgin Mary and the saints as intermediaries between God and man, and by false teaching about the Mass and the role of priests.

Priestcraft, above all, was seen as the hallmark of Roman Catholicism. The priest was seen as a sinister figure who kept a hold on the hearts and minds, and often also the pockets, of his flock by his claim to be a peculiar and indispensable agent of God, without whose ministrations salvation was impossible. There were numerous stories of the deceit practised by priests and by members of religious orders to keep their hold on the Catholic faithful. It was taken for granted that if Roman Catholics were to read the Bible and if the errors of Roman Catholicism were made clear to them, they would naturally throw off their yoke and renounce their bondage.

Although these thoughts were rarely brought to the surface, there was a deep-rooted suspicion and fear of the *foreignness* of Roman Catholicism in the hearts of many English Protestants. The priest, and to a lesser extent the devout layman, was sometimes seen as the agent of a hostile foreign power. There was a folk memory of religious wars and persecution, of the pope's excommunication of Elizabeth I and his encouragement of those who might overthrow or assassinate her. Roman Catholics, therefore, were seen as disloyal. They were a threat to the British constitution and the British way of life. Such views were reflected in the coronation oath. In addition it was widely held that their religion excused Roman Catholics from keeping faith with non-Catholics.

Since they were *Roman* Catholics, and since the position and claims of the pope were to be a major concern in the development of English Roman Catholicism, it will be helpful to look briefly at developments in Rome during our period before returning to the English scene.

Developments at Rome

For most of the nineteenth century the papacy was characterized by two movements. On the one hand there was a dramatic loss of the papal states and a weakening of the pope's political significance; on the other an extraordinary and unprecedented concentration of power within the Church in his hands. With the loss of temporal power came a renewed stress on the spiritual power of the Church, which increasingly asserted itself as an alternative, self-contained, society, fiercely critical of all social, political and intellectual movements outside itself.

The revolutions and demands for liberty and democracy which swept Europe in the nineteenth century were, implicitly at least, anti-clerical. Though revolutionaries often used religious language and were often inspired by Christian sentiments, the Church as an institution was seen as tied to the *ancien régime*, part of the aristocratic and feudal system they wished to overthrow.

The weakening of the temporal power of the papacy was part of a long process. In the Middle Ages the Church had been an immensely important power, and the pope had been recognized, at least in theory, as the supreme ruler on earth. The sixteenth-century Protestant Reformation had destroyed the idea of a united Christian Europe, and had seriously weakened the political power of the papacy. With the growth of nationalism that power had been further limited, in practice if not in theory. Even in nominally Catholic lands secular rulers limited the Church's political influence. National Churches increasingly claimed power for themselves, though allowing the pope a primacy of honour and accepting in principle that disputes would be settled by reference to Rome. This assertion of the rights of national Churches was known as Gallicanism in France and Febronianism in Austria and Germany.

The process was now accelerated. At various times in the early nineteenth century, French, Austrian and Italian armies surrounded the papal territories, which were gradually whittled away by political agreements unfavourable to the papacy. The pope himself became something of a pawn in the politics of Europe and endured a number of humiliating exiles from Rome. The process reached its conclusion during the pontificate of *Pius IX* (1846–78), with the unification of Italy under Victor Emmanuel in 1860 and the seizing of Rome itself in 1870. In the following year, by the Law of Guarantees, the papal lands were reduced to merely nominal holdings. Though Pius IX refused to accept this arrangement he was powerless to prevent it, and he became a 'prisoner in the Vatican'. Theoretically, this situation continued until *Pius XI* (1922–39) secured better terms from the Italian dictator Mussolini by the Lateran Treaty of 1929.

Pius IX was the most influential Pope of the nineteenth century. Though he experienced the almost complete loss of the papacy's temporal power, he was responsible for initiating the movement which greatly strengthened the spiritual power of the papacy over the faithful, and which determined the character of the Roman Catholic Church for the next hundred years.

Pius regretted the separation of Church and state. He saw it as contrary to the will of God. Thus, though he began his pontificate with the reputation of being a liberal and a reformer, when he saw where the dominant political, social and intellectual forces of the time were leading he came to regard them as opposed to God. He could not prevent the advance of liberalism and democracy. What he could, and did, do, as far as possible, was to separate the Roman Catholic Church from modern thought and culture and provide within it an alternative society based on an alternative vision of reality.

The source and framework for this vision came from the medieval world and drew upon the philosophy of *Thomas Aquinas* (1226–74). The Church was seen as a hierarchical structure. Its earthly head was the pope, the representative of Jesus. Through the Church God made his will known. By membership of it men and women were reconciled to God. By its sacraments and obedience to its teaching the faithful were strengthened and directed in this life and prepared for the life to come. The usual channels for sacraments and teaching were the clergy who were the local representatives of the pope.

It was recognized that not everyone accepted this alternative society and this alternative vision of reality, and that national governments were increasingly ignoring it. However, for the faithful, that need not matter. Obedience to the Church rarely conflicted with obedience to the state, and it was accepted that God also worked through the state. However, the Church claimed a higher loyalty because it represented a higher reality. In ths way it was possible to present an alternative ideology without provoking conflict with the state, and in fact offering a judgement on all states.

By its exclusiveness the Roman Catholic Church also offered a judgement on all other Christian Churches and religious bodies. Those non-Catholics who called themselves Christians were technically heretics. They may not be to blame and it could be argued that they were Catholics by intention, even if they would not have described their situation in those terms. Nevertheless, they could only be sure of being within the will of God if they accepted reconciliation with the Roman Catholic Church.

A number of pronouncements during Pius IX's pontificate and beyond emphasized both the Roman Catholic Church's claim to an exclusive role and its separation from modern thought. In 1854, in the Bull *Ineffabilis Deus*, Pius declared the Immaculate Conception of the Blessed Virgin Mary – the belief (already held by the majority of Roman Catholics) that from her conception she enjoyed freedom from original guilt – to be part of Catholic dogma. This declaration strengthened the traditional veneration of Mary, and at the same time added to the authority of the pope in the Church. (In 1950 Marian doctrine was further enhanced by the encyclical *Munificentissimus Deus* of *Pius XII* (1939–58) which declared the Assumption of the Blessed Virgin Mary – the belief that Mary, 'the course of her earthly life having finished, was taken up, body and soul, into the glory of heaven'.) In 1864 came the *Syllabus of Errors*, which condemned as errors, among other things, the separation of Church and state, rationalism in all its forms, freedom of worship for Protestants in Catholic lands, liberalism in theology, Freemasonry and the Protestant Bible Societies. The tone of this document is summed up in the condemnation of the view, 'That the Roman Pontiff can, and ought to, reconcile himself to, and agree with, progress, liberalism and modern civilisation'.[2] In 1870 came the First Vatican Council and the declaration that, when speaking *ex cathedra*, that is, in his official teaching capacity, on a matter of faith or morals, the pope is infallible.

Liberalism in its theological form was further attacked by the encyclical *Providentissimus Deus* (1893) by which *Leo XIII* (1878–1903) attempted to set limits to the critical study of the Bible. Modernism, the attempt by some Catholic theologians to come to terms with modern thought, was outlawed by two documents issued by *Pius X* (1903–14) in 1907, *Lamentabili sane exitu* and *Pascendi dominici gregis*. Meanwhile, Leo XIII had pronounced Anglican orders invalid in 1896.

What these various declarations have in common is first, the assertion of the exclusive claims of the Roman Catholic Church to represent a sphere of reality distinct from the earthly one with which human governments have to do, and, secondly, an opposition to anything in the modern world which may criticize those claims or distract from that reality. It was perhaps the latter concern which lay behind the dalliance of many Roman Catholics with Fascism in the 1930s. It was seen as a bulwark against the worse threat of atheistic Communism. Opposition to Communism has continued to be a major feature of official Roman Catholic teaching.

Roman Catholics and Emancipation

In spite of the English people's antipathy towards Rome, the life of the Roman Catholic community in England before the Emancipation Act of 1829, though 'low key' was not as depressed as Newman, in the passage quoted above, implied. The anti-Roman Catholic laws were not usually enforced. In 1791 the provisions of the Toleration Act (1689) had been extended to cover Roman Catholics. This permitted public worship in registered buildings and gave them a position similar to that of the Protestant Dissenters. More important, the social position of the leading Roman Catholics, the professional advancement made by the growing middle class, and their discreet and unobtrusive way of life, together protected them from too much harassment. They were relatively few in number, quiet and often wealthy.

Roman Catholicism flourished among certain aristocratic families and landed gentry. It was particularly strong in certain enclaves, notably Lancashire and the West Midlands. In such areas there were closely knit communities of Catholics, some of whose members flourished through the industrial revolution, and others of whom were successful in the professions. They included people of local and sometimes national influence. They practised their religion quietly, devoutly and without ostentation. Priests were often employed as chaplains to major families and would serve poorer Catholics in the neighbourhood. The priests themselves did not have excessive influence. This, together with the general quietness of demeanour, appeared, to English eyes, healthier than the more priest-centred, flamboyant version of Catholicism to be found in some Embassy Chapels in London.

Nevertheless, the anti-Roman Catholic laws were on the statute book and Catholics were still prevented from entering Parliament and taking their place in the political life of the country. The Oath of Supremacy included a denial that the pope had any authority 'ecclesiastical or spiritual, within this realm'; holders of public offices were expected to make a declaration denying the doctrine of transubstantiation; Roman Catholics were not officially allowed to serve in the armed forces and could not be called to the Bar; a law forbidding bequests for 'superstitious uses' was sometimes taken to forbid bequests for Roman Catholic uses; and Roman Catholics shared the disabilities of the Protestant Dissenters in repect of education and services of marriage. Furthermore, the existence of such laws enabled agitators to stir up no-popery riots from time to time.

In the period leading up to 1829 a number of forces combined to make emancipation inevitable. They also, incidentally, indicate changes which were taking place in the Roman Catholic community, though the extent of the changes was not apparent until later. Four such forces may be mentioned.

At the most obvious level, by forming committees to influence public opinion, through publications, by soliciting the help of Protestant friends, the Roman Catholics conducted their own campaigns against the legislation which kept them from public life. In particular they drew attention to their loyalty to the crown. In this regard the laity were sometimes willing to make more concessions than the clergy could always approve. Some would even have been prepared to take the Oath of Supremacy, arguing that it merely asserted in rather old-fashioned terms the independence of the state (they might have added that it had been a false assertion of the pope's spiritual authority which had given them such a bad reputation in England). This kind of argument was congenial to laymen who were looking for the status in society which would follow emancipation. The clergy, who would not benefit in the same way, feared that too many concessions would be made. This division between clergy and laity would later be more pronounced.

On what might be termed a philosophical level, Roman Catholics benefited from the arguments used by Protestant Dissenters. Demands for liberty of conscience and assertions that religious opinions should not affect civil liberties were 'in the air'. The Protestant Dissenters expressed this in terms of 'voluntaryism'. Some of them, regarding Roman Catholics as a Dissenting body similar to themselves, felt bound in conscience to argue for their emancipation. The Protestant way of expressing this may not have suited the Roman Catholics but they would naturally be happy to enjoy the benefits.

A more specific factor was the arrival in England of Roman Catholic refugees from France. This was significant in two ways. Such people were seen as victims of the anti-religious forces which had assumed power in France after the revolution of 1789. In face of what was seen as godless persecution the Protestant antipathy to Roman Catholics seemed less important. Generally the refugees were very well received. Secondly, among them were a number of priests, some of whom stayed and established missions, as well as schools and other institutions, thus considerably strengthening the Roman Catholic presence. Incidentally they also introduced devotional practices of a more extravagant nature than was found among English Roman Catholics. This was a foretaste of developments later in the century.

Finally, the most important force leading to emancipation was the Irish dimension. The Act of Union (1801) had made the English Government responsible for some seven million Irishmen, the majority of whom were Roman Catholics. Not only was there an overwhelming case for emancipation in terms of democracy and common sense, there was also the underlying threat of political and social unrest if these citizens appeared to be disenfranchised. Catholic emancipation would no doubt have come quite apart from the Irish dimension, but it is almost certain that it came much more quickly because of it. Within a generation many of those

Irishmen had settled in England, causing a further change in the style of English Roman Catholicism.

Such forces made emancipation inevitable. The question became one of terms. As many Roman Catholics realized, there were genuine problems for the legislators. It was accepted, and continued to be accepted for some time, that the state should be concerned about the religion of the people. If the Protestant Church of England was to be the Established Church of the English people, and for the majority that was not in doubt, and if Parliament was to continue to be the lay assembly legislating for the Church of England, there was an obvious incongruity in the idea of Roman Catholics in Parliament influencing that legislation. Various 'securities' were considered. There was considerable support for the idea that the crown should have the right to veto the appointment of Roman Catholic bishops in England, thus reducing potentially hostile influences on the voters. Another idea was that Roman Catholic clergy should be paid by the crown, thus, presumably, securing their loyalty. Neither idea was adopted. In the end, following the precedent used to deal with the Protestant Dissenters at the time of the repeal of the Test and Corporation Acts in the previous year, Roman Catholics were barred from certain offices of state and those taking public office were to swear that they would not subvert the establishment of the Church of England. In addition, they were forbidden to use any ecclesiastical titles which were already used by the Church of England, and religious orders were restricted or banned. The latter regulation (never put into effect) reflected the peculiarly English suspicion of religious orders in general and the Jesuits in particular.

The Roman Catholic community which was thus brought nearer to the mainstream of English life was already in the process of change. In the eyes of the Roman Catholic Church England was technically a mission field. The English Mission was under the control of the office in Rome of the Sacred Congregation for the Propagation of the Faith, known as Propaganda, an arrangement which formally continued until 1908. This contributed to disputes between the religious orders and the regular, or secular, clergy. The orders argued that, in a missionary situation, they were not under the control of bishops. Until 1840 the country was divided into four administrative Districts, the Northern, Western, Midland and London Districts. In 1840, as Roman Catholicism flourished, four more were created, the Eastern, Central, Lancastrian and Welsh Districts. Each District was under the control of a Vicar Apostolic who had the rank of bishop and who was in theory directly responsible to the pope. In practice there was a permanent agent in Rome responsible for passing information in both directions. Since there were often disputes between the English bishops and between the bishops and the religious orders which led the disputants to appeal to Rome, and since the authorities in Rome did not always have a very clear idea of the situation in England, the agent's task called for considerable diplomatic skill. Beneath the Vicars Apostolic, what were known as parishes were technically mission stations.

This system was clearly out of date. As long as the Roman Catholic community was relatively small and under the influence of aristocrats and landed gentry, it could be made to work. But the situation was changing, and with the change a number of scarcely admitted tensions and conflicts came to the surface. At the simplest level they were conflicts between the old ways and the new, but in fact the new consisted of several distinct but overlapping styles of Catholicism.

The old way was of a broadly homogeneous community, power was with land and wealth, devotion was not obviously emotional, worship was plain and unadorned. Among the new was the way of the Anglican converts, of whom there was a steady trickle. Often highly educated, though not indifferent to emotion, theirs was largely a moral and intellectual quest. They were looking for the 'One True Church'. Believing they had found it, they were often disappointed by the low intellectual level they found among the English Roman Catholic priesthood and they had little in common with the Irish labourers. Some were suspicious of the Italianate devotional practices which were gaining ground; many were frustrated at the reticence and unobtrusiveness of the 'Old Catholics', as the hereditary Catholics and the remnants of the Catholic gentry were called. More significant was the growth of urban Catholicism. This was made up largely of Irish immigrants, and reached its peak in the late 1840s as a result of the Irish famines. For the rest of the century at least the numerical strength of Roman Catholicism depended on Irish immigrants and those born in England of Irish stock. For these people religion and nationalism were bound together. Neither intellectual nor over-emotional, they took their religion seriously. For them it was largely a matter of discipline, of regular Mass and confession. There was a trace of superstition in their respect for the priest. He, after all, was the expert in religious matters, he appeared to be vested with real power in the supernatural sphere, so it was right that he should be treated with reverence. Finally, a different style of worship and devotion had been introduced from the Continent, often directly from Rome. Its appeal was to the romanticism and supposed religious fervour of the medieval period. It spoke of the authority of Rome and gloried in a sense of mystery and splendid ritual and encouraged intellectual and spiritual submission.

By 1850, therefore, the old way was rapidly passing. The gentry were losing control to the bishops and the priests. Of the new ways mentioned it was to be the last that would be most prominent. The scene was set for a more full-blooded, colourful, 'supernatural' Catholicism.

'Papal Aggression' and Ultramontanism

The signal for the new style was the restoration in 1850 of a regular hierarchy of bishops and dioceses to replace the Vicars Apostolic and administrative districts. Both at Rome and in England there had been considerable debate about the move. The Vicars Apostolic generally wanted it because it would make their own positions plainer and give them greater control over the religious orders. The priests wanted it because they hoped to become settled parish priests instead of missionaries technically liable to be moved at any time, and also because they hoped to have some influence on the election of bishops. In Rome it was hoped that a restored hierarchy would strengthen the Church in England by binding it more closely to Roman rule and Roman customs, and also that it might attract more converts from Anglicanism. But some in England and at Rome realized the need to proceed cautiously for fear of causing offence to English Protestant feelings or to political sensibilities. Unfortunately the authorities at Rome were not always well informed about English affairs. Taking advice largely from Italian missionaries in England or from enthusiastic recent converts they were too ready to believe that England was ripe for wholesale conversion, and that the Vicars Apostolic were not sufficiently enthusiastic in taking the opportunities available. When the restoration of the hierarchy took place leadership of the Roman Catholic Church in England was put into the hands of a remarkable man who shared that Roman view, Nicholas Wiseman.

Nicholas Wiseman (1802–65) was born of Irish parents in Spain. His father died while he was young and his mother first took him to Ireland and then, in 1810, sent him to Ushaw College, a Roman Catholic school in County Durham. From there, at the age of sixteen, he went to the newly reopened English College in Rome. For the next twenty-two years Rome was his home.

This long period in Rome established Wiseman's theological and spiritual priorities. Through close proximity to the leading figures of his Church, witnessing its splendid ceremonial and surrounded by evidences of its past and of its devotional life, he became a fervent exponent of papal supremacy and of Roman customs in worship and in Christian life generally. This view, known as Ultramontanism, was a reaction both to the decline in the temporal power of the papacy and to the growth of Gallicanism and Febronianism. At the heart of it is the conviction that Rome alone has the truth, that any deviation from Roman teaching or ways is error, and that the only way to a deepening of the Christian life and a revival of the Church is through a closer allegiance to the Holy See and obedience to the pope.

During his Roman period Wiseman began to develop a reputation as a scholar and teacher. In 1828 he became Rector of the English College and thus the agent in Rome for the Vicars Apostolic in England. His attachment to Roman ways made it difficult for him to appreciate the virtues of the Old Catholics in England, and his relations with the Vicars Apostolic were often clouded by misunderstanding. In particular they were annoyed by his support for the religious orders, and some of them considered his encouragement of prayer for the conversion of England was likely to arouse unreasonable expectations. Nevertheless, he became increasingly convinced that a massive revival of Roman Catholicism in England was imminent.

In 1835 he had the opportunity to tour England. At this time he gave the first really substantial indication of what was to be a major part of his life's work, the ability to commend his faith to non-Catholics and especially to High Church Anglicans. He did this through lectures, but also, more effectively, through his part, in collaboration with Michael Quinn and Daniel O'Connell, in the founding of the *Dublin Review*. For the rest of his life Wiseman was a regular contributor. One of his articles had a profound effect in persuading Newman to abandon his view of the Church of England as a *via media* and moved him towards his eventual conversion to Roman Catholicism.

It was partly with a view to persuading more of the Tractarians that their position should lead them logically to Roman Catholicism that, in 1840, he returned to England as President of Oscott College in Birmingham and as coadjutor Bishop of the Midland District. From this point on he divided his co-religionists. Some were offended by his ardent Romanism, his interest in the Oxford Movement or what they saw as his arrogance and personal ambition. On a practical level they were irritated by his weakness as an administrator. But others were impressed by his charm of manner to his close friends, his deep spirituality and his European reputation as a scholar and ecclesiastical statesman. Of the English Roman Catholic leaders he was by far the best known and most highly respected in Rome, and when the decision to restore the hierarchy was made he was named its head as Cardinal Archbishop of Westminster.

At this point he made an error of judgement which was to cloud his reputation for the rest of his life, but which reflected at least part of his character. While still at Rome, in October 1850, he announced the restoration of the hierarchy in a florid pastoral letter 'from out of the Flaminian Gate' which was to be read in all Roman Catholic churches. Its language was exuberant, triumphalist and quite lacking in tact. He used the language of government and declared: 'Your beloved country has received a place among the fair Churches, which, normally constituted, form the splendid aggregate of Catholic Communion: Catholic England has been restored to its orbit in the ecclesiastical firmament, from which its light had long vanished, and begins now anew its course of regularly adjusted action round the centre of unity, the source of jurisdiction, of light, and of vigour.'[3] As he was to explain later, it was not unusual language for Roman dignitaries, but such flamboyance, such apparent assumption of spiritual, and even temporal, authority, was deeply offensive to many in England.

Earlier that year there had been a long drawn out dispute through the courts about the baptismal teaching of a West Country clergyman, George Gorham. The most offensive aspect of the affair to many was that a matter affecting the teaching of the Church of England should be decided by a secular court. For a time it seemed there might be a serious division within the Established Church, and some High Churchmen did become Roman Catholics because of the Gorham judgement. So Wiseman's letter came at a particularly sensitive time: it looked as if he was trying to take advantage of the confusion within the Church of England.

Soon after the restoration of the hierarchy had been announced Bishop Maltby of Durham had written to the Prime Minister, Lord John Russell, bemoaning the 'aggression of the pope' and *The Times* had criticized it as a 'clumsy joke'. Wiseman's pastoral letter was actually read in English Roman Catholic churches on 17 October. Two days later it was roundly condemned in *The Times* and brought public rebukes from several churchmen and politicians. Particular offence was taken to the choice of Westminster, a name and place rich in historical associations, as the title of the new Archbishop's see. Several critics took the opportunity to criticize the Tractarians for supposedly encouraging Roman pretensions. Among the latter was the Prime Minister who, unwisely, allowed Maltby to publish his reply to the latter's complaint. Russell complained that, 'Clergymen of our own Church, who have subscribed the Thirty Nine Articles and acknowledged in explicit terms the Queen's supremacy, have been most forward in leading their flocks "step by step to the very verge of the precipice".'[4]

Wiseman's response was to publish an *Appeal to the Reason and Good Feeling of the English People* on 20 November shortly after his arrival in London, followed by a series of public lectures. Correctly assuming that on calmer reflection many would feel that the reaction to his pastoral had been extreme, he appealed for toleration, pointing out that his words had been addressed only to Roman Catholics and were solely concerned with the internal organization of that Church. He also made the more polemical point that the Westminster about which he was to be especially concerned as Archbishop was not so much the centre of government but the slums which nestled around the grand buildings. The implication that both those protesting about ecclesiastical rights and the Church on whose behalf they protested were rather less concerned with the slums and those who lived in them was clear enough but left unstated.

The pastoral and the dispute which followed it give a flavour of Wiseman's manner. Even within his own Church he did not please everybody. His fellow bishops felt they were not sufficiently consulted. As the years went by they became increasingly unhappy with his assumption of undisputed leadership and they suffered severely from his incompetence as an administrator. Much of the necessary work of organization, raising money and dealing with secular authorities he left to the bishops. Then he argued with them. He had been responsible for the appointment of Thomas Grant as Bishop of Southwark and of George Errington as his own coadjutor at Westminster. Both were colleagues of long standing but with both he engaged in long, unedifying disputes. But he was increasingly recognized as the spokesman and public face of Roman Catholicism in England.

Under Wiseman the style of English Roman Catholicism changed. In Ultramontane fashion intellectual submission to the authority of the pope became a hallmark and Roman customs flourished. Greater ceremonial was introduced into worship, the position of the priest was exalted, veneration of the Virgin and the saints increased, the use of images and relics as aids to devotion became common and there was a greater willingness to stress ecclesiastical miracles. To the Old Catholics it seemed that the new devotional practices deliberately exalted all that was emotional and un-English. In the realm of architecture, where the English Church had become more ostentatious with a revival of the Gothic style and medieval liturgical practices, some common ground might have been expected. In fact, the Ultramontanes preferred the Roman style. Even in ostentation Roman ways were best.

The result of this movement was to strengthen the position of Roman Catholicism but at the expense of separating it from the rest of English society and bringing about an increase in anti-Roman Protestantism. The English people knew that there was a

Roman Catholic Church in their midst, and the largely Irish urban Catholics found strength and identity through church membership. But the obscurantism and authoritarianism which became associated with Roman Catholicism, underlined by the publication of the *Syllabus of Errors* in 1864 and the declaration of papal infallibility in 1870, created something of a ghetto mentality among Catholics. It may all have made sense from within, but it looked increasingly odd from outside. To be a Roman Catholic was more than ever to belong to a minority culture, strangely different and cut off from the rest of English society.

Preserving the Faith and the Faithful

Under Wiseman's successor, *Henry Edward Manning* (1808–92), a convert from Anglicanism, the character of the English Roman Catholic Church was confirmed on the basically Ultramontanist lines which in many ways it maintained until the Second Vatican Council (1962–5). The Ultramontanist fervour did not always burn equally brightly, but the basic claims were unaltered. Numbers grew. In spite of some converts the growth was largely due to immigration and natural growth, and it was largely among the poorer, less well educated, sections of the community. The growth did not keep pace with population growth but was nevertheless impressive.

The combination of Ultramontanism and the nature of the Roman Catholic community produced two marked features of life and thought. The first, and most distinctive, was the continuing need to make clear the identity of the 'true' Church, both to members and to outsiders. The second was the determination to prevent loss of members, or 'leakage', which in turn led to an increasing involvement with social problems and contact with secular authorities.

The chief means of identifying the Church was the appeal to the authority of Rome. Manning was a diplomatist. He was influential at the First Vatican Council and had helped to persuade, and outmanoeuvre, those who had considered the declaration of papal infallibility inopportune. Henceforth acceptance of the authority of the Church, an authority which was invested in the pope and the bishops, was the doctrine which more than any other ensured both the clear identification of Roman Catholicism and its separation from general intellectual life. Through the Church's teaching men and women were brought into contact with the world of timeless divine realities. Through the priest they received the Eucharist, forgiveness and peace with God and authoritative guidance on moral issues.

A concomitant of this view was a denial of the 'branch theory' which Newman and his friends had held in the early days of the Oxford Movement and to which many in the Church of England still subscribed – the idea that several Christian Churches may be branches, though perhaps not equally sound ones, of the one true Church. For Rome the Church was one, and its unity consisted in submission to Rome. Other bodies were just not Churches. A casualty of this thinking was the Association for the Promotion of the Unity of Christendom. This was formed in 1857, largely due to the enthusiasm of a convert, Ambrose Phillipps de Lisle, who was convinced that a large proportion of the Church of England was longing for reunion with Rome. It was censured by Rome in 1865. When, in 1894, Lord Halifax, an Anglo-Catholic peer and President of the English Church Union, and the French Abbé Portal began to explore the possibility of reunion between the Anglican and Roman Catholic Churches the result was Rome's inquiry into Anglican orders which ended with their being declared null and void by Pope Leo XIII in the bull *Apostolicae Curae* (1896). Subsequent discussions by the same group at Malines between 1921 and 1926 did not proceed far enough to warrant a declaration from Rome, but *Francis Bourne* (1861–1935), who had become Archbishop of Westminster in 1903, made it plain that they did not have his support. Roman Catholics took no part in the early days of the Ecumenical Movement and did not join the British Council of Churches or its local bodies.

The Catholic hierarchy regarded intellectual liberalism with suspicion amounting to horror. The journal *The Rambler*, founded in 1848 and largely a product of educated lay converts, showed unwelcome signs of an independent spirit. It was critical of the intellectual level of English Catholicism, was sometimes irreverent in its tone and made judgements, especially on literary and political issues, not in line with those of the Church. Though it was not officially banned, it was criticized by a number of bishops and its proprietors considered it wise to cease publication in 1864.

Fear of liberalism was also behind the failure for so long to set up a Catholic Hall of Residence at Oxford or Cambridge. The atmosphere was considered to be rationalistic and hostile to Catholicism. There had been plans for Newman to establish an Oratory at Oxford but they came to nothing. With the support of Propaganda the English bishops dissuaded parents from sending their sons to either university. It was not until 1895, after an unsuccessful attempt to establish a Catholic University in Kensington, that it was agreed that some exceptions to the general rule could be made. In the next year chaplains were appointed at both Oxford and Cambridge and subsequently Halls of Residence were established.

Rome's most obvious assertion of authority and its clearest indication of aversion to liberalism was the ruthless suppression of the Modernist movement. Roman Catholic Modernism was many-sided. *Lamentabili sane exitu* and *Pascendi dominici gregis*, the papal documents which condemned it in 1907, attempted to summarize it, but all the leading figures rejected the official portrait of Modernism as a grotesque caricature. Basically, the Modernists asserted the rights of modern intellectual enquiry, especially into the Bible, and claimed that its findings were compatible with Catholic faith. Modernism's chief exponent and victim was the French biblical exegete Alfred Loisy. Loisy's work had previously led to the encyclical *Providentissimus Deus* in 1893 which had attempted to set limits to the work of biblical criticism.

In England *Herbert Vaughan* (1832–1903), who had succeeded Manning as Archbishop of Westminster in 1892, showed little sympathy with intellectual difficulties. He excommunicated the scientist St George Mivart when, having been criticized for a number of articles advocating evolution and questioning the reality of hell, he refused to submit. The joint pastoral letter of 1900 by Vaughan and the bishops of the province of Westminster on 'The Church and Liberal Catholicism' was a bald assertion of ecclesiastical authority. Its chief victim was the Irish Jesuit *George Tyrrell* (1861–1909), the most articulate representative of Modernism in England. Tyrrell had previously asserted the rights of intellectual criticism and now he attacked the pastoral as a wrong use of authority. He refused to moderate his opinions and was deprived of the sacraments in 1907. When he died he was refused Catholic burial. The influential layman Baron *Friedrich von Hügel* (1852–1925) was also critical of a restrictive use of ecclesiastical authority but escaped censure.

An effect of the actions which were taken against the Modernists, both on the Continent and in England, was that Roman Catholic scholars turned their attention away from biblical exegesis and dogmatic theology towards safer areas such as languages and history. This situation was eased by the publication in 1943 of Pius XII's encyclical *Divino afflante Spiritu* which, by acknowledging the existence of different literary types in Scripture, was seen as giving more freedom to Roman Catholic biblical scholars.

The great majority of Roman Catholics, like the majority in other denominations, were not closely in touch with theological arguments or affected by them. For them the local priest, the services of the local church and the local school were of more immediate concern. The shortage of priests was partly made up by importing from abroad, normally from Ireland, and by hurriedly set up training courses which, at least in the early years, sometimes led to the ordination of unsatisfactory candidates. The parish clergy were the people responsible for nurturing the faith and preventing leakage among the largely working-class, often Irish, Catholic community. Their success was shown by the fact that from near the end of the nineteenth century onwards a far greater proportion of working class Roman Catholics remained loyal to their faith than members of other Churches.

Whether it was by accident of circumstances, by design, or, more probably, something of both, a lot of the pastoral work had the effect of increasing the insularity of Roman Catholicism and underlining the sense of its foreignness in the eyes of many outsiders. To them, the local Catholic church was largely a foreign community, led by a foreign priest, loyal to a foreign power and worshipping in a foreign tongue. But these very qualities gave the members of that community a sense of belonging, a loyalty to their cause and a strength beyond themselves. This loyalty was strengthened by the provision of various clubs and guilds in which they found their social life. Since these activities were nearly always led by priests, and since they usually involved some form of religious discipline, at least in theory, the life of the average Catholic was more permeated by religion than was generally the case with non-Catholics.

A particularly marked feature of Roman Catholic life, though in the longer term perhaps a less happy one, was the dependence on and obedience to the priest and the hierarchy generally. There was a clear distinction between the clergy as teachers and leaders and the laity as the taught and led. Control by the clergy perpetuated the insularity of Roman Catholicism. Another important factor was the pressure put on Catholics not to marry non-Catholics. If such a 'mixed marriage' did take place the non-Catholic was asked to agree that the children should be brought up within the Roman Catholic Church.

From the restoration of the hierarchy onwards immense effort was put into the provision of schools for Catholic children, and this, too, had the effect of keeping Catholics 'different'. Wiseman argued that given a choice it was preferable to build a school in which worship could take place rather than a new church. Manning's first three pastoral letters concerned education and, as in so many other things, this set a pattern. Just before the Second Vatican Council opened in 1962 Cardinal Heenan said that the building of schools was the greatest preoccupation of English Roman Catholics. Though, after some initial misgivings, state aid and inspection were accepted, the idea that a common core of Christianity could be taught was not. Hence, at considerable sacrifice, and through complicated negotiations with successive governments, Catholic schools have been maintained. The argument has been that education divorced from positive Christian teaching is inadequate, and that such teaching is best given in an institution which is recognizably linked with the Church and which is pervaded by a Catholic atmosphere.

In educational arguments attention has always been directed to the needs of ordinary working people. These needs have also brought a level of political involvement. While resisting full-blooded socialism great effort has been put into ameliorating the lot of the poor. Manning was an outstanding example. He argued strongly that moral and religious improvement was related to environmental improvement. He associated himself with the Temperance movement. He supported Joseph Arch in his attempt to form rural trade unions, and in 1889 he earned the respect of workers and their leaders by his mediation in helping to end the dock strike of that year. Like many of the Christian Socialists he had a rather idealized view of the guild socialism of the medieval period which was really quite inadequate for the industrial age. Nevertheless, it was fitting that trade union banners should have been carried in his funeral procession.

Subsequent Roman Catholic political thinking in England has tended to accept a stratified society while stressing mutual interdependence and accountability to God. The Church has resisted identification with any one party; both collectivism and uncontrolled capitalism have been criticized. Typically, Roman Catholics have formed their own organizations. Between 1909 and 1967 the Catholic Social Guild promoted education and research into social problems. There have also been such bodies as the Association of Catholic Trades Unionists, which was concerned that the TUC might oppose denominational schools and which developed its own strongly anti-Communist line after the Second World War, the Young Christian Workers' Movement and a Catholic Workers' College designed to promote an approach to industrial problems informed by Catholic teaching. Such organizations, with their tendency to perpetuate Catholic insularity, have been less prominent since the end of the Second World War.

The Second Vatican Council

The Second Vatican Council (1962–5) was a watershed in twentieth-century Roman Catholicism. When Joseph Roncalli (1881–1963) became *Pope John XXIII* in 1958 he was widely believed to be a mere 'caretaker pope'. His personal religion appears to have been quite conservative but he realized the need within the Roman Catholic Church for *aggiornamento* – a bringing up to date – and to that end he called the Council.

The 'bringing up to date' was to involve a radical re-appraisal of many treasured beliefs and attitudes. Among those of greatest importance was the acceptance of other Christian Churches as genuine 'separated brethren', and the abandonment of much of the traditional exclusiveness and triumphalism. The way was opened for the Roman Catholic Church to take part in the Ecumenical Movement. The doctrine of Papal Infallibility was reaffirmed, but

179

cautiously, for there was a reconsideration of the nature of authority in the Church: the bishops, too, when acting together and with the pope have full and supreme power to govern and teach – this is the concept of collegiality. There was a shift from the generally accepted model of the Church as an institution with a settled hierarchy, something like a pyramid with authority coming down from the top, to models closer to biblical ideas, the Church as 'the people of God', as 'the Body of Christ', a 'mystery', models which imply a much greater appreciation of the role of the laity in the Church.

It was not the case that after the Council the Roman Catholic Church was suddenly completely different. There had been a period of development of thought and preparation for change leading up to the Council and some theologians were able to welcome its outcome as a confirmation of what they had been saying for many years. There were also those who would have preferred the Church to maintain a more conservative position, and a small minority who refused to accept the Council's teaching. However, Pope John had certainly suceeded in one of his reported aims, to 'let some fresh air into the Church'. It was now possible to expect a much greater openness to the modern world and perhaps some changes in life-style.

The Roman Catholic Church in England does not appear to have been well prepared for the Council. The twentieth century had been a period of consolidation. Not until 1908 had England ceased to be a missionary area, and not until 1918 had regular parishes been accepted. The pastoral work of containing leakage and the struggle to raise money to build schools and churches had absorbed most of the Church's time and energy. Though from time to time stress had been laid on the world-wide nature of Roman Catholicism the theological developments on the Continent had made little impact, and the life of Roman Catholic communities in Africa, Asia and South America was not widely known. As a result the Council and its impetus to change came as a surprise.

Some critics argue that the renewal of the Church called for by the Council has been sluggish. But there has been movement. A number of episcopal commissions to translate the Council's work into action were established in 1967 and reconstituted in 1983. A

National Council of Priests was formed in 1970 and, in 1980, a National Pastoral Congress consisting largely of lay people was held in Liverpool. Such moves show the possibility of change, though all the bodies mentioned are merely advisory, and authority continues to reside in the hierarchy.

The most immediately noticeable change has been in the liturgy of the Mass, reshaped to encourage the active participation of the laity and now generally said in English rather than Latin. Doubtless something has been lost in terms of mystery, and the former claim that, since they were always in Latin, Roman Catholic services were the same in all parts of the world can no longer be made. But the gain in intelligibility and participation may be thought to make up for that. In addition lay people now take a larger part in church organization at a national and local level. As regards ecumenism, Roman Catholics now more regularly take part in the affairs of local Councils of Churches, and, at a more official level, the Anglican-Roman Catholic International Commission (ARCIC) has reached 'substantial agreement' on almost all the doctrinal differences which caused the division between those two Churches.

Yet what many see as the old insularity and authoritarianism are not easily overcome. It is reported that one Irish bishop returned from the Council and announced that it would make no difference in Ireland. More sensational was the papal encyclical *Humanae Vitae* of 1968 which reiterated the Catholic Church's traditional teaching on the inadmissability of the use of artificial methods of contraception. Many Roman Catholics were bitterly disappointed. In practice, the ban is widely disregarded and surveys of Roman Catholic opinion indicate that it has little support. Perhaps what is most significant is that so many Roman Catholics feel free to take a critical attitude to a teaching so clearly defined by the pope and the bishops, something that would have been inconceivable in 1850.

In the last quarter of the twentieth century the Roman Catholic Church in England is probably less feared and more widely respected than it has been at any time since the Reformation. Though hesitations remain, much of its insularity has gone. With the other Churches it has shared, though proportionately to a lesser extent, a decline in membership. Nevertheless signs of great spiritual vitality are apparent, and the possibility of a fuller working out of Vatican II offers hope for the future.

Notes

1 J. H. Newman, *Sermons Preached on Various Occasions* (Longmans, Green & Co. 1857), p. 200.
2 cited H. Bettenson, ed., *Documents of the Christian Church* (Oxford University Press 1943), p. 381.
3 The whole text is printed in B. Fothergill, *Nicholas Wiseman* (Faber & Faber 1963), pp. 293 ff.
4 cf. E. R. Norman, *Anti Catholicism in Victorian England* (Allen and Unwin 1968), pp. 52 ff. The full text of Russell's letter, pp. 159 ff.

10

The Missionary Movement

The nineteenth century saw a great expansion of the power and influence of the European nations in general and of Great Britain in particular. Following the loss of the American colonies attention turned first to India, the jewel in the crown, and then to Africa, the dark continent. By the end of the eighteenth century British control of the Indian sub-continent was already fairly well established, though it was sometimes exercised indirectly through advantageous treaty arrangements with local rulers or, more usually, through the East India Company which had traded in India since 1600. It was not until 1858 that the Crown officially took over the responsibilities of the Company. Queen Victoria was proclaimed Empress of India in 1876. In Africa there had been trading posts on the West Coast since the fifteenth century. In the late nineteenth century there took place the 'scramble for Africa' among the European nations which resulted in large tracts of that continent being added to the British Empire.

Since the Reformation there had been little missionary work by the Protestant Churches. Where Europeans had settled they had taken their religion, but they had not often attempted to share it with the native population. Thus English settlers in North America, Canada, Australia, New Zealand and the West Indies had been supplied with chaplains. This had been the main work of the Society for the Propagation of the Gospel, founded in 1701, under whose auspices the Wesleys had gone to Georgia in 1735, but such chaplains had been expected to concentrate their ministrations on those of English, or at least European, descent. The Society for Promoting Christian Knowledge, founded in 1698, supported German Lutheran missionaries in East India from as early as 1710.

Exceptional men, such as John Eliot (1604–90) and David Brainerd (1718–47) had worked among the North American Indians, but such efforts were rare.

Now the situation changed. As the spread of British power brought so much more of the world to the attention of the British people, and as the needs of trade made more contact desirable and the industrial revolution made it possible, it was natural that there should also be concern with Christian mission. A large number of societies were formed. The Baptist Missionary Society was first in 1772. The London Missionary Society, founded in 1795, was intended to be a non-denominational society but was soon recognized as Congregationalist. The Anglican Church Missionary Society was formed in 1799 and the Methodist Missionary Society in 1816. Not exactly a missionary society but always closely allied to them, the British and Foreign Bible Society was founded in 1804.

Many more such societies were formed as the century progressed, but they did not indicate at first that a large number of missionaries were being sent out, or even that there was a great interest in the subject. By 1809 the Church Missionary Society had sent only nine missionaries and most of those were German. However, gradually the numbers increased and the interest of the public was gained. Even then that interest was not simply, or not always, evangelistic. Considerations of trade and national prestige played a part, but for the average reader *A Narrative of Missionary Enterprises in the South Sea Islands*, published in 1837 by John Williams (1796–1839), or David Livingstone's *Missionary Travels and Researches in Southern Africa* (1857), would have much in common with the 'Travels' of such gentleman explorers as Mungo Park (1771–1806) who traced the route of the Niger or Sir Richard Burton (1821–90) who made several journeys in search of the source of the Nile. They were all alike books of romance and adventure, introducing the reading public to a strange and exciting world.

Missionary Motives

Why were so many men and women willing to become missionaries? A century after the great expansion of the British missionary movement, when the nation's prestige and the nation's mood is so much different from what it was in the nineteenth century, that question frequently receives a confident and cynical answer. The entire movement can be seen as an adjunct to British imperialism and heavily involved in the interests of British trade. It can be seen as a kind of religious and cultural imperialism, and certainly there is evidence that some of those countries which were on the receiving end of the movement, and which have since gained political independence from Britain, regard it at least partly in that light.

There is no shortage of *prima facie* evidence to support such an unflattering account of missionary motives, but there is much more which indicates that it is a gross over-simplification. For most missionary societies and most missionaries there were probably several motives, but rarely, if ever, would national prestige or trade be an important one. Such considerations might, however, be more significant for those who supported the societies financially.

For many of those who represented their country abroad as administrators, merchants or soldiers, Christianity was part of their culture. Furthermore they had an unquestioning confidence that their culture was superior to any other. In religious terms this is seen largely in the position of the Church of England regarded simply as a national institution, the nation on its religious side. For instance, when its charter was renewed in 1813, the East India Company agreed to support a bishop and three archdeacons, to which were later added a number of chaplains. There were also chaplains in the army. Insofar as such appointments were simply exporting the way of life of the foreign rulers the charge of religious imperialism has weight. Christianity is then seen as the religion of the rulers. It is a relatively small step to go on to argue that if it is spread to the natives it would help to attach the governed to the governors. This view was, unwittingly, strengthened when the government left native education in the hands of the missionary societies.

Even more unflattering to the motives of the missionaries, at least on a superficial level, are those public statements which brought together religion and commerce. John Williams, seeking financial backing for his work in the South Seas, appealed directly to the merchants, 'That the commerce of our country is materially benefited, is evident by the fact that, at the lowest computation, a hundred and fifty or two thousand persons, who a few years ago were unclothed savages, are now wearing and using articles of British manufacture; the cultivation of indigo, cotton, coffee, sugar, arrowroot, coconut oil etc. have been introduced, and it is confidently expected that in a few years the islands now under Christian instruction will be of considerable commercial importance.'[1] We shall see later that Livingstone habitually spoke of Christianity and commerce as if they must naturally go together. Indeed, in his mind they did. It could clearly be argued that missionaries expected considerations of trade to be a motive among their supporters.

However, to leave the question of motivation at that point would be superficial. A number of other factors need to be taken into account. It is significant that most of the missionaries, at least in the early part of the century, did not come from the Church of England, and those who did were supported by the Church Missionary Society, a voluntary body, rather than by the Church itself. Most of them came from the artisan class and were not well educated. They would not have fitted easily into the public school and university world of the colonial administrators, or into the officers' mess. They were not, in other words, obvious bearers of the culture of a ruling class.

Furthermore it is clear that the British authorities positively discouraged rather than supported missionary activity among the natives. This may have been partly because they feared that radical Christianity would lead to criticisms of the administration, but it is certain that they feared it would be seen as a slight on the indigenous religions. When Carey went to India he had to seek support from the Danish authorities because it was refused by the East India Company. In 1858, when the Government of India Act was proclaimed, the Queen's proclamation began with the words, 'Firmly relying ourselves on the truth of Christianity, and acknowledging with gratitude the solace of religion, We disclaim alike the right and the desire to impose Our convictions on any of Our subjects. We declare it to be Our royal will and pleasure that none be in any wise favoured, none molested or disquieted by reason of their religious faith or observance, but that all alike shall enjoy the equal and impartial protection of the law . . .'[2] The Queen herself had added the first two phrases. The government had no wish to upset religious susceptibilities, though it is fair to add that this was soon after the Indian Mutiny which itself was partly caused by clumsiness or insensitivity in that area.

In the light of this official attitude, it is understandable that the missionaries would want to counter any possible accusations that their activities were potentially harmful to British rule and British commercial interests. Arguments such as the one quoted from John Williams should be read in this context. They then appear less extreme than they seem at first sight.

But there were more positive influences at work. The Evangelical revival and the mood of 'seriousness' had penetrated deeply into the national character. Though they were for a long time in a minority a growing number of influential men spoke of British rule in terms of trusteeship. To a later age much of their language appears patronizing, but it shows a growing acceptance of the fact that the privilege of rule carried with it a responsibility to those who were ruled. This attitude of accepting a high responsibility is shown in the lives of many colonial administrators. They saw themselves as committed to passing on the benefits of British civilization, and this was increasingly seen to include the benefits of the gospel as well as the apparently more obvious benefits of justice and efficient administration. Towards the end of the century too there appears to have been a greater degree of evangelical commitment among a number of commissioned officers. Such people would have a more sympathetic attitude to the missionaries.

A more widespread and easily understood motive for supporting missionary work, or indeed for engaging in it, was compassion. There was compassion at what was seen as the wretchedness and suffering of uncivilized savages whose lot could be made easier by the benefits of civilization. To this was often added a sense of guilt evoked by the horrors of the slave trade. The sheer inhumanity of that trade, and the awful cruelty involved in it, had been highlighted by the anti-slavery campaigners. Later, in spite of legislation in the British Parliament, it was realized that it still went on. It was realized too that Britain had benefited from it. Quite apart from that, Britain continued to benefit commercially from her Empire, which meant from the work of native people. Hence insofar as missionary work could be seen as making amends for all that, it had the support of sensitive men and women.

Yet the concept of trusteeship and responsibility or feelings of compassion and guilt can no more provide the deepest motivation for the missionaries than can imperialism and trade. Those who responded to the missionary call would say with the apostle Paul, 'For the love of Christ controls us, because we are convinced that one has died for all; therefore all have died. And he died for all, that those who live might live no longer for themselves but for him who for their sake died and was raised' (2 Corinthians 5.14 f). They were men and women of deep and compelling inner conviction. Soaked in the words and phrases of Scripture, conscious of their own indebtedness to Christ, they 'knew' beyond all doubt that they had been called by God to this task. They had no alternative but to obey. With some this view carried with it the conviction that those who did not hear and respond to the gospel were doomed to eternal damnation. Those who held that view sometimes exhibited a hard sense of moral obligation which was not always attractive. But others felt only the overpowering constraint of the love of Christ. The basic motivation was obedience to God and a commitment to the basic missionary task of evangelism.

As they committed themselves they knew that it was a difficult and costly path to which they were committed. The support which the Missionary Society at home could give was limited. The colonial administration was not welcoming, and there were the obvious problems of a new language and a different life-style. More threatening were the dangers of a hostile reception from those to whom they preached and the effect of unknown diseases such as malaria and yellow fever. Both the potential converts and the diseases exacted a terrible toll. In 1839 John Williams and a companion were clubbed and speared to death and eaten at a cannibal feast on the island of Erromanga. In 1903 P. T. Forsyth, preaching to the London Missionary Society, could say: 'The Central African Mission of the London Missionary Society was begun twenty six years ago. There have been sent out forty one missionaries. Of these, twenty one died after a mission life of about two and a half years, and eight retired from fever. I say nothing of the deaths of wives and children. The percentage of premature loss is fifty three. In about ten years from 1876, the London Missionary Society lost in Central Africa ten men, and nine had to retire – all out of twenty three. Yet the Directors solemnly resolved to prosecute the mission with greater earnestness than ever. This was courage of the missionaries' own kind, and the bold strategy, the audacious prudence of the Holy Ghost, such as the true-born soldier loves. It is the large, exalted, anointed recklessness that took Christ to the cross and won the world.'

The zeal and the suffering of the missionaries was as apostolic as their motivation. Such sacrificial service no doubt worked to the good of British rule and British trade in ways beyond reckoning. But it was offered in a higher cause.

Some Missionaries and Missions

Anything like a full account of the movement is not possible, but a few examples may give a flavour of it.

William Carey (1761–1834) is credited with being the father of the nineteenth-century missionary movement. He typified the lower middle class, artisan, missionary, a man of passionate conviction and a powerful intellect which was trained by his own efforts. He was the son of a parish clerk and schoolmaster who apprenticed him to a shoemaker. Through the influence of a fellow apprentice he had an experience of conversion and, though previously baptized into the Church of England, he became a Baptist and acepted believer's baptism at the age of eighteen. Subsequently he became a Baptist minister and supported himelf by teaching and mending shoes. At the same time he appears to have taught himself Latin, Greek, Hebrew, Dutch and French, thereby laying the foundation for his later reputation as a linguist and showing his prodigious capacity for hard work.

In 1792 he published a modest pamphlet with the title *An Enquiry into the Obligation of Christians to use Means for the Conversion of the Heathen.* The title is significant. Many of his co-religionists argued that God alone brought about conversions and that it was both unnecessary and presumptuous to seek to convert the heathen. In answer to this debased Calvinism Carey drew attention to Jesus' command to his disciples to go out into all the world (Matthew 28.19 f). He followed this by a sermon at Nottingham on the text from Isaiah 54.2 f., 'Lengthen thy cords and strengthen thy stakes'. He urged his hearers (it was a meeting of Baptist ministers) to 'expect great things from God', and to 'attempt great things for God'. As a direct result the Baptist

Missionary Society was formed in the October of that year, and the next year Carey and his family sailed for India.

Because of the East India Company's attitude to missionaries he was unable to operate from Calcutta and was obliged to support himself as manager of an indigo factory at Malda. For much of the year the duties of his position were light, leaving him free for missionary work and for learning Bengali. Six years later another party of Baptist missionaries arrived and established themselves in the Danish settlement of Serampore where they knew they would have more freedom for missionary work than they could expect under British rule. Carey was persuaded to join them there and, together with *Joshua Marshman* (1768–1837), a schoolmaster, and *William Ward* (1768–1823), a printer, made up a notable missionary group, the 'Serampore trio'.

Carey and his companions laid down five important principles which were influential in much later missionary work. The first was widespread preaching. To that end extensive missionary tours were undertaken and missionary bases were established.

Second was the translation of Scripture into the native languages. There were false starts. Carey's first translation into Bengali was not successful. But during the next thirty years Bibles, or portions of Scripture, were translated into over thirty languages or dialects. Considering that none of these men would have been considered well educated in British eyes, their achievement in producing translations, grammars and dictionaries was remarkable.

Third they established a church, in their case on Baptist principles with Ward as the pastor. This was important as it meant that converts could be welcomed into an existing institution which could increasingly be seen as an Indian one. The converts were not left as isolated individual Christians and were not obviously dependent on a foreign, imperialist, institution.

Fourth they made great efforts to understand not only the language but also the thought and life of those to whom they preached. We shall note later that a major problem facing all missionary endeavour was the value to be given to the indigenous culture, and especially its religion. While maintaining the exclusiveness of Christianity, Carey and his companions certainly did not despise Hindu culture. Indeed their sensitivity towards it was both an aid to evangelism and also, eventually, a major force for good in British relations with India.

Finally they committed themselves to the training of an indigenous ministry. To this end they established in 1819 a College at Serampore with a wide curriculum where teaching was to be given in native languages. It had a charter from the King of Denmark and was later to be widely influential in the training of ministers, and others, throughout India. Here we may note that, in preparing for a time when leadership could be passed to Indians, they were far ahead of the thinking of most colonial administrators, though it must be said that the ideal which they had set did not arrive as soon as they may have hoped.

In 1801 Carey became Professor of Sanskrit, Bengali and Marathi at Fort William College in Calcutta. Here he was able to deepen his knowledge of Hindu culture. He spent five years (1806–11) translating the *Ramayana*, an epic poem second only in importance in Hinduism to the *Bhagavad-Gita*. His deep knowledge of, and sympathy for, Hindu literature enabled him to argue that the practice of Suttee – the burning of widows on the funeral pyres of their husbands – while permitted by the ancient writings was not enjoined by them. He was prominent in the agitation against this practice which was officially banned in 1829.

One further achievement of the 'Serampore trio' may be noted. Their example led to an easing of the anti-missionary attitude of the East India Company. They became personally acquainted with some of the chaplains supported by the Company and encouraged them in their work, not only among the English employees but also among the many Indian workers.

David Livingstone (1813–73) was in many ways the epitome of a Victorian hero. A missionary and explorer who appears to have had a love–hate relationship with Africa. An ardent opponent of the slave trade, an imperialist who combined – or confused – British rule with Christian civilization, and a man whose example inspired some of the best minds of his generation. Subsequently his geographical work has sometimes received more praise than his missionary work, and his advocacy of British commerce has been seen as an example of cultural imperialism. Yet his private journals reveal a deep, often emotional, Evangelical piety, together with a strain of fatalism.

Like Carey, Livingstone came from humble stock, in his case a pious home in Blantyre in the West of Scotland. He educated himself through evening classes but was then able to study medicine and theology in Glasgow and London. He first approached the London Missionary Society with a desire to go as a missionary to China, but he was won for Africa by *Robert Moffat* (1795–1883).

Moffat himself was a notable missionary. He translated the Bible into Tswana, the language of the Bechuana people among whom he worked for forty-eight years. He was above all else an evangelist, longing for the gospel to be preached more widely. In this vein he spoke to the younger man of the vast plain to the north of his own mission station at Kuruman, 'where I had sometimes seen, in the morning sun, the smoke of a thousand villages where no missionary had ever been'.[3] Livingstone went to Kuruman in 1841.

Livingstone's first spell in Africa was as part of Moffat's mission, working to the north of Kuruman. He learned the language, and developed an affection for the African which he never lost and which was amply repaid. He also found time to court and marry Mary, Moffat's daughter. But he was increasingly restless and could not settle on one mission station. He made a number of journeys to the north, still, in theory, as part of Moffat's mission. But it could not last. In 1851, having penetrated as far as the Zambesi, he decided to leave the Bechuana and commit himself to exploring that great river.

He remained an employee of the London Missionary Society until 1856. But, though in his own mind he was always a Christian missionary, he was never again based on a mission station with oversight of a mission church. The years from 1851 to 1856 were his great years. Having followed the river to the west, he then crossed Africa from west to east and was convinced, wrongly as it turned out, that in the Zambesi he had discovered a highway for Christianity and commerce. During this time his affection and respect for the African deepened. He was saddened by the primitive living conditions he found, disgusted by what he saw of the religious practices and outraged by the slave trade which flourished in the hands of the Portuguese and the Arabs.

It was his concern for the well-being of the African, his hostility to the slave trade, his deep Christian conviction and his certainty that Christianity and commerce together could transform Africa, which made him a hero on his return to England in 1856. His *Missionary Travels and Researches in South Africa* was published in 1857. During the same year he lectured to enthusiastic audiences throughout Great Britain. Of particular note was a speech to a largely university audience in Cambridge. He offered a challenge and a vision, 'The sort of men who are wanted for missionaries are such as I see before me – men of education, standing, enterprise, zeal and piety ... I beg to direct your attention to Africa; I know that in a few years I shall be cut off in that country, which is now open; do not let it be shut again! I go back to Africa to try to make an open path for commerce and Christianity.' Later, at the Guildhall in Cambridge, where his audience may have been more commercial than undergraduate, he returned to the theme, 'I propose in my next expedition to visit the Zambesi, and to propitiate the different chiefs along its banks, endeavouring to induce them to cultivate cotton, and to abolish the slave-trade: already they trade in ivory and gold dust, and are anxious to extend their commercial operations. There is thus a probability of their interests being linked with ours, and thus the elevation of the African would be the result.'[4] The appeal to commercial interests can easily be criticized, but the 'elevation of the African' was his heart's desire.

He made two further African expeditions, an unsuccessful attempt to open up the Zambesi (1858–63) and an expedition further north around the Lakes Nyasa and Tanganyika (1866–73). During the last period he saw more of the slave trade, and was sometimes himself dependent on the traders. His detestation of it grew. He described it as the 'open sore' of Africa, and his antidote for it was a different, more wholesome, trade. He was convinced that cotton could be produced commercially in this area, and he dreamed of transporting poor workers from Scotland to settle there, thus helping both Scotland and Africa. It was partly because it would be an aid to the development of trade that he searched for the source of the Nile, but his last journals have a sense of fatalism and aimlessness.

He died in his tent alone. The last recorded words in his journal were, 'All I can say in my solitude is, may Heaven's rich blessing come down on everyone – American, English, Turk – who will help to heal this open sore of the world.'[5] He did not know that his constant exposing of the trade, aided by the work of the journalist and explorer H. M. Stanley, who, in November 1871, was the last white man to see him alive, had caused the British government to bring pressure to bear on the Sultan of Zanzibar to persuade him to abolish the trade in his dominions and to close the slave market in Zanzibar. On 5 June 1873, some five weeks after Livingstone's death, a treaty was signed and the market closed.

It is perhaps odd that the Missionary Society which owes its origin to this Evangelical Scot should be the strongly Anglo-Catholic Universities Mission to Central Africa. It was founded as a direct result of his Cambridge lectures. Its first group of missionaries arrived in Africa in January 1861, led by C. F. Mackenzie, who had been consecrated in Cape Town with the rather grandiloquent title 'Bishop of the mission to the tribes dwelling in the neighbourhood of Lake Nyasa and the River Shire'. Livingstone helped them to settle at Magomero and then left them. Sadly the mission was not a sucess, and that may have been at least partly because Livingstone did not give enough direction or practical assistance. The missionaries quarrelled with local tribes and with slave traders. Within a year Mackenzie was dead. His sucessor, W. G. Tozer, withdrew the mission to Zanzibar, much to Livingstone's disgust. But it was the Universities Mission to Central Africa which built a Cathedral in Zanzibar on the site of the former slave market, and which was later able to return to plant and strengthen Christianity in the interior.[6]

With *James Hudson Taylor* (1832–1905) we have a missionary of a different type and a mission in a country less influenced by Great Britain, China.

Taylor was a Yorkshireman whose father, a chemist in Barnsley and a devout Methodist local preacher, had dedicated him to Christian work before his birth. He was converted as a teenager, and became convinced that he was called as a missionary to China. After medical studies in London and Hull, he first went to China in 1853 under the auspices of the Chinese Evangelisation Society.

During the next few years he learned Chinese and engaged in some fruitful evangelistic work. However, his methods, especially his willingness to adopt Chinese dress, were unconventional and not always well received by his colleagues. On his side he appears to have lost confidence in the Chinese Evangelisation Society, which was not particularly efficient and scandalized Taylor when it went into debt, which he considered unscriptural. He left the Society after four years and lived entirely in dependence on God. Often supplies or money were on the verge of running out and he lived a most frugal life, but gifts or fresh supplies always arrived and he was never actually in want. Nevertheless, when illness due to overwork forced him to return to England in 1860 it seemed unlikely that he would ever return to China.

Yet he could not get China out of his mind. In particular he was conscious of the fact that most missionary work, including that in which he had engaged, was concentrated on the coastal regions where Western influence had gained a foothold through commercial treaties forced on the weak Chinese rulers. His interest turned to inland China where the gospel had not been preached.

A well-known passage from his autobiography tells of the decisive moment in his own life and indicates the cast of his mind. His concern for the Chinese who were dying without knowledge of the gospel had affected his health and he had been invited to spend a few days at Brighton. 'On Sunday, June 25th, 1865, unable to bear the sight of a congregation of a thousand or more Christian people rejoicing in their own security, while millions were perishing for lack of knowledge, I wandered out on the sands alone, in great spiritual agony; and there the Lord conquered my unbelief, and I surrendered myself to God for this service. I told Him that all responsibility as to issues and consequences must rest with Him; that as His servant, it was mine to obey and to follow Him – His, to direct, to care for, and to guide me and those who might labour with me.'[7] Thus the China Inland Mission came into existence, and in May of the next year a party of twenty-two, including four children, sailed for Shanghai.

The distinctive feature of the China Inland Mission is that it was a 'Faith' mission. In other words it never asked for money but simply relied upon God to provide. Hudson Taylor never set out the needs of the Mission, but rather the needs of the unevangelized millions in China who, he believed, were doomed to eternal darkness without the gospel. It is a simple fact that adequate resources were always available.

The principles for the conduct of the Mission showed a similar trust in God and a sense of urgency in the missionary task. The mission was to be interdenominational. Members of any denomination were received as missionaries provided they were committed to evangelism and accepted Taylor's conservative approach to Scripture. They were also expected to accept his direction, which was from his base in China not, as with most other societies, from far away London. He did all he could to avoid denominational friction. Men of a similar background were put to work together and, as far as possible, missionaries were only sent to areas where there had been no previous Protestant witness. But no salaries were guaranteed and the basic commitment was to the widest possible preaching of the gospel. It was not the prime task of China Inland Mission missionaries to gather churches and provide teaching and pastoral care, though increasingly the pressure of events compelled them to take up these duties. The missionaries were expected to wear Chinese dress and, as long as the gospel was not compromised, to adopt Chinese habits. However, this appears to have been more as a help to evangelism than out of any deep appreciation of Chinese culture.

The success of the China Inland Mission was phenomenal. Its appeal in England was to the conservative Evangelical wing of the Church. At first the missionaries were of working-class or middle-class background, but its reputation, and its appeal, were greatly enhanced when in 1885 the 'Cambridge Seven', seven young men of social distinction, gave up the possibility of glittering careers to join it.

The best known of the Seven was *C. T. Studd* (1860–1931), an outstanding international cricketer. Studd left China in 1894, but later worked as a missionary in India and Africa, where he died. The others gave at least the whole of their working lives to China. Theirs was no passing emotional commitment. One of them, *D. E. Hoste* (1861–1946) succeeded Hudson Taylor as Director of the Mission in 1903 and led it for over thirty years. He remained in China, suffering internment by the Japanese in 1944, until 1945.

The commitment of the Seven was largely due to the evangelistic missions in Great Britain of the American evangelists Moody and Sankey. Thus home and foreign evangelistic work was linked. More important, it was the concept of individual conversion following a recognition of personal sinfulness which they took with them to China. It is by no means certain that this Western expression of Pauline Christianity was the most appropriate for China.

Education and Medicine

A number of comments on principles and methods have already been made. Those set out by the 'Serampore trio' were generally accepted – widespread preaching, translation of the Scriptures, the establishing of a church, understanding the non-Christian culture and training indigenous leaders. As the movement progressed and the missionaries themselves were more generally accepted, other aspects of the Christian mission in its wholeness received more attention, aspects which later generations might recognize more easily as social work.

The first, and most far reaching in its effects, was education. Given the Protestant missionary's conviction of the importance of the Bible it was obvious that converts and would-be converts should be able to read it. Thus, from the beginning elementary education, at least to the level of basic literacy, went along with preaching. The school stood beside the church on the mission compound.

From these small beginnings secondary and higher education developed. As far as the missionaries were concerned the first aim was evangelism followed by instruction in the faith. However, almost from the beginning it became clear that those who had attended the mission school had a chance of being employed by traders or by the government. Thus education gave a means of social improvement. Central to this, of couse, was the English language, which was essential for those seeking advancement during the colonial period.

English also opened men's minds to the breadth of Western culture and, to their credit, the missionaries were not narrow in their conception of education. Though the Bible and Christianity were central, the curriculum included other literature, and an introduction to the sciences was available in the mission schools long before it was normal in secondary schools in England. This breadth was maintained as higher education developed. In addition there were introduced institutions providing education of a more technical, and immediately useful, nature in such areas as agriculture, animal husbandry and various industries.

The other area to develop was the provision of care for the handicapped and medical work among the sick. This emphasis came later than education. The first missionaries were concerned with the souls of their hearers and, though some of the earliest missionary groups to leave England included men with medical training, as well as supplies of medicines, these were originally for the benefit of the missionaries themselves. However, a realization of the extent of preventible or curable disease, together with a recollection that the command of Jesus to his disciples coupled healing with preaching, made a growing emphasis in this area inevitable.

Like education, medicine could be seen as an adjunct to evangelism, or a way to gain the confidence of would-be converts. But it had deeper roots in the biblical understanding of the wholeness of man as a creature of God and in the Christian ideal of service. The sacrificial work of missionaries among lepers, the blind and deaf, the maimed and the generally outcast of society was in itself a proclamation of the gospel. The small clinic or dispensary, which has given way to the modern hospital, has been a proper and integral part of the missionary movement.

Some Questions and Problems

In many respects the history of the nineteenth-century missionary movement represents one of the wonders of Christianity. It includes stories of almost unbelievable sacrifice and endurance, together with miracles of grace as the gospel was proclaimed in word and action. There were few limits, geographical or social, to its penetration. Yet in its progress the missionaries and their supporters were forced to raise questions concerning the nature of Christianity and its relation to the world to which there are not always obvious answers, and in its 'success' were the seeds of problems which have endured beyond the great period of expansion. Some of these must now be mentioned.

Jesus commanded his disciples to preach the gospel to 'every creature'. It is natural therefore that Carey and his friends should have stressed widespread preaching. The China Inland Mission, with its stress on constantly moving on to those who had not yet heard the gospel, to the neglect of building churches, went a stage further. However, the question arises whether this is in fact the best or most likely way of reaching 'every creature'. It presupposes both an ability to understand the preaching, not just the language but the concepts, and it also seems to presuppose an individualistic way of thinking.

Whether by design or accident many missionaries adopted another approach. *Alexander Duff* (1806–74), of the Church of Scotland, who, in 1830, established a school in Calcutta with English as the medium of teaching and who had a profound effect on later educational thinking in India, was consciously aiming to produce leaders. He, and others, believed that concentration on the relatively few who would be opinion formers was the best way to evangelize the entire society. Similarly, in China, the Welsh Baptist, *Timothy Richard* (1845–1919), aimed to penetrate the intellectual class, with the assumption that they would influence the rest. The aim of reaching the mass of the people through the leaders was implicit in much educational work. In a stratified society it is an understandable policy.

But the strategy of going for the leaders, no less than that of widespread preaching, presupposes an individual decision to accept the gospel. There are, however, well authenticated instances of the Church growing through mass movements. Such a movement took place among the Baganda people of Uganda during the 1890s, and several are recorded among the outcastes (later 'scheduled castes') in India. For those who think of conversion and entry into the Church in terms of personal decision such movements are disturbing. Not all missionaries were, or are, equally convinced of their genuineness or that baptism should be offered. No doubt the conversions involved in such movements are less than perfect and special efforts are called for to provide teaching and pastoral care. But at the heart of such a movement is a different type of experience, unusual to the Western mind. In the cultures concerned they are not aberrant.

The question of the relation of the missionaries to non-Christian cultures arose in other ways, not least concerning the attitude to be adopted to non-Christian religions. The phrase 'the heathen in his blindness bows down to wood and stone' comes from the saintly *Reginald Heber* (1783–1826), who was for three years Bishop of

Calcutta and who had a good reputation among the Indian community. Its dismissive attitude to non-Christian religions, and to non-Christian culture generally, was common among some missionaries. Others were willing to allow some good in them as a kind of preparation for the gospel. The question of whether Christianity comes as a completely new thing, or whether it builds upon some parts of the previously existing culture because it shares some insights with it, remains a live one.

In some areas differences between Christianity and the indigenous culture have forced the missionary beyond academic discussion. Faced with the custom of 'suttee', Christians knew they had to oppose it, and Carey performed a service to Hinduism by showing that it was not in fact commanded. The widespread practice of polygamy has also been opposed, though in Africa it is practised by some professing Christians. In both cases Christianity has stood for the dignity and worth of women, but as far as the second is concerned it may be said to have weakened the indigenous culture, in some instances in such a way that women have been disadvantaged.

The charge of weakening the indigenous culture is brought against the West generally and not just Christianity. Behind, or within it is the dilemma of the developing countries which want, or feel they need, the benefits of Western education and Western technology but realize that, so far, such benefits have only been available when accompanied by cultural trappings. In their eyes Christianity may be seen as part of the cultural trappings. So we return to the accusation made earlier of cultural or religious imperialism.

During the twentieth century this question has increasingly been seen in another way from the point of view of the missionary societies. There has been a widespread weakening of the sort of confidence in Christianity and in their own culture which once inspired the missionaries. Several factors have contributed to this. The growth of Liberalism and Modernism at the early part of the century; the growing awareness of the richness of ethnic cultures in Africa and the East; the revival of the non-Christian faiths and a greater knowledge of them in the West; the realization that the great wars of the twentieth century have been between avowedly Christian nations; and a sense of guilt about British imperialism with a realization of Britain's changed role in the world; all these have had a chastening effect.

A result of this changed mood has been a willingness to support movements for relief and social improvement in what is now known as the 'Third World', but less commitment to evangelism. Organizations such as Christian Aid, or even the Evangelical Alliance Relief Fund (TEAR Fund), find it easier to get support for what are seen as humanitarian causes than do the traditional missionary societies for evangelism.

Finally, there are the problems associated with moving from the status of a mission, supported and administered largely from outside, to that of a self-supporting self-governing Church. At their best the missionary societies have been committed to strong indigenous churches and the training of an indigenous ministry. Only slowly did the fruits of this commitment emerge but, soon after the middle of the twentieth century, it was accepted that the English missionary (and the same applies to other Western missionaries) was in a foreign church as a servant of that church. The change, which is not complete, has called for painful adjustments on both sides but it is increasingly being made to work.

A more difficult problem in this area concerns the nature of the Church itself. At Serampore the Church was Baptist. The chaplains of the East India Company were members of the Church of England, with a few from the Church of Scotland. The Church Missionary Society also spread Church of England principles but of an Evangelical outlook, whereas the Universities Mission to Central Africa was decidedly Anglo-Catholic. Livingstone was a Presbyterian of a moderately Calvinistic temperament. Hudson Taylor moved from a Methodist to an independent Baptist position. Drawing on its local culture, the Church in Africa has produced several movements which the West would call Pentecostal. In addition, the indigenous churches would become aware of other traditions which did not come from the British missionary movement. Perhaps it is not surprising that the Ecumenical Movement began in a missionary context.

Notes

1   E. Prout, *Life of the Rev. John Williams* (1843), p. 505, cited M.

Warren, *Social History and Christian Mission* (SCM Press 1967), pp. 65 f.
2 cited S. Neill, *A History of Christian Missions* (Penguin 1964), p. 323.
3 W. G. Blaikie, *The Personal Life of David Livingstone* (1880), p. 28, cited C. Northcott, *David Livingstone, his triumph decline and fall* (Lutterworth 1973), p. 22.
4 W. Monk, ed., *Dr. Livingstone's Cambridge Lectures* (1858), cited Northcott, op. cit., p. 53.
5 cited Neill, op. cit., p. 370.
6 See O. Chadwick, *Mackenzie's Grave* (Hodder & Stoughton 1959).
7 W. Hudson Taylor, *Retrospect* (China Inland Mission and Religious Tract Society n.d.), pp. 119 f.

11

The Ecumenical Movement

Denominational differences among missionaries, which most of them recognized as a hindrance to their work, merely highlighted the divisions of the Church which had become accepted by the nineteenth century. Since 1054 the so-called Eastern Orthodox Churches, acknowledging a general primacy of the Patriarch of Constantinople, had developed separately from the Churches of the West. In the West the Reformation of the sixteenth century had brought a division between Roman Catholics and Protestants, and soon there were a number of Protestant Churches.

There was, of course, among many Christians an awareness that the Church should be one, and even a sense that at some deep level it really is one. In all its forms it owes allegiance to the same Jesus, nurtures its spiritual life from the same Scriptures, and usually observes, though in different ways and with different understandings, the sacraments of baptism and Eucharist, or Communion. From the latter part of the nineteenth century there grew a desire to give expression to this unity and in the twentieth century it has been expressed in the Ecumenical Movement. The Greek *oikumene* means 'the whole inhabited earth'. It came to mean 'the whole of civilized society' and was used in that sense for those councils of the early Church which sought to get agreement on what should be taught, and practised, as Christianity throughout the world. In the modern use of the word the stress is more on the search for unity.

The Growth of a World Movement

It is customary to date the modern Ecumenical Movement from the World Missionary Conference held at Edinburgh in 1910. There is reason for that, but it is worth noting that there were at least three overlapping movements of thought and experience which flowed into Edinburgh, 1910.

The first of these was the missionary movement itself. As was especially noticeable in the case of the London Missionary Society, those who founded the great missionary societies were more concerned about the preaching of the gospel where it had not previously been heard than they were about establishing any particular form of church government. As early as 1806, in a letter to Andrew Fuller, secretary of the Baptist Missionary Society, Carey had suggested calling 'a meeting of all denominations of Christians at the Cape of Good Hope somewhere about 1810'. Fuller commented, 'I consider this as one of bro' Carey's pleasing dreams', and the idea was not pursued. Nevertheless, missionaries did often meet and, by agreeing areas within which each group should work, went some way to reducing the confusion which denominationalism would have caused to converts.

Equally important was the response to movements of revival in England and America during the nineteenth century. These led to the formation of a number of interdenominational associations, often with an evangelistic aim, and showed men from different denominations that they could work together. The most prominent was the Evangelical Alliance, an alliance of individuals and churches committed to a biblically conservative Basis of Faith, founded in 1846.

But it was the societies of students and young people which were especially active. In 1844 George Williams, a London draper's assistant, founded the Young Men's Christian Association. Founded in London the YMCA flourished in America. It was there too that the Student Volunteer Missionary Union was founded in 1886. An English branch, the forerunner of the Student Christian Movement, began at Cambridge in 1892. It had a less rigid doctrinal stance, and was more committed to ecumenical action, than the Cambridge Inter-Collegiate Christian Union, the oldest of the English student Christian bodies, founded in 1877. In 1895, in Sweden, the World Student Christian Federation was formed to draw together the various student organizations.

All the organizations mentioned shared an evangelistic and missionary interest. Around the turn of the century a number of international conferences were held to promote these aims. In a sense therefore, Edinburgh, 1910, could have been simply one among many. But it had certain distinctive features which together secured its honoured place in the history of the Ecumenical Movement.

In the first place it was fortunate in its chairman, the American Methodist *J. R. Mott* (1865–1955). Mott was basically an evangelist. Converted at a student conference he saw his life's work as evangelism among students and devoted his great organizing skills to that end. He became Secretary to the International Committee of the YMCA and was chief architect and then General Secretary of the World Student Christian Federation. In these roles he travelled the world, speaking at universities and making friends of many who were, or were to become, church leaders and major statesmen. He promoted the interest in missionary work among students and adopted the phrase 'the evangelization of the world in this generation', which was an inspiration to many.

Mott spent nearly two years preparing for the Edinburgh Conference. He determined that it should not be simply an inspirational meeting but a serious consultation of informed delegates. To that end he arranged for eight commissions to research and prepare material reflecting the problems and opportunities of contemporary missionary work. This material was sent to all those attending before the Conference assembled. In addition he used his wide contacts and his powers of diplomacy to ensure the attendance of a wide range of church leaders. Especially notable was the attendance of Randall Davidson, Archbishop of Canterbury (1903–28), and representatives of the Anglo-Catholic Society for the Propagation of the Gospel. Thus a second reason for the significance of Edinburgh, 1910, was that no previous conference of the kind had been so well prepared nor gathered delegates from so wide a cross section of the Church.

Finally, unlike previous conferences, Edinburgh, 1910, appointed a Continuation Committee charged with the task of keeping in contact with the various missionary societies and considering whether another such conference should be held. This committee, the first permanent link between the various societies, was the seed of the later Ecumenical Movement. Mott was appointed Chairman, the Secretary was J. H. Oldham.

J. H. Oldham (1874–1969) was a tireless worker for the ecumenical cause. A Presbyterian who became an Anglican, like Mott his background was in the student movements. He went to India to work for the YMCA, but after three years was forced by ill health to return. Subsequently he was at the centre of missionary and ecumenical work for the rest of his life.

His most obvious gifts were in the area of organization and administration. He had been co-secretary, with Kenneth Maclennan, of Edinburgh, 1910, and was a natural choice as secretary of the Continuation Committee. He held that post until 1938, by which time the Committee had become, in 1921, the International Missionary Council. He was responsible for many ecumenical gatherings, notably the Oxford Conference of 1937 on Church, Community and State. Through his missionary contacts he developed a particular interest in Africa and, in 1925, he was influential in the formation of the International Bureau of African Languages and Literature, of which he became honorary Director. His expertise was recognized by the government and he was a member of a commission on the union of the East African territories. During the Second World War he created the Christian Frontier Council, a body of lay people concerned with the relation of Christian faith to public affairs in industry and the professions, and he launched and edited the Christian News-Letter. He was one of the most influential advisers in the formation of the World Council of Churches, the British Council of Churches and the Commission of the Churches on International Affairs.

But he was more than an organizer. Partly because of acute deafness he rarely contributed to the public assemblies which he organized. But those who knew him well thought of him as a prophet, and his grasp of Christian truth in its relation to personal and political life was made clear in a number of books. While others were optimistic about the progress of the Christian mission he saw the coming dangers of secularism and of political totalitarianism. In the latter regard his friendship with German church leaders and his efforts on behalf of German missionary societies during two world wars did much to keep the confidence of the German church and to maintain its links with the world Church. *The International Review of Missions* which he edited from 1911 was acknowledged for its grasp of world politics as well as for its contributions to Christian missionary thinking. Above all he was a man who made friends with an astonishing number and variety of people and he was thus able to bring together points of view which might not otherwise have met.

We noted that in 1921 the Edinburgh Continuation Committee became the International Missionary Council. This is one of the three strands into which the Ecumenical Movement may be divided. The others are the Faith and Order Movement and the Life and Work Movement. They had a similar motivation – the desire that Christians should unite to bring the gospel to the world. For some time the three strands developed more or less independently, but they shared a number of leading figures and maintained close contact with each other.

Edinburgh, 1910, was officially a Conference of Missionary Societies, the Churches as such were not formally involved. Questions of doctrine and church order on which the various Churches differ, such as the status and function of ministers, teaching on the sacraments or the question of authority, were deliberately not raised. It was accepted, though painful to many, that they could not join in worship at the Eucharist.

Such an exclusion of potentially divisive topics was necessary at the time. Anglo-Catholics such as Gore could otherwise not have attended, and Randall Davidson would not have been there to give the gathering the benefit of his enormous prestige. But such an exclusion could not go on. Missionaries more than most were conscious of the scandal of divisions, and it was becoming clear that the younger Churches, especially in Asia, were impatient with the denominationalism that Western Christians had grown to accept as normal.

One man left Edinburgh determined that the differences between Churches should be brought into the open and discussed. He was an American Episcopalian, *Charles Henry Brent* (1862–1929), who since 1901 had been a missionary bishop in the Philippines. His determination, coupled with great patience, was the force behind the Faith and Order Movement.

His first target was his own Church, and shortly after he returned from Edinburgh the following motion was put to the Convention of the Protestant Episcopal Church of America and passed unanimously, 'That a Joint Commission be appointed to bring about a Conference for the consideration of questions touching Faith and Order, and that all Christian Communions throughout the world which confess Our Lord Jesus Christ as God and Saviour be asked to unite with us in arranging for and conducting such a Conference'.[1] Then the real work began. It was seventeen years before the Conference took place at Lausanne in 1927. During those years Brent, and a remarkable layman, a lawyer Robert Halliwell Gardiner, corresponded with and visited church leaders and theologians throughout the world. Slowly others came to share their vision and a number of discussion documents were prepared for the Conference. A particular achievement was to gain the confidence of German theologians after the First World War.

A conference for 'all Christian Communions throughout the world . . .' should include the Roman and Orthodox Churches. The original invitation was sent (in Latin) to all Roman Catholic Cardinals and Bishops, and in 1919 a delegation visited Pope Benedict XV in Rome. The result was inevitable. Convinced that his Church already possessed all truth the Pope refused to take part. He assured them of his good wishes and they were handed a statement as they left which concluded with his prayer that, 'if the Congress is practicable, those who take part in it may, by the Grace of God, see the light and become reunited to the visible Head of the Church, by whom they will be received with open arms'.[2] After the Lausanne Conference Pope Pius XI issued an encyclical *Mortalium Animos* in which he stated: 'The Apostolic See can by no means take part in these assemblies, nor is it in any way lawful for Catholics to give to such enterprises their encouragement or support. If they did so, they would be giving countenance to a false Christianity.'[3] This was to be the official position of the Roman Catholic Church until Vatican II, though a number of individuals retained a friendly contact.

The attitude of the Orthodox Churches was quite different. In 1919 the Patriarch of Constantinople surprised the Western Churches by issuing his own appeal for closer intercourse and greater understanding between the Churches. There were Orthodox observers at Lausanne, and the Orthodox have continued to play a part in the Ecumenical Movement.

It is never clear what is to be expected of great ecumenical gatherings nor what may be rated as success. It was remarkable that Faith and Order Conferences in fact took place at Lausanne in 1927 and then at Edinburgh in 1937. They enabled views to be clarified and misunderstandings removed. Smaller meetings between the Conferences, at which particular topics were addressed, produced greater trust among theologians of different Churches. An event of particular note was that on the death of Brent in 1929 his role as Chairman of the Continuation Committee was taken by the new Archbishop of York, William Temple. Temple had already been active in Conferences of the International Missionary Council and the Life and Work Movement.

The chief figure behind the Life and Work Movement was the Swedish theologian *Nathan Söderblom* (1866–1931). As a student he committed himself to work for the unity of the Church, but it was always clear to him that such unity was not an end in itself but for the purpose of presenting the gospel to the world. Furthermore he was convinced that the gospel includes principles for the ordering of social and political life. The Church has a responsibility to contribute to the healing of divisions among men, and a united Church would be a better witness to the reconciling power of Christ. Indeed it might be that a way to unity could be found through work to which all could commit themselves, hence the slogan of the movement, 'Service unites doctrine divides'.

In his experience the most frightening illustration of division among men was the First World War. As it began he had just become Lutheran Archbishop of Uppsala and Primate of Sweden. He had previously been pastor of the Swedish church in Paris and then Professor of the History of Religions first at Uppsala then at Leipzig. From neutral Sweden he urged Christians on both sides of the war to work for peace and to affirm the Christian principles on which a just society might be built. His call to Christian leaders to sign a joint manifesto was unsuccessful. Probably many of them felt that he was too far from the realities which they faced to appreciate them properly. But his basic contention that the gospel was relevant to social life, and that Christians have a responsibility to work out that relevance and state it clearly, struck a chord with some. Among them was Temple, at that time Rector of St James', Picadilly, who became a great supporter of the movement.

The first Life and Work Conference was at Stockholm in 1925 under Söderblom's chairmanship. To a later generation neither its debates nor its reports appear particularly remarkable. What was remarkable was that Churches were represented as Churches, including a delegation from the Orthodox Churches.

The next Conference, held at Oxford in 1937, was organized by J. H. Oldham, on loan from the International Missionary Council. Oldham arranged for the preparation and circulation of documents in advance. The theme was Church, Community and State, and in everyone's mind was the growth of the totalitarian state and especially the situation in Germany where the National Socialist government of Adolf Hitler had attempted, with considerable success, to turn the Church into a department of the state. In those circumstances the Conference's stress on the freedom of the Church and its responsibility to take a prophetic role, rebuking secular rulers where necessary and upholding the dignity of man as created by God, was quite impressive.

In the long term the most significant feature of the two Conferences of 1937 – Faith and Order at Edinburgh and Life and Work at Oxford – was that both accepted a resolution that they should combine to form the World Council of Churches. Some work was done at a provisional Committee meeting at Utrecht in 1938, including the appointment of William Temple as Chairman and of W. A. Visser't Hooft as General Secretary, a post he held until 1966. However, the outbreak of the Second World War prevented the actual amalgamation. Throughout the war the organization existed under the clumsy title The Provisional Committee of the World Council of Churches in Process of Formation. It did not finally come into existence until a Conference at Amsterdam in 1948. An equally important milestone was at its Conference in New Delhi in 1961 when the International Missionary Council joined it. Thus the missionary movement which had begun the process at Edinburgh, 1910, took its place in the wider movement which it had, though unwittingly, set in train.

The Changing Nature and Concerns of the Movement

It would be possible to continue to list conferences and committees and thus to cover a great deal of the work of the Movement. However, the bringing together of the three strands we have mentioned into the World Council, and even more the changing world situation, both highlighted some tensions which had appeared just below the surface of the movement and also indicated new spheres of service.

The World Council of Churches is a fairly loose federation of Churches. At Amsterdam its basis for membership was the acceptance of 'Our Lord Jesus Christ as God and Saviour'. At New Delhi this was slightly expanded to become, 'a fellowship of churches which confess the Lord Jesus Christ as God and Saviour according to the Scriptures and therefore seek to fulfil together their common calling to the glory of the one God, Father, Son and Holy Spirit'.[4] This remains fairly broad, and it is to be expected that different member Churches should bring different concerns to the Council's debates.

The major changes of emphasis in the movement since 1910 can be fairly easily listed.

First there is a distinct move from individuals and groups of enthusiasts to Churches. Edinburgh, 1910, was a Conference of Missionary Societies, supported by voluntary associations of an Evangelical nature and by missionary orientated student groups. In such organizations gifted individuals and closely knit groups combining on relatively narrow interests naturally exert influence. Thus a Mott or an Oldham could know personally most people who mattered in the movement, a Brent or a Söderblom could pursue an enthusiasm and persuade other men of influence to join them in promoting it. Gradually the Churches as such became more committed but, at least until the Second World War, there was a sense of men who knew each other as friends working together for a cause, or causes, dear to their own hearts. Then the Churches took over.

The immediate result was a sense of slowing down. Whatever else they may be Churches are also human institutions. They have committees and orders of precedence. They also have ways of understanding the faith and of conducting Christian life which have become hallowed by tradition and which they are inclined to defend. They may also contain within themselves variations of emphasis which certain groups wish to preserve. The result is that they do not move quickly. When it is added that by no means all members of any of the Churches have ever seen the Ecumenical Movement as *the* priority in Christian life, and some have feared that the World Council wished to become a sort of super-church and dictate terms, it is understandable that there should appear to be a slackening of pace.

In this regard the involvement of the Orthodox Churches and the increasing openness of Roman Catholicism after Vatican II did not make for speed. The Orthodox have always been inclined to make prepared statements, especially on matters of Faith and Order, and to decline from associating themselves with final reports of conferences, though taking a full part in discussions. The traditional attitude of Rome and uncertainty about the post-Vatican II status of some traditional Roman dogmas has led to a certain wariness among other Churches, though accompanied by a general delight at the greater openness of the Roman attitude to ecumenism.

A more positive change was a considerable transfer of influence and leadership from the older to the younger Churches. In its early days the movement had been largely white, Anglo-Saxon, Protestant and European. Gradually, and with increasing speed after 1948, this situation changed. The involvement of the Orthodox meant some shift in the balance of power. Then the Churches of Asia, Africa and later Latin America became more prominent. This movement began in the International Missionary Council. It was the missionaries who first acknowledged that their converts had come of age and were Churches in their own right. This was expressed in a slogan from the International Missionary Council Conference at Whitby in 1947, 'Partnership in Obedience'. Both older and younger Churches must work out their obedience to the gospel while maintaining an equal partnership with each other. Sadly, however, some degree of economic dependence inevitably continued and occasionally caused friction.

It was not only that the numbers of representatives from the younger Churches increased. The creation of the Church of South India in 1947 gave the younger Churches a sense of moral leadership. From a manifesto issued by a group of Indian ministers at a Conference in Tranquebar in 1919 had come a movement to unity which eventually led to the creation of a genuinely Indian Church, bringing together former Anglicans, Lutherans, Presbyterians, Congregationalists and Methodists. Though there were some problems of recognition by other Churches, especially the Church of England, this came to be the first successful union of episcopal and non-episcopal traditions. It was followed in 1970 by the Church of North India which was even broader in its contributing traditions. Meanwhile regional conferences of Christians in Asia and Africa, with little or no participation from the West, have become almost commonplace.

The emergence of the younger Churches may be seen as part of a change in the relationship of the Church to the world. For the older Churches it is also part of a change in the status of the West. In 1910 there was a mood of confidence, both about the continued leadership of the West in world affairs and also about the decline of non-Christian world religions. It is often pointed out that the defeat of Russia by Japan in 1905 ought already to have been a warning of coming change. Subsequently there has been the change brought about by the end of colonialism and a reawakening of the non-Christian faiths. It was natural, therefore, that the Churches of Asia and Africa should seek their own expression of Christianity and that more attention should be given to the relation of Christianity to other faiths.

The greater prominence of the younger Churches and, especially, the Second World War brought about a greater involvement with politics and secular life generally. Throughout that war the Provisional Committee of the World Council kept contact with Churches on both sides. Often at great cost, chaplains, Bibles and spiritual support generally were provided for prisoners of war. Help was provided for the growing number of refugees, a work which has sadly had to continue in many parts of the world. There were also many accounts of heroism in attempts to rescue non-Aryans from lands being overrun by Germany.

All this was a far cry from the exchange of theological papers, but it introduced an aspect of the World Council's work which has grown beside the continuing theological debates. At various conferences the World Council has faced theological issues and achieved considerable clarification and agreement. On at least some occasions, however, there have been angry debates on practical responses to the world situation. During the 1960s, and beyond, questions of civil rights in America and South Africa, of racism, of Liberation theology and, perhaps above all, of the glaring inequalities of wealth between the nations of the Northern hemisphere and many of those of the South, had to be faced.

These were the issues which were prominent at the Assembly in Uppsala in 1968. The fact that one of the presidents, Sir Francis Ibiam, was unable to attend because of civil war in Nigeria, and that Dr Martin Luther King, who had been expected to preach at the opening service, had recently been assassinated, gave them a special poignancy. From Uppsala came a serious commitment to the poor of the world and a move from the provision of emergency aid to the encouragement of schemes of development. By no means the only aspect of this commitment, but the one which received most public attention, was the programme to combat racism. This has sometimes involved making grants for 'humanitarian' uses to organizations willing to countenance violence to gain what they believe to be just political ends.

All this raises in an acute form the relationship of the Church to political power. Some critics suggest the Church should never be involved in political issues, but that implies that there are areas of life to which the gospel does not apply and it involves the Church in abandoning its prophetic role. It is of course true that Christian faith or theological expertise are no guarantee of wise political judgement. Usually the World Council, or its member Churches, can call upon expertise in non-theological areas, but the Church's judgements must finally be theologically based. When the Church, or individual Churches, state fundamental principles clearly it is possible that a debate with secular authorities may ensue from which both sides can learn. On a more practical level, the role which the Churches have taken in the history of the former colonial territories, and their continuing influence in those societies, make political involvement almost inevitable.

Behind recent moves in the political sphere lies a theological development and some theological disagreements. The optimistic Liberalism, both theological and secular, of the early twentieth century was severely shaken by world events. For many theologians it was replaced by a theology in which human sinfulness and man's need for divine grace play a more prominent role. With this go two other related but distinct debates. One concerns how far Christians are committed to 'building the Kingdom of God' in this world, or whether they can only wait to receive what God may give in terms of judgement and grace. The other concerns the nature of Christian mission. Is it primarily a matter of changing human systems and promoting the good of humanity generally by establishing just systems of government which will promote healthy and fulfilling life-styles for their citizens; or is it primarily a matter of preaching the gospel to individuals so that each man or woman may come, through a personal response to Jesus, into that relationship with God for which he or she was made? Put another way, is salvation a broad concept which takes in society, or even the whole of creation, or is it a narrower matter concerning the individual and his relation to God?

Probably few Christians would opt for one of the alternatives just posed to the total exclusion of the other. However, debates in the World Council during the 1970s and 1980s have shown that people begin their thinking with different emphases, often based on their own experience and their own situations. Uppsala in 1968 appeared to many to overstress the political dimension to the detriment of the spiritual. Subsequent thinking appears to have modified that approach, while clearly asserting that salvation cannot be understood in purely individualistic terms with no reference to the social and political conditions in which the Church exists. The World Council clearly recognizes that people and Churches experience their faith, and live it, in different ways. This was shown at the sixth Assembly at Vancouver in 1983 which was devoted to a sharing of these different understandings under the general theme 'Jesus Christ – the Life of the World'.

Ecumenism in Britain

British Churches had been affected by the three movements which had been influential in the growth of the Ecumenical Movement. An honourable role in the missionary movement, experience of revival in different forms and the development of student Christian organizations had shown British Christians that it was possible to transcend denominational barriers. Nevertheless, the denominational differences were deeply ingrained. The position of the Church of England was a particular problem. Those of the Free Churches especially conscious of their Reformation heritage were suspicious of the elements of traditional Catholic theology and practice which at least some Anglicans maintained. In addition the link of the Church of England with the state, and the legal and social privileges which flowed from it, had produced in Free

Churchmen a sense that they were not regarded as equals. Among the Free Churches the Methodists were divided, some seeing themselves as nearer to the Church of England, others leaning towards the older dissenting tradition. Meanwhile, within the Church of England there were divisions between Anglo-Catholics and Evangelicals. Rome maintained its traditional exclusiveness. Near the end of the twentieth century it is not possible to say that all these differences have ceased to exist, but there is certainly a greater degree of understanding and tolerance.

Well into the twentieth century the various denominations generally went their own way. For the Free Churches the National Council of Evangelical Free Churches was founded in 1896 and the more representative Federal Council of Evangelical Free Churches in 1919. The two came together to form the Free Church Federal Council in 1939. Between them these bodies provided a forum for the Free Churches and helped them to act jointly in such matters as the provision of hospital and prison chaplains, and sometimes gave them a voice in local government. Some Free Churchmen wanted to move towards a united Free Church, others were content with a looser federation. The latter naturally included those Methodists who feared that a united Free Church would make union with the Church of England more difficult. Meanwhile the divisions which had grown up within Methodism were brought together, somewhat uneasily, in 1932.

For its part the Church of England was secure in its role as the Established Church and as the centre of the world-wide Anglican Communion. But it was not totally indifferent to the problems of division. When the bishops met at Lambeth in 1888 they issued the famous Lambeth Quadrilateral giving the four requirements which they saw as necessary for reunion. These were that all should accept, '(a) the Holy Scriptures of the Old and New Testaments, as "containing all things necessary to salvation", and as being the rule and ultimate standard of faith; (b) the Apostles' Creed as the Baptismal Symbol, and the Nicene Creed as the sufficient statement of the Christian Faith; (c) the two Sacraments ordained by Christ Himself – Baptism and the Supper of the Lord – ministered with unfailing use of Christ's Words of Institution, and of the elements ordained by Him; (d) the Historic Episcopate, locally adapted in the methods of its administration to the varying needs of the nations and peoples called of God into the Unity of His Church'.

Later, in 1920, another Lambeth Conference issued an Appeal to all Christian People to work together for the visible unity of the Church. This time the bishops went out of their way to make it plain that, though they considered the historic episcopate as essential for such unity, they accepted what they called the 'spiritual reality' of other ministries and acknowledged that they had been used by God. They had, however, clearly identified the stumbling block to unity with the Free Churches – the necessity and the understanding of episcopacy.

There were no real moves towards visible unity, but gradually the Churches in Britain learned more about each other, and provided a number of leaders for the world-wide Ecumenical Movement. Prominent among these was William Temple. More than any other church leader Temple gained the confidence of men and women of all denominations. At his enthronement as Archbishop of Canterbury in 1942 he described the Ecumenical Movement as 'the great new fact of our era'. A few months later when the British Council of Churches was formed it was almost inevitable that he should be its first President. In Temple's thinking church unity was not an end in itself but rather a means to Christian mission and service in the world. This emphasis, together with his ability to understand and sympathize with many traditions within the Church, even when he could not always fully agree with them, attracted to the movement many who would otherwise have hesitated to be associated with it. His early death in 1944 was a grave loss to the movement.

The sufferings associated with the Second World War brought the Churches closer together. Co-operation at the local level included organizing the evacuation of children from the major cities to safer areas and practical help for the victims of enemy action. In 1940, with Temple's encouragement, there began a series of 'Religion and Life Weeks'. These were essentially local gatherings in which prominent speakers from various denominations sought to encourage and strengthen Christian commitment and to promote joint activity. Meanwhile Cardinal Hinsley had launched the 'Sword of the Spirit' movement with a similar aim among Roman Catholics. Soon, with Hinsley's support, the two movements were working together. Sadly, on Hinsley's death in 1943, his successor brought this co-operation to an end. Throughout the war the British Council of Churches sought to keep open channels of communication with Christians in Europe, including those in Germany, and at its end took a full part in efforts to provide relief for refugees.

Such practical co-operation deepened understanding between denominations and has continued long after the end of the war. It is seen most clearly in the annual Christian Aid week collections for the poor of the world but is also present in many other local initiatives. Such sharing at the practical level has brought pressure, especially from lay Christians, towards fuller visible unity. But, in spite of valiant efforts, theological difficulties have remained and have continued to keep the Churches apart.

The main theological problem is the question of bishops. Of the four basic requirements for unity laid down in the Lambeth Quadrilateral of 1888 – acceptance of the Scriptures, the traditional creeds, the dominical sacraments and the historic episcopate – non-Roman churches in Britain could accept the first three, with variations of emphasis and understanding, but would have quite serious difficulties about the fourth. The question is, what exactly is meant by historic episcopate?

Broadly speaking Catholic Christians, including the strong Anglo-Catholic wing of the Church of England, take it to mean that for a denomination really to be part of the Christian Church its ministers must be ordained by bishops who were themselves ordained by bishops, and so on back to the first apostles. This is their understanding of apostolic succession. For this point of view bishops are essential to the life of the Church and it is only ministers, or as they would say priests, who have been so ordained who can administer the sacraments. No other ordination or form of ministry is valid. Most people who take this view would agree that God does bless the work of other denominations, but they regard such blessings as 'uncovenanted mercies'. For them other denominations are really outside the body of Christ and church unity can only come about if those denominations accept the role of bishops and their ministers accept episcopal ordination.

Such a view is rejected by the major Free Churches. They point out that in the New Testament the words for bishop and elder (in

Greek *presbyter*) appear to be interchangeable. They may also argue that while the *function* of the bishop, that is pastoral oversight and teaching, is essential, the actual *role* as understood in the Catholic tradition is not. Those who argue in this way are not indifferent to the importance of order and government in the Church, neither do they want to disparage the importance of a specially set aside ministry. But they believe that the authority of the minister comes from a divine call and from his recognition and appointment within the Church, and not from some spiritual gift conferred through episcopal ordination. Nevertheless, many of them would concede that in the history of the Church there have always been men who perform the functions of bishops. It is a source of confusion in debates on church unity that the phrase 'historic episcopate' can be understood both in the strict Catholic sense of apostolic succession, or the conferring of a spiritual gift at ordination, and also in the more general sense of the existence in history of a body of men who exercise pastoral oversight. It is on this point that successive movements towards church unity in Britain since 1945 have come to grief.

What appeared to be a major move towards a breakthrough came with a sermon preached at Cambridge in 1946 by Temple's successor as Archbishop of Canterbury, *Geoffrey Fisher*. Fisher suggested that while the denominations remained separate they should seek ways of moving towards acceptance of each other's ministries and sacraments, and that those Churches which did not have bishops should develop their own forms of episcopacy, or, as the phrase at the time had it, seek to 'take episcopacy into their systems'. It was a premiss of Fisher's sermon, and of subsequent discussions, that the Church of England had a unique role. This was based partly on its historical development in England and its world-wide dissemination, but more on its claim to possess both Catholic and Protestant elements. Thus the Church of England came to regard itself as a 'bridge' church in church unity debates.

As a result of Fisher's Cambridge sermon and the discussions which followed it a number of 'conversations' took place between the Church of England and the major Free Churches. On their side the Free Churches have not objected so much to bishops as to the Catholic understanding of apostolic succession. They have usually been willing to move towards adopting episcopal ordination in the future. The problem has been the initial step, how to get bishops into their system in a way which does not imply any deficiency in their previous ministry or the conferring of a peculiar spiritual gift by the act of episcopal ordination. The proposal normally suggested has been a service of reconciliation which has included a reciprocal laying on of hands with the prayer that all should receive whatever he may lack. The intention has been a kind of pooling of spiritual resources. However, both those of a more Catholic tradition and those of a more Protestant one have seen this as a kind of ordination. The Catholics have not accepted that one not himself episcopally ordained can ordain, and the Protestants have not been able to accept anything which could be taken as the Catholic view of apostolic succession. This dispute brought the failure of moves towards union between the Church of England and the Church of Scotland in 1957 and between the Church of England and the Methodist Church in 1969.

In 1972 there was a successful union; the Congregational Church of England and Wales and the Presbyterian Church of England united to form the United Reformed Church, though not all former members of either party joined. In this case the question of bishops did not arise as both were of the Reformed tradition, but the move gave a new impetus to hopes of a wider reunion. Taking up an idea first accepted by a British Council of Churches Faith and Order Conference at Nottingham in 1964, the leaders of the United Reformed Church invited the other Churches to join in talks planned to lead to a covenant to work and pray for unity. The resulting body, the Churches' Council for Covenanting, produced its proposals in 1980. Once again the chief problem was the validity of the ministry and the form which any service of reconciliation should take. Though the plans were accepted by most Churches they were defeated in 1982 by a combination of Anglo-Catholics and Protestants in the Church of England, largely because the question of whether or not ordination was intended was deliberately left ambiguous.

Nevertheless there have been encouraging signs as well as problems. The new mood in the Roman Catholic Church after Vatican II led to the setting up of the Anglican Roman Catholic International Commission (ARCIC) in 1970. It was able to report 'substantial agreement' on Eucharistic Doctrine in 1971, on Ministry in 1973, on Authority in 1976, and on Justification by Faith in 1986 while at the same time identifying points, such as papal infallibility and devotion to the Blessed Virgin Mary, where more work had to be done. Meanwhile, at the pastoral level Rome has become more flexible on the vexed question of marriage between Roman Catholics and Christians of other communions. A particularly contentious issue which became prominent in the 1980s was the ordination of women. This is practised in a number of Free Churches but is not widely accepted among Catholic Christians. It is a matter on which the Church of England's claim to be a 'bridge' Church may be severely tested.

It is at the practical level that the signs are most encouraging. Since the Nottingham Conference of 1964 the British Council of Churches has encouraged the setting up of Local Ecumenical Projects, that is projects where churches of different denominations work together in a particular area. By 1984 there were over four hundred such projects. They often begin with the sharing of buildings but can go on to shared worship and to joint mission and social responsibility. In such ways the barriers which divided British Christians at the beginning of the twentieth century are being removed. But it is fair to comment that such movements often come from a recognition of the weakness of any particular denomination to carry out work in certain areas alone, rather than from any firm conviction of a theological nature.

Finally, a notable feature of the second part of the twentieth century has been the decline of the SCM. In the 1950s it was still a power to be reckoned with in university circles. During the 1960s it appeared that its influence was directed more to radical politics than to distinctively Christian mission, and by the 1970s it had virtually disappeared. At the same time interest in Christianity among students, following a decline, has flourished. It has flowed into the more conservative Inter-Varsity Fellowship, now renamed the Universities and Colleges Christian Fellowship, and into a non-denominational, charismatic, Christianity. Towards the end of the century problems of church unity do not seem to be a major issue with Christian students; indeed many of the most committed seem impatient of any denominational labels. They are concerned about Jesus, about individual discipleship and, often, about social responsibility. They gladly admit the need for Christian fellowship but they seek it in localities or in sociological interest groups rather than in traditional denominations. It is too soon to say what influence this movement may ultimately have on schemes for church unity.

Notes

1 cited N. Goodall, *The Ecumenical Movement* (Oxford University Press 2nd edn 1964), p. 47.
2 ibid.
3 The whole text is printed in G. K. A. Bell, *Documents on Christian Unity*, Second Series (Oxford University Press 1930) pp. 51–63.
4 N. Goodall, op. cit., pp. 68 f.

12

Movements of Revival and Evangelism

Much of the history of Christianity in Great Britain during the last two centuries may be told in terms of datable public events, the changing relation of the Church as an institution to society, the publication of outstanding books and the impact upon traditional theology of the rise of scientific thinking. But Christians also wish to speak of the activity of God and of man's experience of that activity. They know that the gospel is concerned with the will and the emotions as well as with the intellect. The Church at any time includes many who do not write books or influence public affairs on a large scale, but who believe that they have experiences of God which profoundly affect them and about which they feel obliged to speak to others. Such experiences provide the driving force for the public history of the Church and their effects are part of that history.

The nineteenth and twentieth centuries witnessed a number of movements of spiritual revival. Some critics might see them as symptomatic of a flight from the intellect to the emotions in face of criticisms of traditional Christianity from post-Englightenment thinking. Others might find in them a more genuine expression of New Testament Christianity.

The problem of definition

It is difficult in this area always to use words in a precise way. In particular it is not always easy to distinguish when revivalism passes into evangelism. A revival in its religious sense is normally taken to mean a deepening of spiritual awareness leading to greater fervour in religious practice. In that sense the Oxford Movement was clearly a revival, though the word is more normally found in evangelical circles. It is also normal to say that a revival is a work of God, not of men. In brief, doctrines which have been accepted superficially at an intellectual level become real to a number of people at an emotional level and change their attitude to God. The implication is that revival takes place where there has previously been at least nominal belief. Thus the word 'awakening' is sometimes used instead of revival.

In spite of the insistence on the initiative of God, some teachers have described the human conditions in which revival might occur. They draw attention to such things as a struggle for holiness of life, commitment to prayer and an emphasis in teaching on such doctrines as human sinfulness, the significance of the cross, the need for repentance, conversion and the work of the Holy Spirit. One such teacher was the American *Charles Finney* (1792–1875), whose *Lectures on Revivals of Religion* was published in 1836. Such works led to the possibility of arranging a revival by producing the correct climate and using the correct spiritual or psychological stimuli. Gifted individuals arose who could operate in this area and who were known as revivalists.

Finney and most early revivalists concentrated on the Churches, turning half-hearted or superficial believers into ardent Christians. But soon attention turned to those outside the Churches and to the organizing of large meetings at which the facts of the gospel were presented, and an appeal for commitment was made, to those who may not even have been nominal believers. Thus the words revival and revivalist were used where such words as evangelism and evangelist might have been more appropriate. *D. L. Moody* (1837–99) seems to have thought of himself chiefly as a revivalist, directing his ministry to the Churches, but his friends and advisers increasingly saw him as reaching those outside the Churches. *William Booth* (1829–1912) had experience as a revivalist but deliberately sought to reach those outside the Churches, and *Billy Graham* (b. 1918), more than any before him, developed methods of mass evangelism. While the majority of those who attended the meetings of Dr Graham's last mission in England in 1984 had some connection with a church, the stress was on presenting basic Christian teaching to those unaware of it. Revival had given way to evangelism. But it is questionable whether a strict distinction can be maintained. A church which is unmoved by the concerns of revival within its own ranks can hardly evangelize within a society which lacks even nominal belief.

Revivals and Revivalists

During the eighteenth century there occurred what came to be known as the First Great Awakening. Its most important phase is generally traced to the Congregational Church at Northampton, Massachusetts where it grew during the 1730s under the ministry of the scholar and preacher *Jonathan Edwards* (1703–58). It spread in New England and, to a lesser extent, throughout the English colonies in America. Parallel to it in England was the Evangelical revival associated with the Wesleys and George Whitefield. The two movements were linked through Whitefield's travels in America and by a common indebtedness to European pietism, especially that of the Moravians.

In the last decade of that century America experienced the Second Great Awakening. By then American civilization was moving west. The Churches, at least in the orderly, intellectual, forms found in the east did not keep up with the movement. Instead, on the new frontier a simpler, more emotional, Christianity developed and there grew a tradition of camp meetings. These meetings often lasted several days. They attracted men and women who were conscious of a spiritual need and who were deliberately seeking some kind of spiritual experience.

It was at camp meetings that what later generations came to know as revivalism flourished. There was a conscious stress on experience and preachers set out to induce fear of judgement, relief and gratitude at the realization of divine forgiveness, and the exhilaration and commitment attributed to the filling of the Holy Spirit. Accounts speak of people collapsing, groaning, crying aloud and experiencing visions. Throughout there is a sense of greatly heightened emotion, yet it would be difficult to deny the genuineness of the religion thus generated or its long-continued influence in traditions of simple God-fearing righteousness.

Accounts of such meetings reached England early in the nineteenth century. They were reminiscent of accounts of early Methodist preaching and some Methodists arranged similar meetings. The stress was on preaching of repentance, testimony to conversion and the experience of a new life by some; and the seeking of such experiences by others. One meeting held at Mow Cop in Staffordshire in 1807 became almost legendary within Methodism.

Most Methodist leaders did not approve of such meetings, however, arguing that they were too emotional, and one result was a division within Methodism leading to the establishment of the Primitive Methodists.

A more influential movement, more appropriately called a revival, began in Ulster in the autumn of 1858. In some measure it spread to the rest of Great Britain. It went on for several years and its influence probably continued for two generations, though estimates of its influence vary.

Again it began in America. There, in the autumn of 1857, a number of churches began to hold mid-day prayer meetings. Christians in several cities, often laymen concerned at what they saw as the spiritual dryness of the churches, met to pray for revival. Within months the number of meetings multiplied. Many individuals experienced a renewal of faith and others, becoming concerned about their spiritual condition, turned to ministers and others for help. The spread of the movement excited comment in the press.

News of these events reached Ulster and similar prayer meetings began to take place. It was from one held by a number of laymen in the village of Kells near Ballymena that the movement appears to have spread, first to local churches and then throughout Ulster. Press reports spoke of crowded and prolonged meetings, remarkable conversions and large increases in church membership. Some also spoke of religious mania and uncontrolled excitement, and drew attention to some physical manifestations of weeping, trances and prostrations. On the whole, however, as in America, it was clear that spiritual and moral transformations did take place. When the movement spread to Great Britain there were similar happenings.

As the movement spread a number of revivalists emerged, many of whom were laymen. Some were of high social status such as *Brownlow North* (1804–75), wealthy descendant of a Prime Minister, who turned from a dissolute life to become a notable preacher, or *Reginald Radcliffe* (1825–95) a Liverpool solicitor who became not only a preacher but a supporter of social work among the poor, as well as a sponsor of provision for the social and spiritual well-being of seamen. Others were uneducated working men, some with colourful pasts, such as *Richard Weaver* (1827–96) described as an ex-coal miner and prize fighter, or *Henry Moorhouse* (1840–80) a converted pickpocket from Lancashire who was later said to have influenced D. L. Moody. Among Americans who took part in revivalist work in Great Britain a Methodist couple *Dr Walter Palmer* (1804–83) and his wife *Phoebe* (1807–74) were to be particularly influential.

The emergence of individual revivalists led to the organizing of local revivals or evangelistic efforts, some in churches and others in theatres or the open air. The element of organization meant that some of the spontaneity went out of the movement, and the use of unusual venues, together with the prominence of laymen – sometimes suspected of unorthodox theological views – caused some church leaders who had previously welcomed the movement to become more cautious or even suspicious. The stress on experience, and accounts of prostrations or unusual psychological happenings, added to the suspicion.

The last widely recognized revival in Great Britain occurred in Wales during 1904–5. For some time there had been concern, especially in the Calvinistic Methodist Church, about declining numbers and spiritual vitality. An evangelistic movement, known as the Forward Movement, had been in existence since the 1870s with considerable success in some places. Early in 1904 there were indications of revival at the church of Joseph Jenkins at New Quay in Cardiganshire. But the central figure was to be *Evan Roberts* (1879–1951). A former collier, Roberts was training for the ministry when he came under the influence of Seth Joshua, an evangelist who had recently been at work at New Quay. Roberts claimed to have a vision of a coming revival in Wales and began to gather a group of supporters, including some from the New Quay church. Beginning at his home church in Loughor he set out his concern and laid down four points of Christian discipleship – Christians must (a) put away any unconfessed sin; (b) put away any doubtful habit; (c) obey the Spirit promptly; and (d) confess Christ publicly.

Fairly quickly men and women began to respond to his call. He was invited to other churches and meetings took place which lasted many hours, often well into the night. Roberts' own contribution appears to have been little more than to urge the points mentioned and call for prayer. Often he did not preach at meetings but simply prayed briefly and asked others to do the same. Many responded and the meetings, which had no set pattern, came to include praise, confession and personal testimony. As word spread, including press reports, people first came to see Roberts himself; but then other meetings were held, first throughout Wales, then in the rest of Great Britain and ultimately in many other parts of the world. At its fullest power the revival lasted only a few months, but its influence continued through the lives of those who had been moved by it, some of whom became prominent in religious and social life.

Roberts soon withdrew from public life. He may have been hurt early in 1905 by the criticisms of an Evangelical minister, Peter Price of Dowlais. Price believed a genuine revival was taking place apart from Roberts' activities. He criticized Roberts' claim to speak under divine inspiration and what he saw as the excessive emotionalism of Roberts' meetings. It is not clear whether the ensuing controversy in the press damaged the movement or gave it extra publicity. Roberts retired to live with friends, first in Leicester and later in Cardiff. He preached occasionally but rarely attended large gatherings. He chiefly limited himself to a ministry of prayer.

From these accounts it is possible to make some general observations on the pattern, content and results of revivals. Humanly speaking they begin when a few people are sufficiently concerned about the spiritual state of the Church as they know it to set aside periods for prayer and to invite others to join them. This is accompanied by a concern for holiness of life. Only later do we find Churches joining in, but when they do there is a sense of unity across denominational barriers. The historian of revivals, J. Edwin Orr, gives many illustrations of such unity from both of the revivals mentioned, but it must be noted that those involved normally agreed on a broadly Evangelical theology, few from the Catholic wing of the Church are represented. It may be that the formation of the Evangelical Alliance in 1846, and the inter-denominational prayer meetings it arranged, had prepared the way for this kind of co-operation, but a definite link between the Alliance and the revivals cannot be proved.

In the early, more spontaneous, period of the revival there is a heightened sense of spiritual reality with a recognition of individual sinfulness and a desire to be forgiven and put right with God.

Prayer meetings are crowded and there are reports of groaning and crying aloud in prayer, together with some physical manifestations such as prostrations. At the same time some experience a sense of forgiveness and release, often with a sense of receiving new confidence and power from the Holy Spirit.

At this point there is a difference between the revivals of 1858 and 1904. The first put much stress on biblical teaching. Probably those involved were already more familiar with the teaching of Scripture. Also the revivalists, though they may have blunted the spontaneity of the movement by their attempts to arrange local revivals, did provide a solid diet of simple Bible teaching. It is a common criticism of the Welsh revival that it so concentrated on prayer, praise and testimony that solid teaching was lacking.

In both cases revival was followed by moral reformation and social concern. Numbers in churches and Sunday Schools increased, distribution of Scripture increased and more men and women offered themselves for ordination or missionary service. Drunkenness and violence, especially within families, declined. Many communities recorded a sharp decline in crime. The working atmosphere in some mines and factories was transformed – it is said that some Welsh pit ponies no longer understood the instructions they were given since the miners had ceased to swear and ill treat them! There are numerous accounts of individuals seeking out those whom they had wronged to make restitution and ask forgiveness. A number of missions were established dedicated to the physical as well as the spiritual well-being of the poor and of such special groups as orphans, prostitutes and drunkards.

Finally, a special feature was that lay people, women as well as men, emerged as leaders. Where denominations or local churches stood against the revivals this could be seen, at least partly, as a defence of clericalism.

From Revival to mass Evangelism:
D. L. Moody and Billy Graham

From spontaneous movements of revival emerged first the possibility of producing revival by suitable preparation and teaching, and then the phenomenon of mass evangelism utilizing the gifts of an outstanding individual. In 1869 and again in 1875 groups of Anglo-Catholic churches in London combined to arrange series of midweek meetings. The stress was on teaching, largely on the sacraments, and the aim was to call lapsed or nominal church members to sacramental confession and a renewal of baptismal vows. The example was copied by Anglo-Catholics in urban situations throughout the country. Such people were consciously in the tradition of the Oxford Movement and their model was not Evangelical revivalism but European Roman Catholic missions. It appears to have been the Anglo-Catholics who introduced the word 'mission' in this context. Nevertheless it was among Evangelicals that this kind of work flourished, and from the Evangelical wing of the Church came the two outstanding figures, D. L. Moody and Billy Graham, both American.

Dwight Lyman Moody (1837–99) came from a poor background in Massachusetts. He was poorly educated and never mastered grammar or punctuation. Following a conversion experience in his teens he had a simple but deep Evangelical faith which he combined with outstanding energy and business acumen. By his early twenties he was a successful travelling shoe salesman based in Chicago, spending his spare time in evangelistic work among poor and rowdy children who were otherwise untouched by the churches. Though he once enrolled at a Baptist Theological Seminary, he was never ordained, but his work led first to a flourishing Sunday School and then to an independent church. Meanwhile he became associated with the YMCA and enhanced his reputation by his work for the physical and spiritual needs of Northern soldiers in the American Civil War.

He first visited England in 1867 to meet his wife's English relatives, but his YMCA connections and the reputation of his work in Chicago led to contacts with British Evangelicals. These were strengthened by a second visit in 1872. By then he had a reputation as a revivalist preacher and the possibility of his making a tour of Britain was raised. However, there were misunderstandings and when he arrived in June 1873, accompanied by the singer Ira D. Sankey and their families, no preparations had been made.

Through YMCA contacts meetings were arranged in York and Newcastle. Later in the year they moved to Edinburgh and their fame began to spread. They conducted missions throughout Scotland before visiting Ireland, returning to northern England and then holding a series of meetings in London. The London meetings in the spring and summer of 1875 made them world famous.

In order to reach all classes of society meetings were held in a number of venues. The Royal Opera House in the Haymarket in the fashionable West End was used for meetings attended mainly by the aristocratic and wealthy, and a temporary auditorium was specially constructed on Bow Common in the East End to attract the poorer classes. By the time they left England in July 1875, they had won the support of British Evangelicals and the respect of many others.

Seven years later they returned, this time to better planned missions throughout the country. Perhaps the most difficult and ultimately most effective was a week in Cambridge. Undergraduates who began by mocking their odd accents and lack of education came to respect them. Many young men who became religious and political leaders throughout the world professed conversion during that week, among them the Cambridge Seven who went as missionaries to China.

Moody introduced to British Christianity a new style and methods of mass evangelism. Increasingly he stressed the preparatory work of those who invited him to various centres. The most successful campaigns (he used the military expression from the American Civil War) were those where a team, preferably from a number of denominations, combined in the preparation. During the campaign he also encouraged supporters to hold prayer meetings quite distinct from the main meetings.

It is significant that the central activities are described as meetings. They were not traditional religious services; indeed detractors complained of a lack of reverence and suggested the evangelists had learned from the circus impressario P. T. Barnum. In contrast to the stiff formality, high seriousness and rather ponderous preaching usual at the time, Moody's meetings were relaxed and easily flowing, with a minimum of fuss and solemnity and a stress on participation. They may have appeared rather casual, but the ease with which they flowed depended on the understanding between Moody and Sankey, who shared the leadership.

The use of music, and especially of solo performers who would present a spiritual theme in the verse of a song and encourage the audience to join in the choruses had been developed among American revivalists. Before and after his British campaigns Moody worked with other musicians, but *Ira D. Sankey* (1840–1908), an ex-government clerk who joined him in 1871 was his best known partner.

Sankey and his music made a twofold contribution to the meetings. In the first place they greatly increased congregational involvement. Critics likened it to the style of the music hall, but for many unaccustomed to the ways of churches it became an experience of worship. Secondly the songs both suggested a range of religious emotions and enabled those who sang to express them. The emotions involved ranged from penitence and sorrow for sin, through assurance of forgiveness and commitment to service to expectation of death and longing for heaven. For many the songs were remembered when the sermons were forgotten, and Sankey's *Sacred Songs and Solos* became a best seller. No doubt some of the music was poor and some of the words sentimental and individualistic, but they gave many an opportunity to articulate deep emotions which might otherwise not have been expressed, or even recognized.

Moody's preaching also came as a shock. His sermons were shorter than was usual at the time and his style was conversational and anecdotal. He told biblical stories in a racy, American manner and enabled his hearers to see their own situations in them. He laced his talks with accounts of the personal experiences of his converts and sometimes allowed the converts to speak for themselves. In earlier days his sermons had emphasized the wrath of God awaiting the impenitent sinner, and that note was never completely absent. However, perhaps through the influence of Henry Moorhouse who had visited him in Chicago in 1868, his later stress was more on the love of God calling for the sinner's response.

The most significant and characteristic features of his work were the call to his hearers to make that response and the use of the 'inquiry room'. Usually at the end of an address he asked those who wanted to make a personal commitment to Christ, or who wished for some other spiritual ministry, to stand or move to the front of the meeting. Critics saw this as putting emotional pressure on those who had been moved by the sermon and the worship, and they disapproved of it. Moody argued that if God was speaking through the meetings it was appropriate and spiritually healthy that men and women should have the opportunity to respond. Those who made such a response were then offered individual counsel by trained helpers in an adjacent room or vestry, the 'inquiry room'. It is significant that they were called inquirers and not yet converts since not all of them later claimed to have been converted.

The practice of asking for a personal response is open to emotional manipulation and has been much criticized, but for those who believe in a personal God and claim to be successors of the New Testament, it is difficult to see how it could be omitted. The danger is that those who respond, or those who advise them, should believe that Christian discipleship is complete after such a 'decision for Christ'. Ideally the inquirers would join local churches for further instruction.

As a result of Moody's campaigns Evangelical churches did grow. There was also a growth in Christian social concern indicating that Moody's work was not frothy emotionalism or soft sentimentalism as some critics suggested. Nevertheless, it must be admitted that the influence of the campaigns did not go far outside what might be termed the British Evangelical sub-culture. Though the Anglo-Catholic Liddon commended the Evangelists' zeal and even Archbishop Tait, a Broad Churchman, gave modified approval, most of their support came from the Evangelical wing of the Church of England and from the Nonconformists. There were amazing conversions among the poor in the East End of London, but those most affected were the middle classes, nominal believers or those already on the fringes of the Churches. The great mass of the poor and the working classes were scarcely touched.

Moody has had many imitators and successors. The most significant by far has been *Dr Billy Graham* (b. 1918). Billy Graham's work in Great Britain belongs to a later chapter. Here it must be noted that he adopted Moody's methods while adapting them and developing them to the conditions of a later age. From the time when he sprang to fame in America with a mission in Los Angeles in 1949, his approach has been characterized on the one hand by an apparently simple confidence in the truth of the gospel and the guidance of God, and on the other hand by a businesslike efficiency which Moody could scarcely have imagined.

With Billy Graham revivalism becomes mass evangelism. He has gathered around him a team of experts in various fields and uses the most modern methods of mass communication and organization. In particular great attention is given to thorough preparation for crusades (another military metaphor, taken from American involvement in the Second World War), and to the 'follow-up' of inquirers. The aim is to ensure that local churches are ready and able to receive and care for possible new members. Clearly the emphasis has moved from deepening the faith of nominal believers to presenting the gospel to those who have little or no previous knowledge of it and little or no commitment to the Church.

The Quest for Holiness – the Keswick Convention

The chief stress of nineteenth-century revivalists and evangelists was to produce in their listeners an awareness of personal sin leading to repentance and an experience of forgiveness. The most common range of metaphors was the legal one or the idea of the court room. Sinful man was portrayed as being subject to the punishment of God, the righteous judge, until that punishment was taken by Christ who died in his place. As a result of the work of Christ it was possible for those who accepted by faith the offer made in the gospel to be delivered from the guilt of sin. Many who heard such preaching either awoke to the seriousness of their situation or saw it clearly for the first time. Their horror at the realization of the impending judgement of God, or their over-whelming sense of relief and thankfulness to Jesus who had stood in their place, accounts for the emotion which the preaching sometimes produced. To those self-consciously cool spirits who smile at such emotion, or disparage it, both preachers and converts might have answered in the words of Anselm, 'You have not yet considered how serious a thing sin is'.

The strength of such preaching is its clarity, but that very clarity raised a problem. What was offered was freedom from the guilt of sin. However, as many converts found, freedom from the guilt of sin does not bring freedom from the power of sin. In other words they continued to sin in their lives. Yet if forgiveness means restoration to a life of fellowship with God it is reasonable to suppose that the forgiven life should involve some element of being like God, some aspect of holiness. In addition some passages of the New Testament seem to imply that the believer is free from sin, or should be able to overcome it in his life. For many the difference between the life they suppose they should be living, free from sin, and the life which they know they are living, including sinful thoughts and actions, produces a painful tension. The situation is made worse by the fact that those who are most sincere in their efforts to serve God seem most conscious of their failure to do so completely.

As far as the New Testament is concerned, biblical scholars draw attention to a paradox in Paul's thought and to different ways in which he uses the same expression. In a passage such as Romans 6 he seems to be arguing that in the eyes of God, because of the work of Christ, believers are seen as having died and risen again. In terms of the final judgement they are seen 'in Christ'. However, during their earthly lives they are engaged in a struggle against sin in which they have divine assistance, though it remains a struggle. Such thinking also appears in Paul's contrast between living 'according to the Spirit' and living 'according to the flesh'. Christians are called to live 'according to the Spirit', that is the life which God intends for them with his intentions central. However, they are always inclined to live 'according to the flesh', that is with their own selfish motives central. The Christian life is a struggle for holiness (see Galatians 5.16–25).

If the argument of the last paragraph is accepted Christians do not expect total perfection in this life, though they are committed to struggle for it. By God's grace they can look for a process of transformation, though with some setbacks, until they attain the holiness intended for them. But the argument is not universally accepted. Various teachers and groups have argued that the straightforward teaching of Scripture is that believers should expect and should display some form of perfection or holiness in their lives. Since this is by no means a normal experience following conversion, many have taught that there is a further experience subsequent to conversion, an experience of sanctification or 'second blessing'.

Perhaps the best known exponent of such thinking was John Wesley. His ideas are not absolutely clear. What is clear is that he taught the possibility of what he called 'Christian perfection'. By this he did not mean a blameless moral life but the possibility of a pure heart and motives of love to God and man. What is debatable is whether Wesley believed that such a state came in an instantaneous experience similar to a sudden conversion, or whether it came as the result of a process of growth and struggle. Both views can be supported from his writings. It is important to notice that many revivalist preachers came from a Methodist background, and even those who did not looked back to the preaching of the Wesleys for their example and inspiration. Such preachers also found the idea of a distinct crisis experience separate from conversion congenial to their own thought and methods. Thus in church records of locally organized revivals it is sometimes possible to find two sets of numbers, the number of those who have been justified, that is converted, and the number of those who have been sanctified, that is had a second experience of entering a state of holiness.

The possibility of such a second blessing was prominent in the thought of a number of Americans active in Great Britain during the nineteenth century. Among them were the Methodist couple *Walter* and *Phoebe Palmer*, of whom Phoebe was the most influential as writer and speaker, and the Quakers *Robert* and *Hannah Pearsall Smith*. The latter were responsible for an important convention on the theme of holiness held at Brighton in June 1875, the year of the Moody and Sankey meetings in London. The basic teaching was that an experience of total consecration, and thus of complete inner security, was possible for those who would commit themselves completely to God and allow Jesus to rule in their lives. The usual language was of laying one's all upon the altar.

One result of the holiness movement in Great Britain was the founding, also in 1875, of the Keswick Convention. This was the work of the local vicar, *T. D. Harford Battersby*, who organized the first convention on his own land. Subsequently it became an annual event and the tradition of 'Keswick teaching' became a significant force in Evangelical circles. Its stated aim was 'the deepening of the spiritual life'. At the heart of it was the assertion that just as the experience of conversion came as a response to faith so it was possible for the believer to have a second experience which would give an assurance of total commitment and a subsequent sense of peace and joy. All the believer must do is trust God. Thus the phrase 'resting faith' became almost a technical term. Biblical support was found in Hebrews 4.3.

Keswick attracted many prominent speakers, especially from the Evangelical wing of the Church of England. Many of those who attended claimed to experience the second blessing. In 1878 it began to produce a journal, *The Christian's Pathway of Power*, which later became *The Life of Faith*.

Holiness teaching as a whole had a very simple approach to Scripture and a rather naïve understanding of human experience. However it recognized that those who have had a conversion experience are conscious both that they should lead a holy life and also that they often fail to do so; it seemed to abolish the need for a lengthy moral struggle, which itself seemed to fall back on good works rather than faith; and it made sense of the typical evangelical language of inviting Jesus into the heart or life.

Its critics drew attention to its simplistic approach to Scripture and to spiritual experience. Paradoxically some of those who sought a 'resting faith' far from finding peace found themselves attempting to screw up their spiritual muscles to make an act of commitment or anxiously examining their souls in order to be sure that their commitment was total. Hence the result of holiness preaching could be smug complacency or spiritual tension.

Nevertheless the movement helped many. As it developed the Keswick Convention put less stress on the climactic moment of second blessing and more on a progressive deepening of spiritual life and a growth in holiness which takes account of struggle. The recognition that there can be important spiritual experiences after conversion, and that there are sometimes leaps forward in the struggle towards holiness, became significant in later renewal movements.

William Booth and the Salvation Army
Perhaps the most enduring legacy of the renewal movements of the nineteenth century, and certainly one of the greatest contributions that English Christianity has made to the world, was the Salvation Army. Into it flowed elements of revivalism, evangelicalism and

the quest for personal holiness, largely through the life and work of one man, William Booth.

William Booth (1829–1912) was born in Nottingham, the son of a small scale builder. The business collapsed when William was thirteen and the next year his father died, leaving William apprenticed to a pawnbroker. His work in the pawnshop, first in Nottingham and later in London, gave him an insight into the lives of the very poor and aroused a compassion for them and an ambition to serve them which he never lost.

After a conversion experience as a teenager he began to preach in the streets. His preaching led to some conversions and considerable interest among Nottingham's poor, but it was viewed with suspicion by the Methodist chapel which he had joined. When he moved to London the chapel there was no more encouraging and his membership was withdrawn when it was seen that he favoured a growing reform movement within Methodism. But he found friends among the reformers. Among them he met *Catherine Mumford* (1829–90), whom he married in 1855, and with their assistance he became a minister in the Methodist New Connexion.

He had spells as minister of Methodist chapels in Islington and Gateshead, but his strength was as a revivalist preacher. Both he and Catherine felt that God had called them to such work so that when, in 1861, the Conference of the Methodist New Connexion refused his request that he should be allowed to concentrate on it full-time, and instead suggested that he become President of the Newcastle upon Tyne Circuit, he resigned from the ministry. Together they conducted revivals in Cornwall and the Midlands. From time to time they worked alongside Walter and Phoebe Palmer and it may have been from them that they took the model of a husband and wife team. Certainly Catherine developed a reputation of her own as a preacher and subsequently husband and wife teams became characteristic of the Salvation Army. They had returned to London when a chance meeting with some street preachers outside the Blind Beggar public house in Whitechapel Road led to William being asked to take over the mission of the East London Special Services Committee, an undenominational group which sought to evangelize in the poorest quarters of the East End. It was intended as a temporary appointment, it became his life's work.

The Mission held meetings in a tent on a piece of waste ground. As more people were attracted other meeting places had to be found and the work was divided into various stations. As stations were established in South London and even outside the capital the name became simply the Christian Mission. When the conduct of its affairs, through committees and local congregations in typical Nonconformist fashion, proved inefficient and time wasting, Booth yielded to the persuasion of his closest supporters and took control. From being General Superintendent of the Christian Mission he became, in May 1878, General of the Salvation Army.

The name showed something of the theology and style which the mission had adopted. Booth occasionally quoted some words of John Wesley to his preachers, 'You have nothing to do but save souls ... go always not only to those who need you, but to those who need you most.' He and his followers went to those outside the churches, the poor, the drunkards, the prostitutes, those who knew only grindingly hard work or who had no work at all, those who lived by petty crime and violence. Among such people, normally uneducated, they preached not simply God's judgement but salvation, hope of a fuller, happier, holier life, the life which God intended both in this world and beyond. The way to that life was through repentance, but often long before repentance came the evangelists shared and to some extent relieved the harshness of the lives of the poor.

Men and women were converted. Kneeling at the penitent form they confessed their sins, experienced forgiveness and devoted their lives to God and the gospel. The sins they confessed were not, as often with the middle-class Anglicans of Keswick, minor transgressions of broadly accepted conventions or forgetfulness of a well known creed. They spoke of violence, drunkenness, lust, debauchery, occasionally even murder. They were extremists in their sin, and in their new found freedom and faith they were extremists still. They went to extremes in their advocacy of the extreme, overflowing love of God, and they had results.

Booth encouraged the converts to speak of their new faith and he capitalized on the reputations and past exploits of many. Speakers were advertised as converted pugilists, navvies, barmaids, bookmakers and pickpockets. Those who heard them recognized the genuineness of their experience, though the expression may have lacked theological refinement. They preached in theatres, public houses, market squares or on street corners, wherever a crowd might gather. Odd measures were adopted to advertise meetings. Posters referred to 'Hallelujah Lasses' and sermons were illustrated by mime and acting. Most significant of all, in Salisbury in 1879 a local Methodist, William Fry, with his three sons, played brass instruments at an open air meeting and the tradition of the Salvation Army band had begun. They went for the lowest strata of society, but in doing so also attracted men and women of higher birth and a number of considerable intellectual distinction.

They were not without opposition. Not all who heard them were impressed and arguments could turn to physical violence. Often they were pelted with stones, rotten eggs, vegetables and even dead rats and cats. It took physical and moral courage to endure such attacks in which many Salvationists were injured and their buildings and property damaged. In some places so-called 'Skeleton Armies' of local hooligans looking for a fight would break up processions and invade meeting places. Sometimes the opposition was organized by local publicans, and even some clergymen supported it. Magistrates often considered the Salvationists were the cause of disturbances and banned processions or imprisoned the leaders. Through it all they persevered until many critics were won over by the example of their endurance and others at least recognized that they would not be cowed by violence. Gradually the civil authorities moved against their opponents and secured toleration for them.

Long before that they had begun two different kinds of expansion. In geographical terms the work of the Army began – 'opened fire' was their phrase – first throughout the English-speaking world and Europe, and then throughout the world. During the early eighties there were stations in America, France, Australia, Canada and India. Usually word reached a certain place concerning the English organization and its peculiar style of evangelism, worship and service, perhaps through Salvationists who had emigrated. Then Booth, or his second in command *George Railton* (1839–1913), would arrange for officers to be sent to establish a corps and to train local leaders.

The other expansion, both in England and abroad, was into the social work for which they became famous. It was not that they turned to social concern instead of preaching the gospel, caring for men's bodies rather than their souls. Neither was it that the social concern was a kind of bribe intended to get a hearing for the preaching of the gospel. It was rather the thoroughly biblical conviction that God is concerned for the total man, both body and soul.

Early in their history they had offered shelter for prostitutes and encouragement for those who wished to change their lives. *Bramwell Booth* (1856–1929), William's son and successor as General, worked with W. T. Stead in his campaign against child prostitution. Soon they were involved in such things as providing shelter for the homeless, caring for orphans – Thomas Barnardo was one of Booth's earliest helpers before he branched out to found the homes for orphans which still bear his name – opening cheap eating houses and hostels for working men, helping the families of prisoners and providing homes and encouragement for those released from prison. In 1890 Booth and W. T. Stead published *In Darkest England and the Way Out*. It was an account drawn from the notes of many Salvation Army Officers of the sufferings and deprivations of the poor, together with plans for model factories, a farm colony and a number of settlements in Britain's overseas territories. The grand vision was never realized, but many of the suggestions were adopted and the chronicle of the real conditions in England's slums touched the hearts, and the pockets, of many.

The Salvation Army offered, and continues to offer, a unique blend of joy and discipline. Some of its customs, perhaps especially its military language and style, are bound to the Victorian era. But it continues to attract through its demand for wholehearted commitment, its pursuit of the experience of sanctification, and its reputation for service among the poor and disadvantaged or in any situation of crisis.

Wilson Carlile and the Church Army

During the spring and summer of 1882, at the suggestion of William Thompson, Archbishop of York, conversations were held to consider whether some relationship could be arranged between the Salvation Army and the Church of England. But the obstacles to such a scheme were considerable. Serious negotiations would have had to cover such issues as the position of Booth himself, the question of sacraments, ordination and the ministry of women. There were those in the Church of England who were unhappy about the proposed association while Booth and his closest colleagues feared that protracted negotiations would detract from their work. The idea was not pursued.

Nevertheless, quite apart from the conversations just mentioned, a number of Anglicans saw the desirability of mobilizing lay people for evangelism. Evan Hopkins formed a Church Gospel Army in his parish at Richmond; Canon Atherton, vicar of Bedminster, Bristol, had a Church Mission Army; while an Oxford undergraduate, F. S. Webster, later vicar of All Souls' Langham Place, organized a Church Salvation Army at St Aldate's, Oxford. The organization which came to combine and absorb them all was the Church Army, founded in 1882 under the leadership of Wilson Carlile.

Wilson Carlile (1847–1942) came from a successful London business family of Scottish extraction. As a young man he entered a family business and fulfilled his avowed ambition of making £20,000 before his twenty-fifth birthday. Later he was to say that his business experience was invaluable in organizing the Church Army.

As a young man his Christianity was purely nominal. However, after a serious financial loss had produced a temporary physical collapse, he had a conversion experience while reading a book *Grace and Truth*, which was almost forced upon him by a devout aunt. Though continuing his business career he was increasingly involved in Christian work, at first among the Brethren. An enthusiastic musician, he assisted as an organist at some of the Moody and Sankey meetings in 1875. Subsequently he was drawn to the Church of England by its sacramental worship and its broader contacts with a wider range of people, and in 1880, after the briefest possible spell of training, he was ordained. He joined the staff of St Mary Abbots Church, Kensington, as one of the ten curates who between them represented a wide spectrum of views within the Church of England.

His particular responsibility was for a daughter church, St Paul's. From the beginning he concentrated on the poorer classes and those who did not usually attend church. For them he preached in the open air and held simple evangelistic meetings in the church hall. Like Booth he saw the attraction of processions and music – a clergyman playing the cornet or trombone as he did was a curiosity. Soon he was holding meetings every evening of the week and he had realized that a few sentences from a working man were more effective at such gatherings than a sermon from a clergyman. But, again as with Booth and the Salvation Army, while such activities attracted supporters and led to conversions, they also attracted opposition and led to violence. Eventually, in June 1882, the vicar, Dr Carr Glyn, ordered that the open air work should stop before the violence led to police intervention.

However, Carr Glyn recognized Carlile's special gifts and his concern to train working men as evangelists. It was with Carr Glyn's encouragement that Carlile held consultations with Hopkins, Atherton and Webster, and from those consultations the Church Army was established as a lay movement not limited to individual parishes but available for mission work throughout the Church of England. At first it was a branch of the decidedly Evangelical Church Parochial Mission Society, but from 1885 it was an independent body with Carlile as Chief Secretary. In the same year it was acknowledged and encouraged by the Convocations of Canterbury and York.

The original idea had been that laymen, after a very brief training, should be based in needy parishes to organize other laymen, especially working men, for evangelism. They would always be under the control of the vicar. The needs of the time led to developments beyond evangelism. In 1887 women were appointed, with the title Church Army Sisters, to evangelize among women and children but also to pay attention to the sick. In 1889 some homeless men were admitted to a 'Tramps and Inebriates Labour Home' in which shelter and some employment were provided. The Society was on the path to providing relief and rehabilitation for those in various kinds of need as it has continued to do.

It is inevitable that the Church Army should be compared with the Salvation Army. The organizations rose at nearly the same time, they were both partly inspired by the same revivalist movements, and they were both challenged to meet the same physical and social needs. The style of the early activities, with the processions, music, simple direct preaching and the desire to reach those outside the Churches is also similar, and both movements were forced almost without intending it into social concern. Typical of their age both adopted military terminology.

However the Church Army has features of its own, the chief of which is that it is positively and unashamedly Anglican. From the time of Wilson Carlile its Chief Secretary has always been a clergyman. Its officers must be communicant members of the Church of England and, following training, they are admitted to the office of evangelist. All their work is subject to the approval and direction of bishops and local clergy. Perhaps its greatest triumph is that it draws members and support from all parties within the Church of England. At the end of the twentieth century its major problem may be that too many officers leave the role of evangelist and seek ordination.

Pentecostalism

Central to the revivalist, evangelical and holiness movements of the nineteenth century was the conviction that a Christian could expect a closer relation to God than most conventional church members seemed to experience. Behind this was the suspicion that what had come to be accepted as normal Christian life was somehow less spiritual, less open to supernatural gifts, than the lives of Christians glimpsed in the New Testament. Hence there was an underlying question, what feature or features of New Testament Christianity are absent from the lives of later Christians and their churches, and can that absence be made up.

In broad terms the revivalists and evangelists sought a greater emphasis on the experience of freedom from the guilt of sin and the holiness preachers a greater emphasis on freedom from its power. From time to time among all the movements there were also those who spoke of a distinct experience of the Holy Spirit. Sometimes this seemed to issue in a new power for healing, sometimes in a gift for powerful preaching, but often simply in a new confidence in prayer and worship. It was in search of such an experience, and not just as sensation seekers, that many Christians went to Wales in 1904. It is such an experience, described as baptism in the Holy Spirit, or receiving the Holy Spirit, and recognized as a distinct experience subsequent to conversion, which lies at the heart of the Pentecostal movement.

The phenomenon most closely associated with Pentecostalism is 'speaking in tongues', or simply 'tongues' (known technically as *glossolalia*). The majority of Pentecostalists claim that whenever in the Acts of the Apostles a believer experiences baptism in the Holy Spirit this phenomenon follows. Indeed so close is the relationship that they see tongues as the necessary confirmation of the experience. The basic characteristic of Pentecostalism therefore is a distinct experience of the Holy Spirit subsequent to conversion and confirmed by tongues. The English historian of the movement, Donald Gee, writes: 'In order to safeguard the vital point that the baptism in the Holy Spirit ought to be regarded by Christians as a perfectly definite experience and spiritual crisis for the individual, the Pentecostal Movement has consistently taught that speaking with tongues is the scriptural initial evidence of that baptism.' But he goes on to admit that 'sometimes it may not have been presented wisely or well.'[1]

It is worth pausing briefly on the gift of tongues. It consists of a series of sounds usually of no known language over which the speaker has no control. In the New Testament it seems to appear in at least two forms. There is an initial experience accompanying the coming of the Holy Spirt to an individual which appears to be involuntary. But it also appears from Paul's letters that some Christians have the ability to speak in tongues as a gift which remains with them. In this second form it is as least partially subject to the control of the user in that while he has no control over the sounds made he can choose whether to speak or not. Hence Paul instructs that its use should be regulated. From the New Testament and from later evidence the gift appears usually as a form of communication between the believer and God. It enables the believer to express emotions and make petitions which could not easily be formulated intellectually and put into words. Paul suggests it should be used in private by the individual. But he also assumes that there will be some in the church who are able to interpret the tongues and where an interpreter is present he allows a more public use of the gift.

Interpretation also opens the possibility of a third form of tongues, that is communication of God to the believer, and through him to a wider group. Thus there are accounts of people speaking in actual languages which they have never learned and do not understand. However such a phenomenon may best be put under another of Paul's list of spiritual gifts, that of prophecy.

Speaking in tongues and gifts of healing were experienced during a revival in Dumbartonshire, and became features of the ministry of *Edward Irving* (1792–1834) in London in the early 1830s. Accounts of speaking in tongues and of experiences which may be described as baptism in the Holy Spirit are found in the works of Moody, the Booths and some individuals connected with Keswick, the Salvation Army and the Welsh revival. But Pentecostalism in a form which leads to a denomination, or set of denominations, traces its origins to events in America in the early years of the twentieth century.

On 1 January 1901, students at a Bible School in Topeka, Kansas, prayed that they might be baptized in the Holy Spirit as the disciples were on the day of Pentecost. At her request the Principal, Charles Parham, laid hands on a student named Agnes Ozman and she spoke in tongues. But it was in Los Angeles five years later, among a small group led by a coloured minister, W. J. Seymour, a pupil of Parham's, that a more sustained revival broke out. The little group had previously been put out of a Holiness church and were meeting in a private house. Now they took over a disused Methodist meeting place, and it is to that place, the Azusa Street Mission, that later Pentecostalists trace their origin.

Their numbers grew rapidly and many were baptized in the Spirit and spoke in tongues. Similar phenomena occurred in other local churches and visitors came from all over America and other parts of the world. It was hoped that the revival would flow into the established Churches but that did not happen. The movement was resisted, usually because it appeared over-emotional. In some quarters it was even described as demonic. Thus, in spite of themselves, those who had the experience were forced to adopt an organization of their own, and in 1914 at Hot Springs, Arkansas, the American Assemblies of God was formed.

Among the churches which trace their origins to Azusa Street most speak of a two-stage initiation into Christianity, conversion and the baptism in the Spirit. Others, drawing on the older holiness tradition, speak of three stages, conversion, an experience of sanctification, and then baptism in the Spirit.[2] At their best all are characterized by a confidence that the various gifts mentioned in the New Testament, not just tongues but such gifts as healing, prophecy and discernment, are to be expected in the later Church.

One of those who heard of Azusa Street was *T. B. Barratt* (1862–1940), born in Cornwall but minister of a Methodist Church in Oslo. In 1906 he was in America seeking to raise funds for his work in Oslo. Through others he received the baptism in the Holy Spirit and brought the teaching and the experience back to Norway whence it spread throughout Scandinavia and into Germany.

In England the chief figure in early Pentecostalism was *Alexander A. Boddy* (1854–1930), who from 1886 to 1922 was vicar of All Saints' church, Monkwearmouth, Sunderland. With a group of like-minded parishioners, Boddy had been praying for a deeper spiritual experience. He had visited Evan Roberts in Wales and now he went to Oslo to speak to Barratt. As a result, in the autumn of 1907 Barratt spent some six weeks in Sunderland. Many, including Boddy and his wife, were baptized in the Spirit and spoke in tongues. Subsequently others went to Sunderland to seek the experience and Boddy spoke about it throughout the country. From 1908 to 1914 he held annual conventions in Sunderland each Whitsun. They included teaching on the work of the Spirit and also witnessed a number of healings. Many who were later to be leaders in the movement were introduced to it at Sunderland. It was fortunate that Boddy's bishop, Handley Moule of Durham, looked kindly upon the vicar's rather unusual activities.

Another notable early leader was *Cecil Polhill* (1860–1938), the squire of Howbury Hall in Bedfordshire. He had been one of the seven Cambridge graduates who had gone as missionaries to China in 1885. After working near the Tibetan border he had been invalided home in 1900. Hearing of the events at Azusa Street he had visted Los Angeles and experienced the baptism in the Holy Spirit. On his return to England he contacted Boddy and the two became firm friends. Together they arranged a number of conferences. Polhill also helped the movement financially. He supported its Bible Schools and subsidized students. However, his heart remained in missionary work. He was on the Council of the China Inland Mission until his death, and it was as President of the Pentecostal Missionary Union from its beginning in 1909 until it was taken over by the Assemblies of God in 1925 that he was most active.

As the movement gained in strength but failed to gain acceptance in the historic Churches independent congregations began to be formed. Both Boddy and Polhill remained members of the Church of England. Gee raises the question whether God had intended them as joint leaders of the movement as a separate entity but they failed fully to recognize the fact.[3] Certainly after the outbreak of the First World War and the end of the Sunderland conventions their influence waned rapidly and divisions began to appear in the movement.

The Welshmen *Stephen Jeffreys* (1876–1943) and his brother *George* (1890–1962) both had outstanding gifts as evangelists and preached to mass rallies in Great Britain and abroad. Often their ministry was accompanied by healings. It was to support his early ministry in Ireland that George formed the Elim Evangelistic Band in 1915. From this came the Elim Pentecostal Church. This is a more moderate Pentecostal group which does not insist on tongues as a necessary initial sign of baptism in the Spirit. It is sometimes referred to as 'Four Square' because of the stress in its declaration of faith on the fourfold ministry of Jesus as Saviour, Healer, Baptizer in the Spirit and Coming King. Sadly George Jeffreys himself left that body in 1940 to form the Bible Pattern Church. The main reason was his uneasiness at what he saw as a move towards central organization which was taking control and influence away from local congregations and from lay people. However, other Elim leaders blamed his adoption of the British Israel theory, that is the teaching that the British people are descendants of the ten tribes of Israel who vanish from the pages of the Old Testament after the fall of Samaria in 721 BC.

A smaller group is the Apostolic Church which was formed in 1918, following the failure of an earlier Apostolic Faith Church originally formed in 1908. The re-formed body is largely Welsh with headquarters in Penygroes, South Wales, but it has churches throughout Great Britain and overseas. Its distinctive feature is an hierarchical system of church government, for which it uses all the titles of Christian ministers found in the New Testament with a particular emphasis on prophecy.

It was to meet the challenge of the new groupings that the majority of British Pentecostalist churches agreed in 1924 to follow the American example and adopt a loose federation under the title Assemblies of God. In the next year the Pentecostal Missionary Union was dissolved and its work taken over by the Assemblies of God. It must be stressed that the divisions among the main groups are largely on matters of church government and good relations are generally maintained between them.

On a world scale Pentecostalism has flourished. It is strong in Scandinavia and America. In America it is particularly strong among coloured churches. It is particularly strong in South America and, partly through the work of British and American missionaries, it has flourished in parts of Africa. Such is its strength that when, in 1953, Lesslie Newbigin, a bishop of the Church of South India, deeply involved in the World Council of Churches and with a knowledge of church affairs on a world scale, published a book on the Church, *The Household of God*, he listed Pentecostalism together with Catholicism and Protestantism as the third force in the world Church.

In England, in spite of some gifted evangelists, it has not progressed to the same extent. This could be partly because many of its most able people have gone abroad as missionaries, and partly because its stress on the experience of the Holy Spirit has some-times led it to disparage scholarship and organization. Other contributing factors have been its world-denying ethic, which has led to a lack of engagement with social issues, and the unwilling-ness of many leaders in the older Churches to welcome what they see as its emotionalism. The result is that the movement has become associated with back street missions and small, highly excitable, congregations. However, as we shall see in a later chapter, the rediscovery of spiritual gifts in the historic Churches which began in the 1960s has led to a greater willingness to explore this strand of the Church's life and witness.

Notes

1   Donald Gee, *Wind and Flame* (Assemblies of God Publishing House

rev. edn 1967), pp. 7 f.

2 The best guide to the differing traditions of Pentecostalism is W. J. Hollenweger, *The Pentecostals* (SCM Press 1972). He gives a chart showing variations in two- or three-stage understandings of initiation, p. 24.

3 D. Gee, op. cit., p. 88.

13
Biblical Theology and Redirection

At the end of the First World War thoughts in Great Britain turned optimistically to enjoying a land fit for heroes. The optimism was misplaced. The period between the wars did bring prosperity for some. It was marked by the growth of the middle classes, the spread of suburbia and a further move of population from the country to the town. Others did not prosper. The twenties were a period of economic decline marked by industrial unrest which came to a climax in the general strike of 1926 and the subsequent mining disputes. It was a time of widespread unemployment which particularly affected the mining areas of South Wales and County Durham. There was some economic improvement in the thirties but it was not widespread and merely increased the mood of suspicion and despair among those who did not share it. The Jarrow hunger march of 1936 was the classic expression of those feelings. By that time much of Europe was ruled by dictators and the Second World War was already on the horizon.

Between the wars

In the sphere of religion the mood was mixed. On the one hand there was a sense of disillusionment and an abandoning of at least formal religion. Among many of the self-consciously intellectual the problems which science and biblical criticism had posed for faith were no longer seen as relevant or even interesting problems. Religious agnosticism, coupled with a vague optimism based on an undefined expectation of scientific advance, became the orthodoxy of the twenties. On the other hand the horrors of war which had so shaken the faith of some and exposed the inadequacies of conventional religion had caused others, though doubtless a smaller number, to wonder whether there might be something deeper and more satisfying in Christian belief than the churches had usually

251

provided. The work of the chaplains who had shared the sufferings of the trenches had often impressed the soldiers. In addition, though the decline of the Free Churches had now become marked, the Church of England continued to be a considerable force in public life.

In intellectual terms the mixture of Liberal Protestantism and Modernism continued for a time to dominate religious thought. The Modern Churchmen's Union held its most controversial conference at Girton College, Cambridge, in 1921. Its anti-supernaturalism and reduction of Jesus to the role of a moral teacher led to the setting up of a commission on doctrine in the Church of England. But, in any case, its ingratiating attempts to woo modern cultivated man; its vague spirituality with a tendency to use traditional Christian terms in a non-traditional sense; and, above all, its failure really to come to terms with the tragic elements of human experience which the recent war had demonstrated and which traditional Christian teaching had addressed in such concepts as sin, judgement, redemption and grace, inevitably prevented it from reaching the depths of men's wills and imaginations and getting any kind of hold there. The often quoted words of Richard Niebuhr in criticism of American Liberal Protestantism are applicable to this phase of English Modernism, 'A God without wrath brought men without sin into a kingdom without judgement through the ministrations of a Christ without a cross.' It is noticeable that when a number of British intellectuals, such as T. S. Eliot and C. S. Lewis, moved back to Christian faith it was a more orthodox Christianity with a stress on supernaturalism and the transcendence of God to which they were attracted.

Nevertheless, the Church was not moribund. Archbishop Randall Davidson tried, though unsuccessfully, to mediate in the general strike and, at the local level, churches of all traditions worked hard to alleviate the harshness of unemployment and played their part in sustaining communities. In the field of housing, perhaps the greatest single social need of the day, the Anglo-Catholic successors of the Tractarians were prominent in the formation of trusts and associations which, if they did not transform the slums, provided many examples of what could be done. At the same time the Industrial Christian Fellowship, founded in 1918 on the basis of the Christian Social Union, carried on pastoral and evangelistic work among industrial workers and attempted by argument and persuasion to improve working conditions when that seemed necessary. In all these areas the leaning of many Church leaders towards at least a moderate socialism was clear.

A major achievement of the immediate post-war period was the passing of the Enabling Act in 1919. For some time pressure had been building up concerning the relation of the Church of England to Parliament. Few wanted disestablishment, but there was concern in at least two areas, the role of non-Anglicans or even unbelievers in the control of the Church through Parliament and the sheer difficulty of getting ecclesiastical measures debated because of the pressure on Parliamentary time. The Enabling Act created the Church Assembly, consisting of clergy and a number of laity, and set up Parochial Church Councils made up of baptized Anglicans. Church Assembly had the power to legislate in certain areas and make proposals to Parliament which became law if they were not challenged within thirty days.

The most notable example of Parliament continuing to use its power came in the debates on the revision of the Prayer Book. In 1927 Church Assembly proposed a revision of the Book of Common Prayer. In some of its language and in permitting reservation of the sacrament the revised book reflected the growing influence of the Anglo-Catholic movement. There is little doubt that Anglo-Catholicism was strong among the clergy and that the Evangelical wing of the Church was in decline. However the laity were not so Anglo-Catholic. The Prayer Book measure was challenged in both Houses of Parliament. The Evangelicals who organized the opposition were able to rely on the sympathies of Free Churchmen and the residual anti-popery feelings of the nation, and the measure was defeated. In the following year the bishops gave permission for the new book to be used where the Parochial Church Council agreed to its use, but it never won the affection of the majority of worshippers.

Prominent in the struggle for greater autonomy for the Church, though not particularly involved in the Prayer Book controversy, was William Temple.

William Temple

During a period of about thirty years *William Temple* (1881–1944) built up a reputation as the most prominent Christian leader and thinker in England. He had a remarkable breadth of interests and abilities as philosophical theologian, church statesman, administrator, devotional writer and speaker, and apostle of Christian Socialism. To these he added perhaps his greatest gift, the ability to see several sides of an argument and to win the support and enthusiasm of men of different persuasions. He had the weaknesses of his strengths. He was not a controversialist and rarely, if ever, stood alone on any issue. He sought synthesis and consensus above all and, especially in drafting reports of the many conferences with which he was involved, could be relied upon to find the right phrase to please most parties, sometimes at the expense of decisiveness and clarity. His contributions can be seen in three overlapping areas: as a leader of the national Church, as an ecumenical statesman and as a Christian thinker and apologist.

All his life he was essentially an establishment figure. Son of an Archbishop of Canterbury, he followed a sucessful career at Rugby and Oxford by being a philosophy tutor at Queen's College, Oxford, public school Headmaster at Repton, Rector of the fashionable St James's, Piccadilly, Canon of Westminster, Bishop of Manchester and Archbishop in turn of York and Canterbury. His predecessor at Canterbury, *Cosmo Gordon Lang* (1864–1945), had damaged his reputation by appearing to court favour with the rich and powerful. No doubt he did so at least partly to extend his range of influence. But Lang, Glasgow-born son and grandson of ministers of the Church of Scotland, had had to fight hard to establish himself in that world. Temple accepted it as his birthright. His home, his intellectual and administrative gifts and his natural charm and easy public manner, which disguised the fact that though a life-long teetotaller he suffered badly from gout, all marked him out as a natural leader.

He saw the advantages of a National Church which could represent the whole nation in its religious capacity. At the same time he grasped the fact that the Church *of* the Nation needed a measure of freedom if it was to speak *to* the Nation. Hence he took the lead in the Life and Liberty movement which led to the

Enabling Act of 1919, but he was careful never to push the demands of freedom to the point of disestablishment. That would be to reduce the Church of England to the status of a sect and weaken its influence.

From the beginning of his career Temple was a convinced if somewhat idealistic Socialist, as his father had been. From 1908 to 1924 he was President of the Workers' Educational Association. He did not, as he might, hold this merely as an honorary position but travelled the country campaigning on the Association's behalf and speaking at its courses and conferences. From 1918 to 1925, unusually for a bishop at the time, he was a member of the Labour Party. Among his close friends he included R. H. Tawney, an exact contemporary at Rugby and Balliol, J. H. Oldham and later Stafford Cripps who became Chancellor of the Exchequer in the 1945 Labour administration.

In 1908 he was present at an influential conference at Matlock when the SCM, until then predominantly a missionary orientated body, first took social concern seriously. Later he was chairman of a large Conference on Politics Economics and Citizenship (COPEC) which met at Birmingham in 1924. Critics complained that the Birmingham conference lacked realism and produced little of value. However it was Temple's chairmanship which restrained it from being even more wildly idealistic and optimistic and it did show a level of social concern among Christian people and help to create an atmosphere receptive to change.

His later work in this area, the study of unemployment, *Men Without Work* (1938), produced by a committee he had established, a further conference at Malvern in 1941, and his book *Christianity and Social Order* (1941), all show a deepening and narrowing of his concern. By his own admission he became less optimistic. The experience of the thirties had shown the intractable nature of many social issues. Involvement with the international Church impressed on his mind the dangers of the European dictatorships. Above all he had learned, particularly from Reinhold Niebuhr, that Christian social thought had to take account of the element of sin in individuals and social systems. In *Christianity and Social Order* he shows the influence of Stafford Cripps. There he offers specific suggestions in narrower areas and takes up the medieval search for 'middle axioms', that is statements which may offer working guidelines between fundamental Christian statements of faith and the complexities of individual problems. He contributed to one of those problems by working closely with R. A. Butler in the preparation of the 1944 Education Act.

His ecumenical work has been noted earlier. Representing the SCM he was an usher at the great Missionary Conference at Edinburgh in 1910, and he showed his skill in drafting reports at the Jerusalem Missionary Conference of 1928. On the death of Charles Brent he became chairman of the continuation committee of the Faith and Order movement in 1929. His ability to see all sides of a question and to gain the confidence of representatives of different theological positions was invaluable. He was chairman of the Faith and Order Conference at Edinburgh in 1937 which agreed to combine with the Life and Work movement to form the World Council of Churches and it was almost inevitable that he should be elected chairman of the provisional committee. Sadly he did not live to see its official inauguration at Amsterdam in 1948. However, he had performed a signal service by supporting the appointment of W. Visser 't Hooft as its general secretary when some others thought he was too young and some that he was too Barthian. In fact Visser 't Hooft held the post for twenty years with great distinction.

In England Temple established good relations with Cardinal Hinsley, especially in the first few years of the Second World War, as well as with the Free Churches. More than most holders of the position he was accepted as Archbishop of the entire nation.

It is part of the office of a bishop to teach the faith and Temple excelled as a teacher. His *Readings in St John's Gospel* (1939, 1940) became a minor classic of devotional literature, and his major theological works *Mens Creatrix* (1917), *Christus Veritas* (1924) and *Nature, Man and God* (1934) were major attempts to justify, or at least to explain, historic Christianity in philosophical terms and were written with a confidence which was rare at the time. But here there is something of a paradox. As an individual counsellor, as an evangelist among students and as an apologist on the BBC he undoubtedly encouraged and strengthened the faith of many. Yet his own intellectual position as presented in his major academic works seems to have been slightly at variance with the one found in his more popular writing and speaking. The latter is much more straightforward and biblical. His philosophical position was growing out of date almost as he wrote, and towards the end of his life he admitted as much.

It is no insult to Temple to describe his work as a late flowering of Hegelianism in the idealist form which it had taken in England, especially at Oxford. Basically he was an immanentalist. He believed that a philosophical view of the world disclosed four gradations of reality – matter, life, mind and spirit. Humanity represented what might be called the high point of reality as far as we can know it, and man is at his best, his most human, in his exercise of mental and moral, or spiritual capacities. From this position he argues it is reasonable to suppose that the world shows evidence of purpose, that it owes its existence to an intelligent creator, and that man shares some qualities with that creator.

Where Temple goes beyond philosophical idealism is in his insistence on the incarnation. The coming of the Logos into the world may be seen as the fulfilment of God's immanence in creation. It is not something which had to happen, but having happened it can be seen as rational. Conversely the incarnation provides the principle for a rational understanding of the world which would otherwise be lacking. This is basically a patristic argument much used by the *Lux Mundi* group. By a similar argument the whole of creation can be seen as potentially revealing, or potentially sacramental. The potentiality becomes real in the incarnation and in the Church's sacraments. Those to whom the revelation has become real and who share the sacramental worship of the Church look at creation in a new and different way. In all this, Christianity is presented as offering an explanation of the world in terms of the best philosophy that the world has available. It does not challenge the world and its philosophy.

Whatever criticisms may be made of his philosophy, Temple's life and preaching were a commendation of Jesus. He lived into a time when many of his contemporaries had become disillusioned and were searching for some spiritual meaning to life. To them he preached the challenge to follow Jesus. Something like this traditional Evangelical appeal is present in the pastoral letter issued jointly by Lang and Temple as new Archbishops of Canterbury and York respectively in 1929. It called for a greater emphasis on Bible study and prayer as the basis for a more confident proclamation of the gospel, and acknowledged the materialism of the age and the 'dullness of spirit (and) languor of worship' in many congregations.

Temple's appeal as an evangelist was most clearly present in his work with young people, especially students. His biographer refers to the closing meeting of a university mission to Oxford in 1931 as the congregation sang the hymn 'When I survey the wondrous cross'. 'Before the last verse, Temple stopped the singing and said, "I want you to read over this verse before you sing it. They are tremendous words. If you mean them with all your hearts, sing them as loud as you can. If you mean them even a little, and want to mean them more, sing them very softly." There was dead silence . . . and then – to hear Isaac Watts' words:

> Were the whole realm of nature mine
> That were an offering far too small;
> Love so amazing, so divine,
> Demands my soul, my life, my all.

whispered by the voices of 2,000 young men and women was (in the recollection of one of them) "an experience never to be erased from my memory until the whole tablet is blotted".'[1]

In 1922 Randall Davidson had set up a commission on doctrine in the Church of England. The first chairman, H. M. Burge, Bishop of Oxford, died in 1924 and Temple took his place. In the preface to the commission's report, published in 1938, he acknowledged the change which had taken place in theology since the commission began its work. There had been a move from a theology based on the incarnation and seeking to provide a rational explanation of the world, 'a Christocentric metaphysic', towards one which put more stress on a gospel of judgement and redemption, a theology which challenged and condemned the self-sufficiency of modern cultivated man and offered him salvation through repentance and commitment. The time when Christian apologists could attempt to make grand metaphysical maps of reality in the idealist fashion had passed, at least temporarily. Intellectually Temple had spent his life attempting to construct such a map, trying to relate faith to contemporary philosophy and to find in Christ the key to the rationality and unity of the world. A.

M. Ramsey, an admirer, comments: 'Nothing, therefore, in his last years befitted his greatness more than the humility with which he acknowledged that his quest had failed, and that other tasks were superseding it.'[2] The immediate future lay with neo-orthodox biblical theology whose chief exponent was Karl Barth.

Karl Barth and the return to Biblical Theology

Though it is widely acknowledged that, beginning with his commentary on *The Epistle to the Romans* (1919), the work of *Karl Barth* (1886–1968) marks a significant redirection or new beginning in twentieth-century theology, he was not at first widely read in England. Scottish theologians, always closer to German thought and more receptive to dogmatic or systematic theology, were quicker to recognize his significance. It was not until 1933 that E. C. Hoskyns produced a translation of *Romans*, in fact of Barth's second edition of 1922. By that time Barth had not only produced the first volume of a *Christian Dogmatics* in 1927 but had already decided to revise it, and in 1932 had begun his massive *Church Dogmatics* which was not complete at his death. His admirers claim that English speaking theologians have still not fully come to terms with him, though it must be acknowledged that this is partly due to the sheer amount and somewhat repetitive nature of his writing. What did emerge quickly and fairly clearly was that here was a fundamental challenge to the methods and conclusions of the then dominant theology, and a challenge which was expressed with considerable passion.

Barth was trained in the Liberal Protestant tradition which was very much under the influence of Schleiermacher and attempting to speak to modern culture in its own terms. For nearly twelve years he was a pastor of the Swiss Reformed Church, mainly at Safenwil in the Aargau. Subsequently he was professor of theology at Göttingen (1921–5), Münster (1925–30) and Bonn (1930–5) until he was compelled to leave Germany because of his opposition to the Hitler regime. He spent the rest of his life in Basel where he was professor of theology until he retired in 1962.

In the development of his theology the years he spent as a pastor were crucial. It was the task of having to preach regularly to normal Christian people in the everyday stresses of their lives, and then when they were faced with the horrors of world war on their doorsteps, that forced him to ask what the Christian Church really had to say to such people and such circumstances. He concluded that the Liberal theology which he had been taught, and in which he had excelled, had nothing to offer. He thus began a search, through fringe theologians of a Pentecostalist orientation, through the Reformers and Fathers, and above all in the New Testament. The result was his commentary on *Romans*.

The Liberal tradition had come to equate Christianity with the best of human, especially German, culture. From Schleiermacher onward it had turned away from ideas of supernatural revelation and had appealed instead to subjective human experience, urging men and women to be loyal to their own highest moral aspirations. The Bible had come to be seen as a collection of literature in which certain high points of man's religious quest had been recorded and as valuable for its moral and religious insights. In England the phrase attributed to Jowett, 'The Bible is a book like any other and must be studied like any other', and the attitude it implied had led to the limitation of biblical studies to the application of historical and literary criticism. In other words, theological students felt their treatment of the Bible was complete when they had considered the date and authorship of the various books and identified various types of material.

Barth challenged this man-centred approach with its too easy acceptance of the assumptions of the Enlightenment and its flight from the supernatural. But he was not, as is sometimes implied, merely an iconoclast protesting against the work of his teachers. Indeed his references to them often show admiration and affection. He simply asserted that a study of the Bible, and of the Christian tradition, which learned from the *methods* of the Enlightenment but was not blinded by the *assumptions* of the Enlightenment produced a startlingly different picture.

In his early work, and as he most affected British theology, Barth was more a prophet than a theologian. He established his own position, and was characterized by others, by his opposition to the current Liberal Protestant teaching. He showed that as far as the Bible is concerned Christianity is primarily about God and his acts in revelation and not, primarily, about man and his feelings. Hence he put a stress on God as God, the 'wholly other' not a kind of end-product of man's higher aspirations. He emphasized the holiness and majesty of God, and reintroduced ideas of man's fallenness and sin, and his need of grace. Conversely he criticized the appeal to human morality and religion as at best an attempt to build up a claim against God or to hide from him in subjectivism and at worst as an attempt to do without him. In particular he criticized natural theology, the attempt to argue from the world to God, or to build a picture of God from human intelligence, as a product of human pride and an attempt to make God the object of the theologian's study. For Barth God is always the subject, the initiator of the relationship between himself and man, and he compared any attempt to move in the opposite direction to the religion of the law against which Paul had protested.

At this point, largely because of the situation in which he was working, there is a tendency in Barth, and even more in some of his followers, to stress the element of judgement and the inadequacy of contemporary theology. But Barth was not merely saying that man cannot on his own find God, that his best efforts to do so fall under the judgement of God, and that man is subject to sin and depravity. Such assertions could never be the substance of Christian preaching and in all his work Barth is above all else a Christian preacher. The central point which emerges from his rediscovery of the Bible is the assertion that God has moved towards men in the person and work of Jesus Christ. There God has revealed himself. In biblical language there God has spoken, and his speech – his Word – is primarily action on man's behalf. That is the grace of God, his sheer unmerited kindness in action. Indeed it could be argued that it is only those who have been claimed by God, and begun to experience the freedom which he gives them to develop with Jesus into the man or woman whom he intends them to be, who have any real understanding of the sin and judgement from which they have been redeemed. This action or Word of God which is uniquely present in Jesus is present in a secondary sense in Scripture and in a third sense in Christian preaching. All are ways by which the grace of God is expressed to men.

As his thinking developed, and particularly after his work on Anselm, *Fides Quaerens Intellectum* (Faith seeking understanding) published in 1931, Barth worked out a dogmatic theology with Christology as its centre. In it he takes account of the fact that not only does God *not* speak in any other way but in Christ, but that he *does* really speak in Christ. Therefore it is possible to speak of a definite objective revelation based on the divine initiative. This is theology from within the Church. Thus Barth is not indifferent to rationality but he asserts that those who have experienced grace have moved beyond the man-centred rationality of the Enlightenment and can use their renewed rational gifts to understand and explain their faith.

The later developments of Barth's theology did not have a great influence on British theology. What was noticed was the passionate protest against Liberalism, the transcendent view of God and, especially, the approach to the Bible.

Over several generations the work of biblical criticism had drawn attention to the human elements of the Bible, what might be called its historical conditioning. In the excitement of these discoveries what seemed to be overlooked was the writers' claims that they were witnessing to divine acts. Their work proceeded from the conviction that God had acted, and that they were compelled to write as they did, both drawing attention to God's acts and explaining the significance of them. In other words, the biblical writers were writing theology. That being so, it is a misunderstanding to treat the biblical writings merely as a collection of sources whose significance is exhausted by means of literary and historical criticism. This is an instance where the *methods* of the Enlightenment, the methods of biblical criticism, can be helpful, but where the reader who accepts the *assumptions* of the Enlightenment, which tend to rule out any divine action, is unable to penetrate to the meaning of what he is reading.

A renewed attention to the theological content of Scripture is at the heart of what came to be known as the Biblical Theology movement. It is understandably connected with the name of Karl Barth but it is wrong to suppose that all those involved in it would agree with Barth's theology in detail, or indeed with each other. What its representatives share is the conviction that the Bible is basically a book of theology. Such a conviction breaks down the barrier which had almost imperceptibly grown up between biblical scholars and the theological teaching of the Church. The latter, though often apparently battered by modern thought, had generally hung on to a supernatural element.

The single great effect of this movement was to undermine the Liberal Protestant conviction that it was possible to get behind the New Testament documents to a Jesus who had been a simple ethical teacher. Underlying this conviction was the assumption that Christian teachers from Paul onwards had elaborated and falsified both the picture of Jesus himself and his teaching. Such thinking had led to a distinction between the historical Jesus and the Christ of faith. But to recognize the New Testament writings as theological documents meant that such a distinction could not be defended. As far as our documents are concerned the historical Jesus and the Christ of faith are the same person.

In Britain this argument had been advanced while Liberalism was at its height by the Free Church theologians *James Denney* (1856–1917) and *P. T. Forsyth* (1848–1921), both of whom had argued for a theological reading of the New Testament. However its best known exponent was to be an Anglican New Testament specialist.

Edwyn Clement Hoskyns (1884–1937) taught the New Testament at Cambridge from 1921 until his death. He was one of the group of Anglo-Catholic theologians who produced the collection *Essays Catholic and Critical* (1927). Consciously in the tradition of *Lux Mundi*, this group sought to keep the strengths of the immanentalists without losing confidence in a transcendent God. Hoskyns' contribution was an essay on 'The Christ of the Synoptic Gospels'. His argument was that the most rigorous application of the critical tools available showed a Jesus who was conscious of the messianic significance of his mission and who claimed that in his person and work the reign of God was breaking in to history. Later, in *The Riddle of the New Testament* (1931), written with his pupil Noel Davey, he argued that the rest of the New Testament writings applied this thesis; they were in agreement with the Synoptic Gospels and not introducing new and alien ideas. For Hoskyns the supernatural element was not something added by Paul and his successors; it impregnated all strata of the tradition. From the beginning Jesus' person as God in action was part of the gospel. He called his hearers not to high ethical endeavour but to a decision about himself, to accept the forgiveness of God and the new relation with God that he brought. Such a decision brought men into the Church.

Soon after, C. H. Dodd's *The Apostolic Preaching and its Development* (1936) argued that at the heart of the New Testament was preaching (*kerugma*), a proclamation of the acts of God. It was this element rather than the teaching (*didache*) which was basic.

This revival of Biblical Theology might have taken place without the work of Barth. Hoskyns' Anglican admirers seem anxious to argue that he was not a Barthian though he translated Barth's *Romans*. As a matter of fact it was clearly influenced by Barth. Its result was a much more positive approach to Scripture. For a generation or more many ministers of all denominations had unfortunately seemed to consider it a mark of academic integrity and sophistication to speak of what they disbelieved about the Bible. Their training had too often presented biblical criticism in a negative way. The disastrous effects of that approach continued in self-consciously enlightened modernity on the one hand and rigidly defensive literalism on the other. But there was some recovery of confidence. On the pastoral level the Bible Reading Fellowship, founded in 1922 at St Matthew's Church, Brixton, encouraged private devotional reading. On the academic front it once more became customary to see the Bible as a whole and attention was given to major themes found in both Testaments, such as salvation, covenant and the people of God. At the same time the British tradition of biblical scholarship, never really dormant, flourished anew in men such as H. H. Rowley, Vincent Taylor, T. W. Manson and W. Manson.

The German Church struggle

One of William Temple's memorable sayings was that the Christian Church exists for those outside it. He meant that the Church must present the gospel as God's offer of forgiveness and reconciliation in ways appropriate to its own time and culture. But in stressing the needs of a particular culture there is a danger that the Church will simply cater for those religious instincts which that society is willing to acknowledge. The Church can then become subservient to its society and the gospel can be distorted and merged with the general culture. The danger is greater if any particular culture has been genuinely influenced by the gospel and contains some Christian elements.

Part of Barth's early work was to protest against the identification of Christianity with nineteenth-century German Liberalism. Others followed him in stressing the freedom of the Word. *Emil Brunner* (1889–1966) differed from Barth in that he wanted to keep a limited and carefully qualified place for natural theology, a 'point of contact' in man to which the gospel appealed. The dispute between them was bitter, perhaps partly because they had been close, and it was exacerbated by the political circumstances to be considered shortly. But they had much in common and in England Barth and Brunner were usually seen as joint exponents of the theology of the Word. In America the brothers *Reinhold Niebuhr* (1892–1971) and *H. Richard Niebuhr* (1894–1962) protested against the way the gospel had been emasculated in their country by its forced association with American Liberalism. Both were concerned about the relation of the gospel and the Church to contemporary culture and Reinhold in particular drew attention to the absence of a realistic doctrine of sin in the optimistic stress on progress in much American Christianity. Now, in Germany, there emerged a more obvious attempt to subordinate the Church to a certain view of society and to distort the gospel.

In January 1933 Adolf Hitler became Chancellor of Germany. His 'National Socialist German Workers Party' (the Nazis) led a number of smaller parties in opposition to the Communists. Though his progress to power had been accompanied by violence and corruption he did have a large measure of popular support. After the First World War Germany had been humiliated by the Treaty of Versailles. There had followed a period of confusion and decline, considerable growth of Communist influence, conflict between many smaller parties, general lack of direction and widespread immorality. The financial collapse of 1929 added mass unemployment and rapid inflation. In such circumstances Hitler could well appear as a national saviour and he attracted the support of many idealists.

Hitler's policy was based on the Nation, the Race and the Leader (Führer) principle. He spoke of restoring the pride of the German nation and reclaiming the land which had been taken from it at Versailles. He argued that the Aryan (German) race was biologically superior to any other, a master race. Further, he argued that to achieve full national and racial potential loyalty should be invested in one absolute leader, and that was to be himself.

His ideas were attractive. He offered order after a period of chaos, he advocated discipline and moral purity, and he was building the nation's economic strength. Many were willing to overlook the less desirable aspects of his rule, which in any case were not fully apparent at first. By propaganda, intrigue and violence he won the support of most sections of society and silenced his critics. In particular he moved against the Jews. He blamed them for most of the nation's ills and produced false scientific evidence to show that they were an inferior race and a source of corruption. They were deprived of legal rights, dismissed from their jobs and, later, sent to concentration camps. Some six million Jews perished during the twelve years of Hitler's rule.

When he first came to power Hitler's apparent idealism and appeal to what were seen as traditional German virtues were attractive to conservative churchmen of all denominations, and he was willing to use their support. He established a concordat with the Vatican which gave the Roman Catholic Church certain privileges if it refrained from involvement in politics. Meanwhile he assured the Protestants that he valued their moral influence. Some Protestants were persuaded that Christianity could be combined with National Socialism and Hitler supported this group, the so-called 'German Christians', while he moved against dissidents in the Church. He established Ludwig Müller, a supporter, as Reich bishop and later set up a Ministry for church affairs with wide powers of control over church government and finance.

The ease with which most of the Protestant Church capitulated to Hitler is partly explained by the apparent attractiveness of his policies, especially his opposition to Communism. But it is largely the result of the Lutheran teaching that God appoints civil rulers and that rebellion will make matters worse. Lutheran Christians therefore tend to try to improve a situation from within and, of course, to pray for civil rulers. In Luther's defence it must also be pointed out that he, and the other Reformers, assumed he would be dealing with a 'Christian Prince' who would pay some attention to church leaders. He also specifically allowed rebellion when a ruler deliberately transgressed the first commandment.

But a number of Protestants did correctly read the signs of the times and fought against them. An eloquent, unbiased, witness to their bravery was the Jewish physicist Albert Einstein who wrote, 'Being a lover of freedom, when the [Nazi] revolution came, I looked to the universities to defend it, knowing that they had always boasted of their devotion to the cause of truth; but no, the universities were immediately silenced. Then I looked to the great editors of the newspapers, whose flaming editorials in days gone by had proclaimed their love of freedom; but they, like the universities, were silenced in a few short weeks ... Only the Church stood squarely across the path of Hitler's campaign for suppressing the truth. I never had any special interest in the Church before, but now I feel a great affection and admiration for it because the Church alone has had the courage and persistence to stand for intellectual and moral freedom. I am forced to confess that what I once despised I now praise unreservedly.'[3]

In truth the German Church struggle was, for the most part, on the limited front of ecclesiastical, spiritual and theological freedom in the face of Müller's attempts to force it to support Hitler and acknowledge that he was sent by God for the hour. One form it took was the practice, taken from the Reformation period, of issuing Confessions of faith, hence the title 'Confessing Church'. In the circumstances such Confessions expressed defiance of the Nazi regime. The most famous, written by Karl Barth, came from a synod at Barmen in 1934. Its flavour comes in some sentences from the first article; 'Jesus Christ, as he is attested to us in Holy Scripture, is the one Word of God which we have to hear and which we have to trust and obey in life and in death. We reject the false doctrine, as though the Church could and would have to acknowledge, apart from and besides this one Word of God, still other events and powers, figures and truths, as God's revelation.'[4]

There were numerous other acts of defiance. Pastors refused to read official pronouncements from their pulpits, theological teachers refused to take the oath of loyalty or begin lectures with the Nazi salute, theological faculties did not accept that non-Aryans should be dismissed from teaching posts or that the Old Testament should be dropped from theological courses or used as a vehicle for anti-Semitism. A Pastors' Emergency league was formed, many humble pastors were harassed, dismissed from their posts, imprisoned or in some cases killed because their preaching was considered hostile to the government. As theological seminaries were closed, underground ones were formed to train pastors for the Confessing Church and to offer encouragement and support.

The Confessing Church has been criticized for restricting itself to church affairs or for not realizing earlier that more overt political resistance would be needed. Nevertheless what it did demanded rare courage and gave it some right to be heard, in Germany and beyond, when the Second World War was over.

Among the many martyrs of the Confessing Church was one who achieved fame after his death and whose story illustrates the complexity of the situation. *Dietrich Bonhoeffer* (1906–45) came from a liberal, agnostic, family with wide-ranging connections in German political and academic life. He became a theologian and came under the influence of Karl Barth. During the 1930s he was able to travel for study and work and he visited Italy, America, Spain and Great Britain. He argued the cause of the Confessing Church at a number of ecumenical gatherings and was elected to the Council of the Life and Work movement. In that capacity he established a close friendship with George Bell, Bishop of Chichester.

Within days of Hitler coming to power Bonhoeffer had criticized the Leader principle in a radio broadcast which was cut short before its conclusion. He organized an underground seminary which eventually had to be abandoned to avoid the attention of the Gestapo. In 1939 when war was inevitable and it was thought that his life might be in danger, Reinhold Niebuhr arranged his appointment to a post at Union Theological Seminary, New York, but, though he did take it up he soon became convinced that he should be in Germany and he returned there before war broke out. The Nazis thought his ecumenical contacts could be useful and he became a civilian agent of the *Abwehr* (the counter-intelligence department). In that capacity he was allowed to travel outside Germany and in 1942 he met Bell in Sweden.

In fact, together with other members of the *Abwehr* and some highly placed service and political figures, he was engaged in secret resistance activities and was involved in the plot to assassinate Hitler. For a Lutheran and a man conscious of all that he owed to his own nation it was a remarkable decision deliberately to set out to take the life of the head of state and to be involved in the deceit and subterfuge of resistance work. Through Bell the conspirators sought assurances from the British government that, after the assassination, a non-Nazi administration in Germany would be able to negotiate peace terms. They were not successful, the Allied powers were intent on securing unconditional surrender and Bell was not able to convince the British government that there was sufficient support for such a plan in Germany. In fact Bell's speeches in the House of Lords arguing that there were 'good Germans' were regarded with suspicion.

The assassination attempt, which took place on 20 July 1944, failed. The chief conspirators were not at once implicated but most of them were already under suspicion by the Gestapo. In the autumn files were discovered and Bonhoeffer and his friends were arrested, charged among other things with arranging the release and escape of Jews bound for the concentration camps. He was executed at Flossenberg on 9 April 1945.

Apart from his political significance, which was really rather slight, or even the value of his theological writings, Bonhoeffer's life illustrated the vitality of the Confessing Church and the resilience of its theology. The letters he wrote from his last imprisonment and other papers prepared at that time were later published to wide acclaim. In England, as the Second World War came to an end there was an almost romantic appeal about the German Church struggle. Perhaps partly born of despair of other hopes there was a willingness to pay attention to the theology which had sustained it.

Notes

1 F. A. Iremonger, *William Temple, Archbishop of Canterbury* (Oxford University Press 1948), p. 378.
2 A. M. Ramsey, *From Gore To Temple* (Longmans 1960), p. 160.
3 cited A. C. Cochrane, *The Church's Confession under Hitler* (Pittsburgh, Pickwick Press 2nd edn 1976), p. 40.
4 The full text of the Declarations, Resolutions and Motions of the Synod is printed in Cochrane, op. cit., pp. 237–47.

14
To Secularism and Beyond

The opportunity to reorganize British society, for which many who described themselves as Christian Socialists had longed for years, appeared to have arrived in 1945. A Labour administration came to power immediately after the Second World War, but in unpropitious circumstances. A long and difficult period of reconstruction lay ahead, and with it some reassessment both of Christianity and socialism and of the relationship between them.

Though in the euphoria of victory it may not have been apparent, two world wars had drastically altered Britain's status as a world power. Almost at once, with the granting of independence to India in 1947, the process of dismantling the Empire and moving towards a Commonwealth began. The opportunity to take a leading role in the formation of a new Europe was, at least temporarily, allowed to pass in 1949.

At home there were distinct gains as the Welfare State began to become a reality. Great strides forward were made in such fields as health and education and generally the Churches welcomed such moves. Though some pointed out that the welfare provided was largely economic and material, with the danger of sapping the individual's independence, the provision of religious education in schools was seen as contributing to the nation's spiritual well-being. Nevertheless, for many there grew a sense of disillusionment. The New Jerusalem did not look like providing a sense of security for its inhabitants. Use of atomic power at Hiroshima and Nagasaki had produced a sense of disenchantment and uneasiness. There was an awareness that a war of unimaginable horror was a possibility, and for the first time in centuries Britain would be in no position to do anything about it.

Intellectually, confident agnosticism still had considerable support. In academic philosophy a relatively small book, *Language,*

Truth and Logic (1936), by *A. J. Ayer* was the best known product of the school of linguistic analysis and was immensely influential. Its argument, broadly, was that statements which could not be tested by the rules of science, language or logic simply had no meaning. Since theological statements could not be so tested there was no point in arguing whether or not they were true, they were simply meaningless. As the debate proceeded it was noted that moral and aesthetic statements also appeared to be ruled out, and attempts were made to argue that statements could have meanings in their own contexts without referring to objective realities. Some philosophers of religion were occupied with this debate into the 1960s.

On the other hand in the post-war years there was also something of a religious revival in intellectual circles. The Biblical Theology movement gained strength; lay theologians such as C. S. Lewis and Dorothy Sayers were widely read; university faculties of theology began a period of expansion; and academics in other fields, such as the Oxford mathematician *C. A. Coulson* and the social anthropologist *E. E. Evans-Pritchard*, were willing to speak of their Christian faith. Particularly influential among students was the Inter-Varsity Fellowship of Evangelical Christian Unions (IVF). Claiming that the SCM had moved too far from its original evangelistic and missionary orientation into the realms of sociology and politics, the IVF came into being in 1928. By the 1950s Christian Unions were established in most British universities. Later, responding to the changes in higher education, it became the Universities and Colleges Christian Fellowship (UCCF) in 1974. It has helped to ensure that Christianity continues to be a live option among students.

As memories of the war and its necessary austerities receded the nation entered a period of unprecedented affluence. It was accompanied by some movement towards materialism and secularism. For many, particularly the young, the 1960s were a time of experiment and questioning which could easily be interpreted as rebellion. Accepted standards and institutions were indeed challenged, sometimes aggressively, with the assumption that they were obstructive and should be swept away, at other times with a more reasonable request that they should justify their existence in a new world. On the whole there was a move away from absolute standards. It was a period of permissiveness and individuality. The Church, in all its forms, and Christianity itself, were questioned and often found wanting – though Jesus was frequently admired and exempted from the criticism. At the same time there was an increased concern for the poor expressed through a variety of relief agencies, an increased fear of nuclear war, together with the Campaign for Nuclear Disarmament, and an increased interest in a more diffused spirituality expressed by some in experiments with drugs and by others in explorations of non-Christian religions or strange occult sects. All these trends have continued.

In retrospect the 1960s came to be seen in many respects as merely an exciting radical interlude. Subsequent years witnessed an economic decline and something of a restoration of traditional values. But there was not the conservative backlash which some had feared. Some changes were permanent. The search for affluence and for security measured by possessions continued. Neither Christianity nor any other spiritual system could expect to be accepted without question, and its ethical precepts, especially in the realm of sexual ethics, were not unchallenged. At the very least modes of expression had to be changed. But by the late 1970s it was no longer common to find the very possibility of spiritual values being denied, and a new openness to religion was widespread. Material change and progress there had been, but spiritually the mood was not so different from the late 1940s.

Billy Graham – Evangelism and Social Concern

After the Second World War it was natural that the Churches should make some effort to respond both to the growing sense of disillusionment and to the apparent openness to Christian commitment, particularly since in most denominations, but especially in the Church of England, the number of conservative Evangelicals was increasing markedly. In 1945 Church Assembly produced a report *Towards the Conversion of England*, emerging from a commission established by Temple in 1943. It was widely read and debated, but the general impression was that, while it had helpfully diagnosed the effects of secularism and materialism on the national mood and identified a sense of spiritual emptiness, it was less helpful in suggesting positive action. What it had suggested was greater devotion within the Church and a large advertising campaign. The first is always needed and the second was too expensive. Its lasting contribution was to publicize a much admired and widely quoted definition of what evangelism is: '. . . so to present Jesus Christ in the power of the Holy Spirit, that men shall come to put their trust in God through him, to accept him as their Saviour and serve him as their King in the fellowship of his Church', which actually came from the Archbishops' Committee of Inquiry on the Evangelistic Work of the Church of 1918.

One response was the Mission to London of 1949 inspired by *William Wand*, the Bishop of London. In its preparation, with its encouragement of local church involvement, its use of the laity, its stress on prayer and its widespread publicity, it anticipated many of the emphases, if not the style, later associated with Billy Graham. Its weakness was probably a diffusion of aims. As well as offering the unbeliever the challenge of conversion it also attempted to show the relevance of Christianity to the life of society. The latter, though admirable in itself, seems to have deflected attention from the former. Men are usually more willing to talk about social issues than they are to talk about their own standing before God. At its conclusion Wand admitted that the mission had strengthened the faithful but hardly affected those outside the Churches.

Whatever the value of *Towards the Conversion of England* and the achievements of Bishop Wand's Mission to London, modern large-scale evangelism is inextricably linked to the name of Billy Graham. A campaign in Los Angeles in 1949 had made the former youth evangelist and President of a Bible School in Minneapolis a national figure. His Greater London Crusade held at Harringay arena during the spring and early summer of 1954 gave him an international reputation. Subsequently he has preached throughout Europe, in India and the Far East, in Africa, Australasia and even in Eastern bloc Communist countries. He has been a friend of several American Presidents and honoured by other world leaders. Through his vast meetings, often in sports arenas, and through television and radio networks it is probable that his preaching has been heard by more human beings than that of any other evangelist, so that he has become one of the best known Christian figures of the twentieth century. But most of that was still in the future when he arrived in England in February 1954.

The Greater London Crusade had been planned by English Evangelicals who had been impressed by reports of Billy Graham's work in America and who believed that the mood in England was ripe for such a venture. But they had not been able to carry the majority of English Church leaders with them and rumours of Graham's American activities, not all of them accurate, had produced some hostile press reports. In the event, with the Archbishop of Canterbury and the Lord Mayor of London at the concluding meeting, and that meeting attended by 120,000 people at Wembley arena and a further 65,000 at an additional meeting at the White City, the crusade was considered a great success. Many who had been critics were won over by Graham's own personality and evident sincerity. But reservations have remained. In his subsequent visits to England, and in his wider international work, he has never quite had the wholehearted support of English Christians. The same criticisms recur and it is worth considering them.

Underlying them all is what might be called an English distaste for the American packaging and slickness of the missions. This was particularly pronounced in 1954. It was perhaps compounded by a half-conscious resentment of American leadership in general as the realization spread that America had assumed the role of world leadership which Great Britain had previously exercised. It has continued as critics have drawn attention to the now almost world-wide activities of the Billy Graham Evangelistic Association, and especially its supposed wealth. It is assumed in England that religion should be associated with poverty! More obviously there has been unease at the businesslike methods – the long preparation of the Churches before a mission begins, the smooth, almost show business style of the meetings, the counsellors, the decision cards, the follow-up and the general stress on size and numbers. In fact a new element was introduced during the Greater London Crusade, the use of land lines to relay central meetings to distant venues.

But it is not easy to see why these methods should not be used. Billy Graham himself stresses the importance of a team approach, and he means not only those who are seen, like Cliff Burrows who conducts the meetings or George Beverley Shea his best known soloist, but also those whose talents lie in organization behind the scenes. The major problems are the danger that the personality of the preacher should become more important than the message, and the dangers of insensitivity, inflexibility or even corruption which come with any large organization. In fact the flamboyant style of the fifties was quite quickly toned down.

A more theological criticism is of fundamentalism. Here the problem is to know exactly what is meant by the term. Historically it relates to a series of twelve books under the general title *The Fundamentals* published in America around 1910. They were composite volumes written by eminent Evangelical scholars from America and Great Britain. In essence, in opposition to what they described as Liberal theology, the writers wished to assert what they saw as fundamentals of Christian orthodoxy, such as the deity and virgin birth of Jesus, the miracles, a substitutionary view of atonement and the resurrection. A fundamentalist could, therefore, be one who holds such views. Often, however, it means one who asserts the literal truth of Scripture and simply refuses to concede the right of biblical critics to work on it, thus giving to the actual words of the text some supernatural status. With this there is also sometimes the implication that the one described as a fundamentalist is unscholarly, bigoted and harsh in his judgements of those who disagree with him. When it is added that there is a wide spectrum of views between those mentioned it is clear that the description fundamentalist is not always clear or helpful.

As far as Billy Graham is concerned the criticism seems to be at least an accusation that he is unscholarly in his approach to theology generally and to Scripture in particular. There is little doubt that he would support the kind of position put forward in *The Fundamentals*, and his frequent use of the phrase, 'The Bible says ...', followed by the quotation of a text shows a distinct leaning towards a literal interpretation. Nevertheless this could be understood as a kind of preacher's shorthand meaning something like, 'the teaching of the Bible is ...', and it must be remembered that a conservative approach to the Bible, which takes account of the various types of literature, is not of itself unscholarly. Billy Graham's career has precluded him from being a scholar in a strictly academic sense, but his speaking and writing indicate a widely read and thoughtful man. Traces of a harsh attitude of the sort which may accompany fundamentalism in its narrower sense may have been present in some of his earlier preaching but they have not survived. Like Moody he appears to have moved from a stress on the judgement of God awaiting the impenitent sinner to a stress on the love of God waiting for the sinner's response.

Thirdly there is the criticism, to which evangelism of this sort is always open, of over-emotionalism. Some emotion is quite proper in preaching the gospel, indeed it would be odd if it was entirely absent. But does Billy Graham use excessive emotional pressure, in effect manipulating his hearers? He concludes his sermons by inviting those who wish to make a decision for Christ, or who are seriously considering that step, to leave their seats and move to the front of the arena where they will be met by counsellors. It is argued that only excessive emotional pressure would make people do such a thing.

In fact those who have worked with him claim that Billy Graham has a distinct spiritual gift in this area and that it is that gift rather than any psychological manipulation which accounts for the numbers who respond. Some even express surprise at the lack of emotion. During the Harringay crusade one of the British organizers is said to have remarked that had he ended his sermon by reading the multiplication table and then given the invitation people would still have come forward. During the 1966 crusade at Earls Court the entertainer Cliff Richard was invited to speak at a meeting and decided he should familiarize himself with the procedure. Later he explained, 'I went to a meeting a couple of days earlier and was thoroughly impressed by his vocal presence, but when he made his invitation I remember thinking that no one would go forward as there had been no emotional stress or pressure ... if I had been a non-believer I would have been impressed by the man but not necessarily moved enough to go forward. To my amazement, hundreds – in fact, I believe it was 3,000 that night – went forward.' Finally, speaking of a meeting at Durban, South Africa, in 1973, Bill Burnett, later Archbishop of Cape Town, recalled that the sermon 'didn't come anywhere near me. But then he wasn't talking to me. What he had to say left me totally untouched. I was absolutely astounded when I saw how many people came forward to be counselled, because the way I was feeling, nobody would have moved.'[1]

The last criticism is perhaps the most serious. It is that he so stresses the element of personal decision for Christ that what should be an important part of Christian discipleship becomes the whole. Christianity is thus reduced to an individual believer's experience of God understood in terms of realization of personal sin followed by acceptance of forgiveness and reconciliation. Those who have passed through such experiences then urge them upon others and, ideally, develop their own relationship with God through Bible study and prayer. In all this, it is argued, the great themes of the Church and sacraments, and the understanding of discipleship as including practical concern for the well-being of other human beings and the whole of God's creation are lacking. For all the large numbers involved the Billy Graham style of evangelism can be seen as essentially sectarian, promoting a doctrinally and socially narrow, individualistic and world-renouncing version of Christianity.

There is certainly some truth in this picture as far as it concerns his early career. But it is not true of his later position. Behind the change are important developments of thought within the Evangelical wing of the Church on the relation between evangelism and social concern.

During the early part of this century there was a stress on what was called in America the 'Social Gospel'. In America the leading exponents were *Walter Rauschenbusch* (1861–1918) and *Washington Gladden* (1836–1918). The Kingdom of God was almost equated with social improvement and there was an optimistic expectation that such improvement would occur and continue. Something of the same kind of thinking, though in a more chastened mood, could be found in the thinking of the World Council of Churches (WCC) until the 1960s. Salvation was seen in terms of development and ideas of sin and conversion, in the traditional sense of those terms, were no longer central. Indeed they were sometimes reinterpreted into social terms in such a way as to distort their biblical meanings.

In response those who were unhappy with what they saw as a reduction of the gospel to social improvement concentrated on what they termed proclamation evangelism, calling on men and women to make an individual response to God in repentance and faith. This wing of the Church, the Evangelical wing, developed a pessimistic view of society and concentrated on snatching people from it in spiritual terms rather than improving their lives within it. The result was that the holistic approach which had kept a close relation between evangelism and social concern, illustrated for instance in the early revivals and many early missionaries, was lost. In its place came a polarization, proclamation evangelism *or* social concern.

Incidentally, a major contributing factor to this polarization was the integration of the International Missionary Council (IMC), into the WCC in 1961. Because the WCC can only admit *Churches* into membership many non-denominational missionary societies which had been part of the IMC were excluded. The WCC lost what could have been a helpful influence and the Evangelicals who had supported the now excluded societies formed a negative impression of the WCC. The polarization was underlined.

Billy Graham seems to have begun by accepting this polarization. His gift was clearly proclamation evangelism and he was suspicious of those who appeared not to value it highly. In particular he was wary of the WCC which he suspected of being over-concerned with social issues. But as his work developed it took him to many parts of the world. He saw the poverty of the Third World and the problems of apartheid in South Africa (his meetings were multi-racial and desegregated), and he met Christians living with those problems. Furthermore he was often welcomed, supported and encouraged by churchmen who would not obviously be labelled Evangelicals. His own thinking and that of his advisers, who now included Christian leaders throughout the world, moved to a greater recognition of the place of social action.

An important watershed was an international conference on world evangelization held at Lausanne in July 1974. The Billy Graham Evangelistic Association was responsible for the organization and much of the financial provision but Billy Graham himself remained largely in the background. The majority of the nearly 4,000 delegates were from the Third World and knew the significance of social concern. At its conclusion the conference accepted a covenant, drafted largely by the Anglican *John Stott*, which both affirmed the traditional biblical emphases of proclamation evangelism and also stressed the importance of Christian social action. It also set up a continuation committee which subsequently sponsored world and regional study groups on a range of theological, cultural and social issues. Lausanne, and especially the covenant and the continuation committee, may be seen as an attempt to recover the holistic approach of earlier Evangelicals and to establish a relationship between proclamation evangelism and social responsibility.

The Greater London Crusade was an important indication of the growing confidence of Evangelicalism in Great Britain. It was now set on a period of growth. Over the next generation, while maintaining its traditional emphases on such matters as the authority of Scripture and individual conversion, it set aside its somewhat negative attitude and become much more active in the life of the Churches and in exercising social responsibility. For the previous half century Evangelicals had been known largely for the things which they denied, opposed, or at least suspected, such as popery, any kind of ritualism, biblical criticism, Liberal theology, the social gospel and the WCC. They could have been caricatured as defensive, narrow and cultureless, relics of a decaying Protestantism. They now became much more outward looking and optimistic.

The crusade of 1954 was itself a boost to their numbers and confidence. Together with later Billy Graham crusades it helped to provide Evangelical leaders. At a popular level it was responsible for beginning the magazine *Crusade* which was widely read by evangelical Christians until the early 1980s. More important however was the steady work of the IVF, now UCCF, in public schools and universities. Many who became evangelical leaders in their denominations, and in the maze of small interdenominational causes which make up the Evangelical constituency, were brought to faith and had their first experience of leadership and responsibility through the student Christian Unions. Meanwhile the Evangelical Alliance provided a common forum and rallying point.

During the 1960s Evangelicals demonstrated their new strength and confidence. Many Anglo-Catholics and formerly confident liberals, previously the stalwarts of Christian Socialism, were shaken by secularism, the rejection of transcendence and formal religion, characteristic of that decade. A number of them adopted both radical theology and radical politics. Others retreated into a more arcane Anglo-Catholicism or became Roman Catholics. But Evangelicals in the Church of England showed their increase in confidence by becoming more positive about the sacraments, more concerned about liturgy and more committed to social action. The high point was a conference at the University of Keele in April 1967, which showed a new openness to ecumenism and to other points of view within the Church of England.

A most important figure in British Evangelicalism since the Second World War has been John Stott. From 1950 to 1975 he was rector of All Souls, Langham Place, which became a centre for Evangelicals in London. As a scholar, preacher and Evangelical statesman he has won the confidence of his fellow Evangelicals and become a trusted adviser to younger leaders, as he is to Billy Graham. His many books provide spiritual direction, biblical exegesis and an armoury of theological argument. Increasingly they have turned to cultural, ethical and social issues, and he was influential in persuading Evangelicals to move away from narrowly theological concerns to take more seriously the worlds of politics and sociology. This wider thinking is expressed in his support of the London Institute of Contemporary Christianity, a kind of Evangelical 'think-tank'.

Stott's involvement with Billy Graham illustrates the link between American and British Evangelicalism. But the link should not be overstressed. American Evangelicalism is non-denominational or flourishes among what, in English terms, would be called the Free Churches. In England a high proportion of Evangelicals and a higher proportion of leaders come from the Church of England. This also indicates that the Evangelical constituency in Britain is not uniform. There are shared basic convictions, but there are also wide differences of opinion. This is shown most clearly by denominational allegiance, but there are other differences. For instance some have been quite critical of Billy Graham and his methods, and some have been much less affected by the move to greater social involvement which has moved the majority.

The Secularizing of Doctrine

The Evangelicals, like most Christians, used the traditional language of the Church. They spoke of God as a person separate from the world, of Jesus as Son of God who 'came into' the world, and of a relationship between God and the believer which could be expressed in personal terms. A particular feature of the 1960s, and lingering far beyond that decade, was the assumption among some influential religious thinkers that such language had to be abandoned. Instead, they argued, Christianity had to be expressed in secular terms, that is in terms limited to this world. Such thinking came to public notice when *John Robinson*, a Cambridge New Testament scholar who had become suffragan Bishop of Woolwich in South East London, popularized it in a small paperback *Honest to God* (1963).

Robinson's starting point appeared to be some phrases from Bonhoeffer's *Letters and Papers from Prison* (1953). Bonhoeffer was critical of the kind of religion which appealed to man's weakness and which cut him off from the world. In the past, he argued, men had turned to religion mainly for help and explanation of the puzzling and frightening features of the world, and some kinds of religion and some religious practices reinforced that way of thinking. In contrast to that he looked forward to an expression of Christianity which would take account of man's increasing scientific knowledge and technological control of his environment, and which would not shield him from the world but help him to express his faith within it. Hence he used such expressions as 'man come of age' and 'religionless Christianity'. Bonhoeffer was taking up Barth's criticism of religion as man's search for God on his own terms. He was also, presumably, writing under some strain and, sadly, he did not live to develop his ideas. However his own spiritual life certainly included such traditional religious practices as prayer and the idea of the believer's relationship with God. These more traditional aspects of his thought were not always recognized by those who quoted from *Letters and Papers from Prison*.

But Robinson was also consciously drawing upon the work of two major theologians, Rudolf Bultmann and Paul Tillich. Both had been influenced by Barth's criticism of Liberal Protestantism, but both had then developed their own theological positions which were quite distinct from his.

Rudolf Bultmann (1884–1976) was primarily a New Testament specialist and a leading exponent of form criticism to the Gospels.

At a time when others were trying to find the Jesus of history he argued that the Gospels were not meant to provide historical or biographical material. The Gospels, he suggested, are made up of small units of previously oral tradition. These units were preserved by the early Church in order to be used – in worship, in sermons, in teaching and in controversy. What we have, therefore, is not a biographical account of Jesus of Nazareth but a collection of sermon and teaching material used about him. Therefore the question to be asked is not, 'What was Jesus like?', or 'Did this or that incident really happen?' Such questions simply cannot be answered. The real question is 'Does the message of salvation contained in the New Testament preaching work?', and to that question the answer is 'Yes, it does!' In other words, the real Christ is the preached Christ.

Bultmann argues that the basic New Testament message is a call to decision. Christian preachers call on men and women to cease living one kind of life and open themselves to another. That other life, the Christian life, is made possible by their response to Jesus as he is made known in preaching. However, the way in which this is expressed in the New Testament is foreign to the twentieth century. The New Testament writers used the thought forms of their own day. They thought of heaven above and hell below, and found it relatively easy to speak of angels and demons, miracles and supernatural forces. From the world of Jewish apocalyptic they took the idea of the age to come which had already invaded this age, so that men could live from above or from below, 'according to the spirit' or 'according to the flesh', and even those who sought to open themselves to Jesus were in danger of being conformed to this world. Such language is not natural or easily understood in the twentieth century. The problem, therefore, is to present the same call for decision in terms which are more natural and more easily understandable for the twentieth century.

Bultmann makes two suggestions to be applied at the same time. He suggests that the New Testament message should be disentangled from the thought forms of the early Christians, which he refers to as myth. In other words the language of heaven and hell, angels, demons, miracles found in the New Testament should not be kept, but the essential teaching about Jesus and the challenge he offers to men and women should be presented in twentieth-century terms. He refers to this process as demythologizing. He insists that he is not making belief easier by reducing the number of things to be believed. Rather he believes that he is making it in a sense harder by insisting that those who hear the preaching should really be faced by Jesus' challenge without their attention being distracted by other matters such as the possibility of miracles.

At the same time he introduces the language of existentialism. This approach to philosophy stresses the importance of individual commitment. One who simply lives according to the conventions of his day and society is not, says the existentialist, living authentically. Authentic existence involves the individual's making his own personal commitment to each action as it occurs. Bultmann argues there is a parallel between the existentialist call to decide against conventional existence and live authentically, and the call of the New Testament preachers to decide against the life of this world and commit oneself to the life which Jesus offers. He is not saying that Christianity *is* existentialism, but that twentieth-century Christians can make use of this particular insight.

Paul Tillich (1886–1965) is less biblical than Bultmann. Robinson took up two of his key ideas. The first is that modern theology must begin from the questions which men ask. It must not present a fully worked out metaphysical picture of reality with a 'take it or leave it' attitude. Instead it must explore the fundamental questions or areas of concern which worry modern man and show how the Christian gospel sheds light upon them. This is popularly described as a theology from below as opposed to a theology from above.

Secondly Tillich argues that twentieth-century man is concerned about what would traditionally be called religious questions, but that the way in which Christianity is usually expressed is not helpful to him. Robinson particularly draws attention to Tillich's argument that all men have experiences which may be described as experiences of depth. These are moments when they feel they are penetrating below the superficial level on which life is often lived. In such moments men may feel that they are closer to making sense of the world or that they have intuitions which, even if only for a fleeting moment, shed a new light on the rest of their experience. In Tillich's words men can draw from such intuitions 'the courage to be', and they should be interpreted as experiences of God. Thus men should not be asked to look for God as a transcendent person above them, they should be encouraged to recognize him in experiences within or beneath their normal experience. So the metaphor of height is replaced by one of depth.

Robinson dissociated himself both from Bultmann's extreme scepticism about the historical reliability of the Gospels, and from the detailed working out of Tillich's position in his *Systematic Theology* (1953, 1957, 1964), but he used ideas from both. He argued that the idea of God as a person separate from the world, and language which implied some 'other' world in which God was to be located, distinct from the world of nature and history was no longer tenable. Instead God should be understood, in Tillich's terms, as the 'Depth of Existence' or the 'Ground of Being'. God thus understood is encountered as the continuing creative source of the world, and he is encountered especially in human relationships when they are genuinely personal. What is needed for the encounter is the kind of vulnerability which Jesus demonstrated in entering in to such personal relationships in a spirit of self-giving love.

It is clear that the kind of commitment, an existentialist commitment to the world and to other people, and the subsequent experience of depth which Robinson describes could not be limited to conventionally religious people. Furthermore, if this is the way to God it raises questions about the uniqueness of Jesus, the practice of prayer and the normal understanding of Christian morality. Robinson described Jesus as 'the man for others' (a phrase from Bonhoeffer) and one who because he was totally open to the Ground of Being could be described as 'transparent to God' or 'a window into God'. Later, in *The Human Face of God* (1973), he argued that Jesus differed from other men only in the degree to which he was open to God, a position reminiscent of Schleiermacher. On Robinson's grounds prayer could have been mainly meditation but he preferred to link it with practical social engagement rather than with petition or withdrawal from the world. Morality became situation ethics, that is not a predetermined code but a responding to each situation in love.

Many who felt the attraction of a spiritual interpretation of life but who could not accept orthodox Christianity as they understood it were happy to accept this approach. Many more, including a large number within the Churches, seemed immensely grateful that the questions had been raised and pleasantly surprised that ideas such as these were current among theologians. For such people Robinson had clearly opened a potentially profitable debate. Others, both Christians and non-believing philosophers, argued that his position was basically atheistic.

A more measured response came from the many theologians who pointed out that the kind of belief in God which Robinson was denying, apparently in the belief that other Christian teachers taught it, was in fact very simplistic and one-sided. The first half of his book, with the assumption that most of his fellow Christians believed in God as a father figure literally 'up there', was little more than a caricature and, coming from a bishop, caused much offence. Generally speaking, orthodox Christian teachers, following the Bible, have presented a far more dynamic view of God than Robinson allows. They have traditionally asserted that human language, simply because it has developed to meet human needs and uses, cannot adequately describe God. It is against that background that personality has been used as the best, or least misleading, language available. But it is not asserted that God is simply *a* person like any other. All language about God is metaphorical. The metaphor of depth is no less misleading than that of height. Loyalty to Scripture and the breadth of the Christian tradition would find room both for immanence and transcendence while preserving the essential biblical idea of the freedom of God.

What the furore about *Honest to God* illustrated was the gulf between the thinking of academic theologians and that of the general public, whether Christian or not. A similar situation was revealed fourteen years later with the publication of a composite volume purporting to give the most recent thinking on the person of Christ. *The Myth of God Incarnate* (1977), edited by John Hick, consisted of ten related essays by seven authors. It was more technical than *Honest to God* including some fairly specialist arguments on biblical and intertestamental thought, on Platonism and semantics.

Basically it made two points: first Jesus did not claim to be God and secondly the very idea of incarnation is just not thinkable for twentieth-century man and therefore must be ruled out. Jesus is presented as a man intensely conscious of God in whom the unity of divine and human, potentially open to all, was realized in a special way. His attitude to others was a parable of God's love reaching out to the world. He brought a vital awareness of God's presence, claims, promise and power. Those who met him 'caught' something of his relationship with God br̩ ꞓ kind of 'spiritual contagion' and found themselves bound up with him into the community of 'agape', outgoing love, which is the Church. The myth of the incarnation arose from his followers' attempts to do justice to their experience of him in the intellectual categories available in their own culture.

The book was not well received. It was pointed out that it did not reflect the views of the majority of scholars in the field and appeared to have a radically sceptical approach to the historical reliability of the New Testament. The essayists attributed anything which did not support their own position to later interpretation by the early Church. A number of works were written in refutation but the most telling criticism came from a work which did not specifically have *The Myth of God Incarnate* in mind. The distinguished Cambridge New Testament scholar C. F. D. Moule, in *The Origin of Christology* (1977), argued that the early Church's teaching about Jesus was basically already present in the earliest records we have of Jesus' own teaching.

The secular approach continued to have followers. One of the contributors to *The Myth of God Incarnate*, Don Cupitt, gave his own quite sceptical version of the findings of biblical criticism and the history of relations between science and religion in a series of television programmes entitled *The Sea of Faith*, and explained the logic of his own move to atheism in a book he called *Taking Leave of God* (1980). But by the later 1970s most academic biblical scholarship was showing more confidence in the broad historical reliability of the texts and a number of academic philosophers and scientists were showing more openness to a Christian view of the world.

Charismatic Renewal

While some British religious leaders looked for a secular understanding of Christianity, a quite different movement began to be felt. The experience of baptism in the Holy Spirit and of spiritual gifts (charismata) normally associated with Pentecostalism began to appear in the older mainstream denominations. At least three influences contributed to the emergence of the movement in British church life in the 1960s.

Internationally Pentecostalism had become much better known and respected. Some Pentecostal Churches had even joined the WCC. Particularly influential in this regard was *David du Plessis* (born 1905). As early as 1936 du Plessis, then secretary of the Apostolic Faith Mission in South Africa, had been told by *Smith Wigglesworth* (1860–1947), a forceful and eccentric Yorkshireman with an extensive ministry of evangelism and healing, that God would use him to take the message of Pentecostalism to the other Churches. At that time it seemed unlikely since, on his own admission, du Plessis was then a rather narrow Pentecostalist who felt that other denominations were false churches. In 1949 he was secretary to the Advisory Committee of Pentecostal World Conferences and living in America. During that year, while recovering from a serious car crash, he became convinced that the time for the fulfilment of the prophecy had come. Subsequently he became deeply involved in ecumenical work and was even invited to Rome as an observer at the Second Vatican Council. His policy was simply to speak of the baptism in the Spirit rather than of Pentecostalism as a denomination and he found many churchmen of other denominations eager to hear what he had to say. Not all his fellow Pentecostalists were happy with his activities and his ministerial credentials were withdrawn in 1962, but he continued with an international preaching and teaching ministry. More than any other individual he contributed to the partial removal of the barriers of ignorance and suspicion which had grown up between Pentecostalists and the mainstream Churches.

Secondly, throughout the 1950s, and before du Plessis's name was widely known in Great Britain, there was a fresh stirring of interest in the Pentecostal experience and in spiritual gifts generally, especially the gift of healing. In various parts of the country small groups, often drawn from Pentecostalist churches and from the Christian Brethren, began to meet for study and prayer concerning revival, in which they included the rediscovery of the gifts. Gradually these groups became known to each other through personal contacts, conferences and the magazines or newsletters which they issued. A similar interest in healing and prayer for revival was growing among Evangelical Anglicans and a number of individuals began to speak of being baptized in the Holy Spirit and receiving the gift of tongues.

The third influence, which brought the others together and made them more public, came from America. There a similar movement became public rather sensationally in 1960. On Passion Sunday, 3 April that year, *Dennis Bennett*, rector of St Mark's Episcopal Church, Van Nuys, California, a highly respectable church of 2,500 members, explained from his pulpit that he and some members of the congregation had been filled with the Spirit and spoken in tongues. He was obliged to resign. The incident was widely publicized, including articles in *Time* and *Newsweek*, and some of Bennett's supporters began to publish a magazine, *Trinity*. Through this publicity those in Great Britain heard of the wider movement, the British press unearthed some similar incidents, and as they reacted to the news those who were sympathetic to the experiences described began to discover each other. At least from 1963 a number of American visitors helped to spread and strengthen the movement throughout Britain. Other notable American influences were a convention of the Full Gospel Businessmen's Fellowship International (FGBMFI), an association of prosperous Pentecostal laymen, which met in London in 1965, and the book *The Cross and the Switchblade*, an account of the work of a Pentecostalist minister, David Wilkerson, among young criminals and drug addicts in New York.

A leading English spokesman and organizer of the movement was *Michael Harper*. In 1964 Harper resigned his curacy at All Souls, Langham Place, where his vicar, the influential John Stott, had opposed the idea of a post-conversion baptism in the Spirit, and formed the Foundation Trust as a service agency for the charismatic movement. The Trust produced a magazine, *Renewal*, and organized a number of conferences which were ecumenical in membership and, especially in the 1970s, grew rapidly in size. It was these conferences which particularly brought the movement to the attention of British Christians and introduced many of them to baptism in the Spirit and to charismatic worship. Its aim was to promote renewal in local churches but not to encourage people to leave their local congregations or denominations. It closed in 1981 partly to avoid giving the impression of organizing the Holy Spirit and partly because it felt its work was done. By then separate groups had been formed in the various denominations.

The central teaching of the movement is that baptism in the Spirit and the spiritual gifts mentioned in the New Testament can be experienced by Christians in the twentieth century and should be expected. In particular it has drawn attention to the pattern of Christian worship found in 1 Corinthians 14 with the suggestion that something like it should be reflected at least in some points in contemporary worship.

The movement has tended to use the language of the Pentecostal denominations formed early in the twentieth century. For their part some Pentecostalists assumed that those now experiencing baptism in the Spirit would join them. Members, and some leaders, of the other denominations, who already regarded Pentecostalism as a somewhat odd and emotional sect and who had no personal experience of the new movement, were not clear how the whole situation should be interpreted. Their confusion may have contributed to some later misunderstandings.

Some influenced by the new movement did become Pentecostalists, among them a few Anglican clergy and ordinands, and accepted Pentecostalist theology. This includes belief in a two or three stage initiation into Christianity and an insistence on tongues as a necessary indication of baptism in the Spirit and an empowering for service. There is also, generally, a limitation of the gifts to those mentioned in 1 Corinthians 12.8–10. Others, perhaps influenced by the Brethren's understanding of the Church which had been a concern of some pioneers of the movement, later stressed that element and moved into the House Churches or the movement of Restorationism.

The majority have adopted a less dogmatic approach and have tried to integrate the new movement into the lives of the mainline denominations. Baptism in the Spirit is interpreted variously, as a new stage in spiritual development, a leap forward in an on-going quest for holiness, or a release of spiritual riches already potentially present. At the same time many leaders dropped the phrase 'Baptism in the Spirit', preferring 'filling by the Spirit' or some less precise phrase. In any case it is not said, though it may sometimes be implied, that those who have not had the experience are not fully Christian. Tongues is recognized as one gift among others and the range of gifts is extended beyond those mentioned in 1 Corinthians 12.8–10 to others mentioned in the New Testament (see e.g. Romans 12.5–8; 1 Peter 4.7–11).

The movement has brought a deepening of faith to many and a greater expectancy in Bible study and prayer. New forms of music and a fuller participation in worship, including gesture, dance, drama and the gift of prophecy have been introduced to many congregations. In particular it has helped to break down denominational and theological barriers, for though it began in Evangelical circles it has influenced all sections of the Church and is particularly strong in Roman Catholicism.

Sadly it has also brought problems. A clumsy enthusiasm on the part of some exponents and a deep-seated fear on the side of those unprepared for it have both contributed to divisions in some congregations. Critics have accused it of anti-intellectualism and a flight from the problems of the world into a spiritual ghetto. Others have complained of emotionalism, élitism and an unbalanced acceptance of the demonic. It has, however, drawn attention to the considerable gap between the expectations of divine activity which most Christians and most denominations claim in their liturgies, hymns and official statements, and those which they actually have. That gap may be the biggest of the problems it has revealed.

It is claimed that an increasing number of younger church leaders and of those training for the ministry have been influenced by the movement. It has produced an increased engagement with the world in terms of evangelism and, in some cases, tackling such social issues as drug abuse. It may come to be seen as the most significant movement in British Christianity in the second half of the century.

Note

1 J. C. Pollock, *Billy Graham, Evangelist to the World* (New York, Harper and Row 1979), pp. 120, 258, 35.

15
Conclusion

It would be clear to any observer of English society in the later years of the twentieth century that the position of the various Churches in the life of the nation and the status of the Christian religion in its thought are far different from what they had been at the beginning of the nineteenth century. While the self-confident secularism and materialism found in earlier years of the century are rarely found, those who would like to speak of a Christian society are in a minority. Some speak of a multi-faith society, others of a post-Christian one. But traces of the earlier situation survive and there is vigorous life in the Churches.

Decline and hope

The Church of England remains the Established Church, with the sovereign as its official head on earth. The move to greater practical autonomy represented by the Enabling Act of 1919 has continued. In 1970 the role of the laity in Anglican church government was increased by the introduction of synodical government. This provides for the election of clergy and laity to synods at deanery and diocesan level and ultimately to a General Synod composed of three 'houses', bishops, clergy and laity. Such a system provides for wider representation and discussion, but hardly for speed of action or decisive leadership.

Since 1975 Synod has been able to authorize alternative forms of worship and some experimentation has taken place. This has incidentally led to expressions of support for the services of the Book of Common Prayer of 1662. As a result, while the order of service used in any parish church is agreed by the incumbent and the Parochial Church Council, the availability of the traditional service is guaranteed by law. Perhaps more important was the decision in 1976 that when a bishop is to be appointed a church committee, including representatives of the diocese concerned, should submit names to the Prime Minister. But the final appointment remains in the hands of the sovereign advised by ministers of the day.

However the impact of the Church on society is not measured simply, or even chiefly, by decisions in Parliament or by administrative arrangements. It comes through the unsensational work of ministers and members of all denominations and through the influence of those who associate themselves with the various Churches. The trend for such people to be found mostly among the suburban middle class has continued. Thus a particular area of concern has been the inner cities as the Churches there have continued to struggle to attract and minister to the urban poor. Here a report produced in 1985 by a Commission on Urban Priority Areas set up by the Archbishop of Canterbury may prove to be a landmark.

This report, *Faith in the City*, could be seen as a late flowering of Christian socialism. It describes the continuing movement of the educated and successful away from the inner cities to the suburbs. This, together with a decline in the type of industry and the need for unskilled labour which had produced the rapid growth of industrial cities in the nineteenth century, has meant that those left in the inner cities are often those who simply could not get away from them, which includes a high proportion of the old and those from ethnic minority groups. Using statistical evidence and first-hand experience the report draws attention to the very high levels of poverty, homelessness or unsatisfactory housing conditions, and unemployment in the inner cities with their inevitable results in strains on family life and extra demands on public welfare services.

It is not a particularly emotional report, but it draws attention to economic decline, physical decay and social disintegration. The picture which emerges is of a sharp polarization of society. From a social or political viewpoint the central issue is one of power or powerlessness in the social system. On the one hand there are those who either have some power and influence, albeit small, or who can at least manage to live in the system without too much distress; on the other there are those without power or influence, or easy access to them, who feel that they are virtually excluded from power and who find it increasingly difficult to lead decent and honourable lives within the system. More important is the realization that those in the second category, which includes the majority of those living in the inner cities, are increasingly without hope of any change in the situation. This results generally in a widespread cynicism and particularly in a distrust of authority, especially the police.

The report recommends that the Church of England should give more attention to the problems of the inner city in the training and deployment of ministers and the use of funds. It calls for close co-operation with other agencies in education and social welfare projects and for a willingness to comment constructively and, where necessary, critically on relevant national and local political issues. It suggests that the government should co-operate with voluntary bodies working in the field and asks that greater priority be given to housing, to support for the socially disadvantaged, and especially to the problems of unemployment. In all it amounts to a request for a massive redistribution of resources, with an underlying questioning of the structures of society which have made such a request necessary. It was seen by some sections of the press as too socialist in orientation and critical of the Conservative government of the day. This was denied, but the report may have contributed to the same party's decision to make the inner cities a major concern when it was re-elected for a third term in 1987.

In considering the position of the Church in late twentieth-century Britain it is worth reflecting that, though it is critical of the performance of the Church of England, and by implication of the other churches, *Faith in the City* was able to call on the experiences of churchmen actually working in the inner cities and to point to signs of Christian life there. It is probable that, quite apart from its underlying theological assumptions about the justice of God and his concern for the poor and underprivileged, no other national body could have produced such a report. Though often weak and not always obviously effective the Church is still present where men and women are dispossessed and suffering, as well as in the more prosperous suburbs. As evidence for this one may point to a large number of, usually small, organizations committed to specifically Christian motivated social work in urban settings, a number of whom are united in the Evangelical Coalition for Urban Mission. Behind this is a renewed willingness for Christians to think seriously in social and political terms, as shown by the journal *Third Way*, which was established by an Evangelical group in 1977 but attracts readers from other traditions.

Nevertheless, at a time when the Christian Church in many parts of the world is growing rapidly, the numbers of those who associate themselves with the various Churches in Britain appears to continue to decline. But the evidence is not straightforward or easy to interpret.[1]

In 1985, the last year for which substantial evidence is available through public opinion surveys and statistical returns from the Churches, nearly half the population saw itself as Christian though not attending church regularly (that is more than once a month on average) or belonging to a particular congregation. The large majority of those would be people who were baptized as infants. In addition 15% of the population (17% in 1980) were actually members of churches, having made some definite effort to join one. Of the latter only about half attend regularly. Against that must be set an increasing number who do attend regularly and involve themselves in the life of a particular congregation but who either have not yet taken the step of joining or who feel that belonging to a particular denomination is irrelevant. It must be noted that in all denominations there are a number of local churches which are growing.

There does seem to be an openness to Christianity in at least some sections of modern Britain. The greater confidence of the Evangelical wing of the Church has been noted, as well as the boost it has received from the charismatic movement. An expression of it was an interdenominational project under the title 'Mission England' which ran from 1982 to 1985.

The two most visible manifestations of this were a 'Mission to London' held at various centres within the capital and focusing on the Argentinian evangelist Luis Palau, and a tour of various provincial centres by Billy Graham under the title 'Mission to England'. Different estimates have been given for the numbers attending, and of course some individuals attended many times and at several venues, but it is likely that one and a half million people heard the preachers, of whom some 10% responded, either professing conversion or seeking spiritual advice. Nevertheless the organizers of the entire project suggest that its greatest benefit came through the work of training and preparation in local churches. Many local churches spoke of an increase in membership and numbers attending church and a deepening of spiritual life. It is clear that, while numerical decline is evident, the evidence of growth in interest, numbers and confidence in some sections of the Church cannot be ignored.

It is clear that many of the more hopeful signs are outside the mainstream Churches. We may conclude by mentioning two of them.

Black-led churches

Recent surveys of religious life and affiliation in Great Britain have had to take account of a remarkable growth in black-led churches (their own usual title for themselves). Many of the black immigrants who arrived during the twenty years after the Second World War came from Christian backgrounds. Churches founded by white American or British missionaries had played a major part in their education and social lives. While some found a spiritual home in one or other of the indigenous churches many did not and they set about establishing churches of their own. Often this began with a few friends, or a few families, meeting in a home to sing hymns, pray and read the Bible together. It led in some cases to the formation of churches which sometimes became affiliated to denominations with headquarters in the immigrants' home country, and sometimes formed small independent denominations of their own.

The most obvious characteristic of such churches is their African or Westindian[2] origin. Leadership in this country is almost exclusively black and local. The leaders have almost invariably emerged from the immigrant communities. They are men and women who understand and share the lives of their people and who are trusted because of the shared background.

Theologically black-led churches are usually in the Pentecostal-holiness tradition. Worship is likely to include speaking in tongues and prophecy and to involve a high degree of congregational participation. During a service two themes are present. First there is a sense of unity, an affirmation of group solidarity. It is the Church as a body, an entity with a life of its own transcending that of individual members, which engages in worship. The individual is caught up in something larger and more significant than himself. Secondly, there is an openness to the supernatural and an expectation of the exercise of spiritual gifts. This naturally involves experiences of individuals, but they are made possible through the support and security offered by the group and are seen as expressions of congregational solidarity.

This solidarity, the sense of belonging, is found in the lives of these churches outside worship as well. It expresses itself in generosity between members and prompt support in any kind of distress. In age, illness or bereavement a church member is rarely deserted. It is also found in world-renouncing ethics which may be seen as an attempt to defend the society of the church from pollution. Alcohol, tobacco and sexual laxity are especially frowned upon; dancing, cinema, theatre and public entertainment generally, tend to be regarded with suspicion. Alongside world-renunciation the church provides an alternative society. The young church member, open to temptations which would draw him away from the values of his Christian culture, is offered another life-style focused on the church. The church not only offers more than the usual round of devotional and social meetings, increasingly it is offering educational opportunities to supplement those provided by the state.

There can be no doubt of the growth and impact of the black-led churches among at least some sections of the immigrant community. Between 1970 and 1980 their membership doubled, usually by the conversion of second generation immigrants. In addition it is estimated that the numbers who attend worship and other church functions could be as much as five times the official membership.

Critics sometimes complain of an element of exclusiveness in these churches. It has not always been easy for those in the indigenous churches to make contact with them. Exclusiveness may partly be explained on cultural and historical grounds. Generations of oppression are not lightly put aside. It must also be remembered that the black-led churches were often formed because black immigrants did not feel welcome in indigenous churches, and that they often exist in parts of the inner city which the more prosperous white churches have left. Indeed they sometimes worship in the actual buildings left by white churches which have moved to the suburbs. The development of black-led churches is thus part of a wider cultural, social and economic division within society.

A more positive reason for apparent exclusiveness is a different conception of Christian life and faith. Black-led churches stress the difference between believers and unbelievers, church members and the world. To become a Christian, to enter the Church, is to have crossed a line. One mark of this is a different quality of life. For most members this does not appear to be forced. God is very real to them and the experience of spiritual gifts is natural. Generally they do not see the same sense of reality in the indigenous churches, which they refer to as so-called churches or nominal churches, and so they have not always been eager to associate closely with them.

Black-led churches differ among themselves on points of belief and ritual. The most prominent difference of belief emerges over baptism. Some, known as 'Jesus name' or 'Jesus only' churches, baptize in the name of Jesus only, not in the name of the Trinity. Their argument is that this was the custom of the early Church as found in the Acts of the Apostles, and that the doctrine of the Trinity is not clearly stated in the New Testament. In terms of ritual some have the custom of 'washing the feet of the saints', men and women separately wash each other's feet in accordance with Jesus' example in John 13. On the whole the members are not sophisticated theologians and will follow closely the teaching of their own pastors and leaders.

The possible role of black-led churches in providing social and political leadership among black immigrants in the inner cities is widely recognized. But it may be that their longer-term significance for British Christianity will be in the spiritual realm. As they grow in confidence and take a fuller part among the British Churches, others could learn from their liveliness in worship and their all encompassing attitude to discipleship.

House Churches – Restorationism

By far the liveliest section of the Church in Britain at the end of the twentieth century is the so-called 'House Church Movement'. Its numbers are estimated to have grown from 20,000 in 1975 to 75,000 in 1985, but it is only possible to speak of estimates since there are several groupings within the movement and they do not think of themselves as one denomination. Indeed they consider the existence of denominations to be a mark of apostasy and sin.

The title House Church Movement comes from the origins of the movement. It was first widely recognized as a distinct phenomenon in the early 1970s. At that time it was generally seen as a result of the charismatic movement in the mainstream denominations. The general view was that some people had become unhappy with the life of their local churches and had begun to meet in private houses for worship and the exercise of spiritual gifts. However, the origins of the movement are earlier and help to explain some later emphases.

When treating the charismatic movement we noted the growth of small groups from Brethren and Pentecostalist backgrounds from at least the early 1950s. It is probably best to recognize those groups as central to the House Church Movement. The charismatic groups breaking off from mainstream denominations were added later. In this way a number of virtually independent small churches came into existence strongly influenced by but not identical to the charismatic movement. Many, though not all, of these churches have adopted the theology and life-style known as Restorationism. Subsequently some congregations have left the established denominations to join the movement and others have adopted Restorationist theology, or some of it, while remaining within the denominations. At the same time they have outgrown private houses and now have, or sometimes hire, their own buildings.

The central principle of Restorationism is a drive to restore the Church to the experience of life which it knew in the New Testament. It is asserted that the Church as a whole fell from this pure state after the New Testament period and denominations are generally seen as a result of that fall, though it is not normally denied that some truths have been maintained by the denominations and that genuine Christians are found within them. Some movements in Church history, such as the Montanists of the second century, the Reformers of the sixteenth, and especially the Anabaptists of that time, the revivalists of the eighteenth century and the Pentecostalists, are recognized as earlier movements of Restoration which were only partially successful. Real Restoration means to bring the Church back under the immediate authority of God.

The importance which is placed on the immediate authority of God is stressed by both advocates and critics of the movement. It is partly expressed through the spiritual gifts to which Pentecostalists and the charismatic movement have drawn attention. Thus the dispensationalist view that such gifts were intended for the early Church only and should not be expected in the modern Church is denied. But authority is also expressed through the ministries which God has appointed in the Church and through the Church as a body when it recognizes and is guided by those ministries. The key scriptural passage is Ephesians chapter 4, especially vv. 11–12, 'his gifts were that some should be apostles, some prophets, some evangelists, some pastors and teachers, to equip the saints for the work of ministry, for building up the Body of Christ.' As with the spiritual gifts it is asserted that these offices are to be expected in the modern Church.

The stress on the Church and the ordering of its life reflects the Brethren strand in the origins of the movement. It also shows an appreciation of the importance of the corporate nature of Christianity. With all this is the conviction that the return of Christ is near and that the characteristic feature of the days preceding his return is a pouring out of the Holy Spirit for the establishing of God's Kingdom before the return of the King. The role of the restored Church, or perhaps better the Church in the process of being restored, is to announce the coming of the Kingdom and by the quality and order of its life to show, even if only by dim anticipation, the community life which will characterize the Kingdom.

Most interest and controversy has centred on the restoration of apostleship. Restorationists accept that the original twelve apostles are unique. However, they note that in the New Testament there are others who perform apostolic functions – they establish churches, give directions on the life of the local church, and are asked to adjudicate in matters of dispute even to the point of excommunication. They are men with a trans-local role whose authority is recognized by the leaders and members of local churches. Such apostles, it is argued, will always be found in the Church and should be recognized because of their gifts.

As local churches are called to submit to the apostles so church members are called to submit to local leaders. Prospective members usually take a rigorous commitment course in which the importance of subjection to God's authority through his appointed ministers is stressed. It is this feature of the movement, designated discipling, shepherding or covering, sometimes with slight variations of meaning, which is most open to abuse or misunderstanding. Some Restorationists teach that every believer must be 'covered' by a higher authority and that to be outside this chain of authority is disobedience. Clearly this could be a harsh and restrictive system and there have been criticisms of its abuse, but in practice it is based on personal relationships freely entered and often spiritually helpful.

Restorationists display what earlier generations referred to as 'seriousness' in their Christian discipleship. They have no doubt that God speaks, that he makes demands and offers. Those who join them find an experience of forgiveness and a sense of direction which pervades the whole of their lives. Above all they have an experience of acceptance and belonging.

Critics complain that the stress on authority and demand for obedience stifles the freedom of members and makes genuine discipleship impossible. It is argued that the movement grows less by evangelism than by attracting discontented members from other churches. Since some of those discontented members have often been influenced by the charismatic movement it could be that Restorationists are in fact robbing other churches of potential leaders.

It is also sometimes suggested that Restorationists are indifferent to social problems, that they think of Christians as being saved 'out of' the world rather than taking responsibility for it. That is not quite true. There are many examples of Restorationist churches setting up or supporting organizations to help those in various kinds of need, and within congregations there is a strong sense of mutual support and generous assistance to fellow members. However the movement appears to pay little attention to broad political issues or to the structures of society. It is not unfair to describe most congregations as broadly middle class and comfortable.

Conclusion

It is too soon to know whether Restorationism will fall into the error it criticizes in others and become a denomination. While it has much to teach the mainstream denominations in terms of commitment and discipleship, it could also learn from them in matters of biblical and theological scholarship and recognition of some of the problems of the modern world. Sadly the movement seems likely to develop outside the mainstream of British church life, and to pay more attention to the variations within its own ranks – often flowing from the personalities and gifts of individual leaders – than to make a fuller contribution to the wider life of the Church.

The black-led churches and Restorationism are the clearest signs of life and growth in contemporary British church life, but they are not the only ones. The charismatic movement goes on. Willingness to be involved with society grows. Churches of all denominations and traditions show signs of confidence and growth. The numbers of those training for Christian ministry seems to be increasing. All are signs of life, and perhaps signs that a long period of decline is near its end. For all that has changed and may change in the expression of Christianity and its relationship with the world around it, the witness of church history is that Christianity has within it the resources for life and renewal.

Notes

1 See Peter Brierley, ed., *UK Christian Handbook* (Marc Europe 1983, 1984, 1987). The following paragraph is dependent on the 1987/88 edition (1987).
2 The conflated word 'Westindian' is used to describe a culture still close to its Caribbean origin but so heavily influenced by the indigenous British culture that it really belongs to neither, thus forming a distinct sub-culture.

Appendix 1:
Church Leaders

Anglican Archbishops of Canterbury

Charles Manners Sutton
1805–28
William Howley 1828–48
John Sumner 1848–62
Charles Longley 1862–68
Archibald Campbell Tait
1868–83
Edward White Benson
1883–96

Frederick Temple 1896–1902
Randall Davidson 1903–28
Cosmo Gordon Lang 1928–42
William Temple 1942–44
Geoffrey Fisher 1945–61
Arthur Michael Ramsey
1961–74
Donald Coggan 1974–79
Robert Runcie 1980–

Roman Catholic Archbishops of Westminster

Nicholas Wiseman 1850–65
Henry Manning 1865–92
Herbert Vaughan 1892–1902
Francis Bourne 1903–35
Arthur Hinsley 1935–43

Bernard Griffin 1943–56
William Godfrey 1956–63
John Heenan 1963–76
Basil Hume 1976–

Appendix 2:
Development of the World Council of Churches

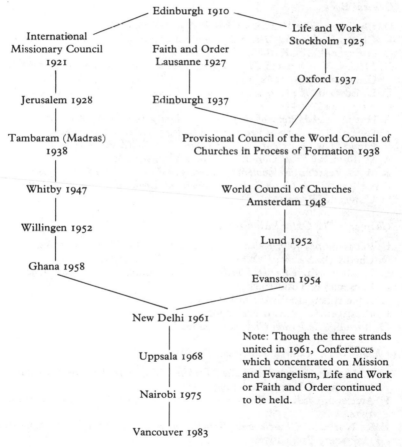

Edinburgh 1910

International Missionary Council 1921

Life and Work Stockholm 1925

Faith and Order Lausanne 1927

Oxford 1937

Jerusalem 1928

Edinburgh 1937

Tambaram (Madras) 1938

Provisional Council of the World Council of Churches in Process of Formation 1938

Whitby 1947

World Council of Churches Amsterdam 1948

Willingen 1952

Lund 1952

Ghana 1958

Evanston 1954

New Delhi 1961

Uppsala 1968

Note: Though the three strands united in 1961, Conferences which concentrated on Mission and Evangelism, Life and Work or Faith and Order continued to be held.

Nairobi 1975

Vancouver 1983

The chart is an extension of the one found in N. Goodall, *The Ecumenical Movement* (2nd edn 1961), p. 15. Only the major Conferences are noted.

Bibliography

Main sources and suggestions for further reading.

General Books

O. Chadwick, *The Victorian Church*. 2 vols, A & C Black 1966, 1970.

K. Clements, *Lovers of Discord: twentieth-century theological controversies in England*. SPCK 1988.

H. Davies, *Worship and Theology in England*. Vols IV and V, Princeton University Press 1962, 1965.

D. L. Edwards, *Leaders of the Church of England 1828–1978*. Hodder & Stoughton 1978.

A. Hastings, *A History of English Christianity 1920–1985*. Collins 1986.

A. Heron, *A Century of Protestant Theology*. Lutterworth 1980.

R. Lloyd, *The Church of England 1900–1965*. SCM Press 1966.

A. M. Ramsey, *From Gore to Temple*. Longmans 1960.

B. M. G. Reardon, *Religion in the Victorian Age*. Longmans rev. edn 1980.

P. A. Welsby, *A History of the Church of England 1945–1980*. Oxford University Press 1984.

Chapter 2 The Oxford Movement

G. Battiscombe, *John Keble, a study in limitations*. Constable 1963.

O. Chadwick, *Newman*. Oxford University Press 1983.

L. E. Ellsworth, *Charles Lowder and the Ritualist Movement*. Darton, Longman & Todd 1982.

J. H. Newman, *Apologia Pro Vita Sua*. Fontana edn 1959.

G. Prestige, *Pusey*. Mowbray 1982.

G. Rowell, *The Vision Glorious*. Oxford University Press 1983.

Chapter 3 The Church and Social Problems

K. S. Inglis, *Churches and the Working Classes in Victorian England*. Routledge & Kegan Paul 1963.

H. McLeod, *Class and Religion in the Late Victorian City*. Croom Helm 1974.

E. R. Norman, *Church and Society in England, 1770–1970*. Oxford University Press 1976.

E. R. Norman, *Christian Socialists*. Cambridge University Press 1987.

R. H. Preston, *Religion and the Persistence of Capitalism*. SCM Press 1979.

A. R. Vidler, *F. D. Maurice and Company*. SCM Press 1966.
(See also Chapter 15)

Bibliography

Chapter 4 Religion and the Advance of Science

I. G. Barbour, *Issues in Science and Religion*. SCM Press 1966.
R. J. Berry, *God and Evolution*. Hodder & Stoughton 1988.
J. Dillenberger, *Protestant Thought and Natural Science*. Collins 1964.
J. C. Greene, *Darwin and the Modern World View*. New York, Mentor Books 1973.
R. Hookyas, *Religion and the Rise of Modern Science*. Scottish Academic Press 1972.
J. Polkinghorne, *One World, the Interaction of Science and Theology*. SPCK 1986.
R. Stannard, *Science and the Renewal of Belief*. SCM Press 1982.

Chapter 5 Biblical Criticism

J. Barton, *Reading the Old Testament*. Darton, Longman & Todd 1984.
C. Blomberg, *The Historical Reliability of the Gospels*. Inter-Varsity Press 1987.
R. Gnuse, *The Authority of the Bible*. New York, Paulist Press 1985.
R. M. Grant (with D. Tracy), *A Short History of the Interpretation of the Bible*. 2nd rev. edn, SCM Press 1984.
I. H. Marshall, *Biblical Inspiration*. Hodder & Stoughton 1982.
C. Tuckett, *Reading the New Testament*. SPCK 1987.

Chapter 6 Reactions to Scientific and Biblical Criticism

J. Carpenter, *Gore, A Study in Liberal Catholic Thought*. Faith Press 1960.
M. A. Crowther, *Church Embattled*. David & Charles 1970.
P. T. Marsh, *The Victorian Church in Decline*. Routledge & Kegan Paul 1969.
A. Symondson, ed., *The Victorian Crisis of Faith*. SPCK 1970.

Chapter 7 Liberalism, Modernism and Reaction

A. von Harnack, *What is Christianity?* Philadelphia, Fortress Press; reprinted 1986.
D. E. Miller, *The Case for Liberal Christianity*. SCM Press 1981.
B. M. G. Reardon, *Liberal Protestantism*. A & C Black 1968.
B. M.G. Reardon, *Roman Catholic Modernism*. A & C Black 1970.
A. M. G. Stephenson, *The Rise and Decline of English Modernism*. SPCK 1984.

Chapter 8 The Free Churches

D. W. Bebbington, *The Nonconformist Conscience*. Allen & Unwin 1982.
C. Binfield, *So Down to Prayers*. Dent 1977.
D. M. Thompson, *Nonconformity in the Nineteenth Century*. Routledge & Kegan Paul 1972.

Bibliography

Chapter 9 Roman Catholicism

A. Archer, *The Two Catholic Churches*. SCM Press 1986.
B. C. Butler, *The Theology of Vatican II*. Darton Longman & Todd, rev. and enlarged edn 1981.
P. Hebblethwaite, *Runaway Church*. Collins 1975.
J. D. Holmes, *More Roman than Rome*. Burns & Oates 1978.
E. R. Norman, *The English Catholic Church in the Nineteenth Century*. Oxford University Press 1984.
D. F. Wells, *Revolution in Rome*. Tyndale Press 1973.
M. Winter, *What Ever Happened to Vatican II?* Sheed & Ward 1985.

Chapter 10 The Missionary Movement

P. Cotterell, *The Eleventh Commandment*. Inter-Varsity Press 1981.
J. Murray, *Proclaim the Good News*. Hodder & Stoughton 1985.
S. Neill, *A History of Christian Missions*. Penguin 1964.
S. Neill, *Salvation Tomorrow*. Lutterworth 1976.
L. Newbigin, *Unfinished Task*. SPCK 1985.
Dr and Mrs Howard Taylor, *Biography of James Hudson Taylor*. Hodder & Stoughton 1965.
M. Warren, *I Believe in the Great Commission*. Hodder & Stoughton 1976.

Chapter 11 The Ecumenical Movement

J. Coventry, *Reconciling*. SCM Press 1985.
R. Davies, *The Church in Our Time*. Epworth 1979.
R. Davies, *The Testing of the Churches, 1932–1982*. Epworth 1982.
N. Goodall, *The Ecumenical Movement*. Oxford University Press 2nd edn 1964.
N. Goodall, *Ecumenical Progress, A Decade of Change 1961–1971*. Oxford University Press 1972.
J. Matthews. *The Unity Scene*. British Council of Churches 1986.

Chapter 12 Movements of Revival and Evangelism

F. Coutts, *No Discharge in This War*. Hodder & Stoughton 1974.
W. Hollenweger, *The Pentecostals*. SCM Press 1972.
J. Kent, *Holding the Fort*. Epworth 1978.
D. Lynch, *Chariots of the Gospel*. Worthing, H. E. Watter 1982.
J. I. Packer, *Keep in Step with the Spirit*. Inter-Varsity Press 1984.
J. C. Pollock, *Moody Without Sankey*. Hodder & Stoughton 1963.
C. Whittaker, *Seven Pentecostal Pioneers*. Marshall Pickering 1983.
(See also Chapters 14 and 15)

Chapter 13 Biblical Theology and Redirection

G. W. Bromiley, *Introduction to the Theology of Karl Barth*. T & T Clark 1979.

Bibliography

A. C. Cochrane, *The Church's Confession under Hitler*. Pittsburgh, Pickwick Press 1976.

R. Gutteridge, *Open Thy Mouth for the Dumb*. Blackwell 1976.

C. W. Lowry, *William Temple, an Archbishop for all Seasons*. University Press of America 1982.

B. Ramm, *After Fundamentalism*. New York, Harper & Row 1983.

D. M. Roark, *Dietrich Bonhoeffer*. Waco Tx, Word 1972.

J. D. Smart, *The Past, Present and Future of Biblical Theology*. Philadelphia, Westminster Press 1979.

Chapter 14 To Secularism and Beyond

D. Cupitt, *The Sea of Faith*. BBC 1984.

P. Hocken, *Streams of Renewal*. Paternoster Press 1986.

J. Newport, *Paul Tillich*. Waco TX, Word 1984.

J. C. Pollock, *Billy Graham, Evangelist to the World*. New York, Harper & Row 1979.

V. Pratt, *Religion and Secularisation*. Macmillan 1970.

W. Schmithals, *An Introduction to the Theology of Rudolph Bultmann*. SCM Press 1968.

(See also Chapters 12 and 15)

Chapter 15 Conclusion

Archbishop of Canterbury's Commission, *Faith in the City*. Church House Publishing 1985.

J. Habgood, *Church and Nation in a Secular Age*. Darton, Longman and Todd 1983.

R. H. Preston, *Church and Society in the Late Twentieth Century*. SCM Press 1983.

D. Sheppard, *Bias to the Poor*. Hodder & Stoughton 1983.

A. Walker, *Restoring the Kingdom*. Kingsway 1985.

N. Wright, *The Radical Kingdom*. Kingsway 1986.

(See also Chapters 3, 12 and 14)

Index

This selective index includes only the most significant persons and subjects covered in the text.